T0360977

REGIONAL DEVELOPMENT IN AN AGE OF STRUCTURAL ECONOMIC CHANGE

Regional Development in an Age of Structural Economic Change

Edited by
PIET RIETVELD
Department of Economics
Free University
Amsterdam, The Netherlands
DANIEL SHEFER
Center for Urban and Regional Studies
Technion - Israel Institute of Technology
Haifa, Israel

Routledge
Taylor & Francis Group

LONDON AND NEW YORK

First published 1999 by Ashgate Publishing

Reissued 2018 by Routledge
2 Park Square, Milton Park, Abingdon, Oxon, OX14 4RN
711 Third Avenue, New York, NY 10017, USA

Routledge is an imprint of the Taylor & Francis Group, an informa business

Publisher's Note
The publisher has gone to great lengths to ensure the quality of this reprint but points out that some imperfections in the original copies may be apparent.

Disclaimer
The publisher has made every effort to trace copyright holders and welcomes correspondence from those they have been unable to contact.

A Library of Congress record exists under LC control number: 99076364

ISBN 13: 978-0-367-00018-9 (hbk)
ISBN 13: 978-0-429-44268-1 (ebk)

Contents

Figures, Tables and Maps

Contributors

Oedzge Atzema
Faculteit Ruimtelijke Wetenschappen
P.O. Box 80115
3508 TC Utrecht
The Netherlands

Piet Boomsma
Willemskade 40
8911 BC Leeuwarden
The Netherlands

Frank Bruinsma
Department of Regional Economics
Free University
De Boelelaan 1105
1081 HV Amsterdam
The Netherlands

Daniel Felsenstein
Department of Geography
Hebrew University of Jerusalem
Mount Scopus
Jerusalem
Israel

Aliza Fleischer
Development Study Center
P.O. Box 2355
Rehovot
76122 Israel

Daniel Freeman
Computerized Economic Models
11 Rupin Street
Rehovot
76353 Israel

Amnon Frenkel
Center for Urban and Regional Studies
Technion – Israel Institute of Technology
Haifa
Israel

Marina van Geenhuizen
Faculty of Technology, Policy and Management
Delft University of Technology
P.O. Box 5015
2600 GA Delft
The Netherlands

Andaki Kangasharju
School of Business and Economics Research Center
University of Jyväskylä
Finland

Hans Kuiper
Erasmus University
Burg. Oudlaan 50
3062 PA Rotterdam
The Netherlands

Peter Nijkamp
Department of Regional Economics
Free University
De Boelelaan 1105
1081 HV Amsterdam
The Netherlands

Piet Rietveld
Department of Regional Economics
Free University
De Boelelaan 1105
1081 HV Amsterdam
The Netherlands

Daniel Shefer
Center for Urban and Regional Studies
Technion – Israel Institute of Technology
Haifa
Israel

David Shefer
Center for Urban and Regional Studies
Technion – Israel Institute of Technology
Haifa
Israel

Esther Sultan
Statistics and Data Bases Division
Israel Ministry of Tourism
24 King George Street
Jerusalem
94262 Israel

Preface

Spatial economic systems are never in equilibrium and they are always subject to unexpected shocks and long term technological progress. These long term developments are especially important since they can have profound effects on the relative position of regions within any economic system. These effects, moreover, can work in two different ways. It may be that existing core regions are best positioned to exploit the opportunities (and resist the threats) of structural economic change. On the other hand, a long term historical perspective reveals that there have been clear shifts not only in the world economy but also in the relative position of regions within countries.

Such structural shifts encompass a variety of economic, technological, social and demographic changes – such as increasing immigration flows from suppressed and/or low income regions to liberal and high income regions; the growing importance of knowledge related activities, changing consumer tastes (such as the increasing importance of leisure activities and tourism), and the creation and deterioration of key infrastructure systems and facilities. Each of these changes can have a profound effect on the well-being of regions but the mechanisms are often difficult to trace and unravel.

The present book originated in May 1997 with a two-day workshop on how structural economic changes impact regional growth and development. The meeting of regional scientists, economists and geographers from Israel and the Netherlands took place in Tel Aviv, a city that illustrates the potential – and importance – of adjusting to rapid structural economic change. Founded only some 90 years ago, Tel Aviv has become a large, vibrant and dynamic financial and cultural urban centre.

A selection of the papers presented at the Tel Aviv meeting is included in this book. We thought the workshop was very interesting and stimulating; we hope that readers will have a similar experience.

We want to thank the organizers of and the participants in the Tel Aviv workshop for their individual efforts and contributions. We also want to acknowledge the skilful editorial assistance provided by Ms. Dianne Biederberg in preparing and completing this volume for publication.

Piet Rietveld   *June 1999*
Daniel Shefer

1 Spatial Consequences of Structural Change

PIET RIETVELD AND DANIEL SHEFER

1.1 Introduction

During the past decades regional economies have been influenced by various structural forces. A major force is *globalization*. Economic activities tend to take place more and more at the international level. This does not only hold true for the markets of goods and services implying trade, but also for financial markets and international investments. Globalization has various effects (cf. OECD 1997) including increasing specialization of regions, increasing inter-dependencies, new patterns of spread of technologies and changes in the product mix of regions.

The globalization is partly due to *changes in the cost of transport and communications* (cf. Janelle 1969). The process of decrease of costs of transport (and the increase in the quality of transport services) has already started long ago. It has led to a very large reduction in transport costs and hence to opportunities of specialization and large scale production. The decrease in communication costs has led to better possibilities of coordination of production and distribution processes at various places.

Another important factor concerns changes in the *position of the public sector*. In many countries governments have tried to reduce their involvement in economies by deregulation, changes in the social welfare system, reduction of trade barriers, etc. These changes tend to lead to a smaller emphasis on considerations of equity in policies of the public sector. At the regional level these policies tend to increase regional discrepancies in welfare levels. A special case related to the international detente since the last decade is the reduction of defence expenditures that had far reaching effects on certain regions relying on the defence sector (either as a location of defence related research, or as a region hosting large military camps, ports and airports).

Technological change leads to the destruction and creation of many jobs at various places (Bertuglia et al. 1997). Regions face opportunities for attracting firms making new products, but also run the risk that firms already settled there are forced to leave the market because they cannot stand the competition of firms from elsewhere producing new products. The long run cyclical movements of the economy lead to continuous processes of relocation of firms since in each phase of the life cycle of the products made, they may need another environment (Vernon 1966 Nijkamp and Rietveld 1987).

Demographic change and international migration are important phenomena that have long run consequences in many economies. An economy of a country like Israel has grown tremendously during the last decade owing to the large scale immigration of mainly highly qualified workers. On the other hand, a good number of rich countries in the world are facing considerable difficulties in absorbing immigrants from poorer countries such as the developing countries and Eastern Europe. These migration flows have led to particular spatial patterns of inflow and diffusion of ethnical groups, especially impacting urban economies. Existing tendencies of dual labour markets have been reinforced by the massive inflow of lowly qualified foreigners.

The list above indicates that regions are exposed to various forces, some of them continuous (like transport cost improvements), some of them with a shock character: like sudden changes in political systems (Eastern Europe) or changes in the regulatory regime in sectors. In the next section we discuss to what extent such changes may be expected to lead to changes in the relative position of regions.

1.2   Convergence versus Divergence in Regional Systems

When analysing the development of a system of regions in the course of time one can use the following two points of view:
- divergence versus convergence: do the relative differences increase or decrease?
- positive rank correlation versus negative rank correlation: do the relative positions of regions change considerably in the course of time.

Thus, four different cases can be distinguished when one wants to study the relative positions of regions in time (see Table 1.1).

Table 1.1 Change in relative positions of regions

	rank correlation: positive	rank correlation: negative
convergence	I	II
divergence	III	IV

These four cases can be illustrated by means of Figure 1.1. Clearly in reality there can also be intermediate situations (convergence – equal inequality – divergence, and positive – zero – negative correlation). For the sake of simplicity these intermediate cases have been omitted in Table 1.1 and Figure 1.1.

The convergence idea has been strong in the standard stylized model of neoclassical economics (Richardson 1973; Sala-i-Martin 1996).

Changes in all kinds of external conditions will lead to changes in the economic conditions of regions, and may thus in the short run lead to divergence. However, if markets are flexible, interregional trade and interregional mobility of labour and capital will make sure that after the initial turbulence a process of convergence will take place. Indeed, nowadays tendencies can be observed that markets become more flexible: trade barriers tend to become lower, international investments grow rapidly as a consequence of outsourcing strategies, information technology leads to an improvement of the functioning of international markets (Nijkamp 1998).

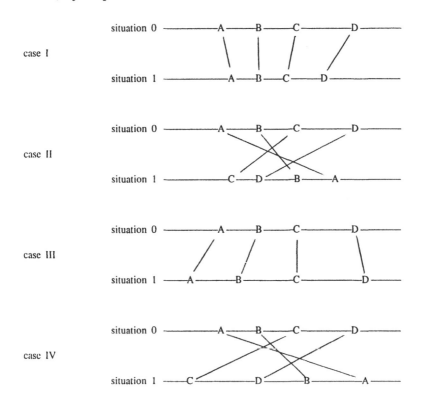

Figure 1.1   Changes in regional positions in a four region system

The divergence case has also a long tradition in regional analysis. For example Myrdal (1957) has formulated the principle of cumulative causation indicating that a small initial advantage of a certain region may bring about a process of cumulative steps taken by the private sector leading to an increasing advantage in the course of time. As long as congestion does not lead to countervailing forces, backwash effects will be dominant. The work of Krugman (1991) although using a different terminology can also be seen in this tradition: economies of scale and agglomeration lead to processes where particular regions are able to become successful producers of certain products. Small advantages or coincidences may play a decisive role in which region will eventually be the winner.

It must be emphasized that the above formulation of the issue of convergence and divergence is stylized. The cases are not as polar as suggested here. Empirical work by for example Kuznets (1955), Williamson (1965) and Ram (1995) leads to the conclusion that in the long run interregional differences tend to follow a pattern of divergence, followed by convergence. The interesting question is of course which mechanisms are behind this and the possible role of long run structural changes in such a switch of regime.

The other dimension concerns the stability of the relative positions of the regions. Of course this depends strongly on the length of the time span considered. It is not difficult to document cases where there have been clear changes in the relative position of regions. For example, certain regions being early in the process of industrial revolution because of presence of raw materials are now depressed regions having difficulties in adjusting to the new situation that these raw materials can easily be imported. And in the very long run of many centuries there have been major shifts in the position of large cities having prime positions in the world economy (see for example Wallerstein 1974).

Nevertheless, it is also clear that despite many structural changes in economies there is a remarkable constancy in the relative positions of cities and regions in spatial systems. This suggests that the development of a region does not only depend on the forces being active, but also on the initial conditions. Some theories have been developed to understand this stability. For example, *evolutionary theories* of development (Nelson and Winter 1982) underline that bounded rationality plays a large role in the behaviour of firms. This creates a tendency that firms attach themselves to fixed routines, not only in their behaviour of product and process innovation, but also of locational choice. The importance of innovation for the long run development of firms means that firms prefer to locate in regions with a workforce and culture that is favourable. Regions with a differentiated production structure are considered to be more attractive than regions with a more monocultural orientation (Jacobs 1984; Lambooy et al. 1997). These factors imply that regions that have already achieved a prominent position may be expected to maintain such a position. This inertia is again reinforced by the favourable infrastructure positions these regions usually have: the infrastructure once supplied to a region given a certain stage of economic development will remain of importance for next stages. This leads to a pattern of path dependence (David 1985, Gifford 1996): once for some possibly rather trivial reason a region has an advantage in infrastructure terms, economic forces will tend to reinforce this initial advantage.

The two dimensions of Table 1.1 are not entirely independent. The theories supporting the divergence view imply that rank correlations are

4

high (case III). It is difficult to find proponents of case IV. In the convergence supporting theories there is not a clear link between the two dimensions, however. The reason is that here the historical aspects do not play such a large role. When in an equilibrium model there is a unique equilibrium the initial conditions do not matter. This means that the convergence oriented theories are rather silent about the relative positions of particular regions in the course of time.

1.3   Themes Covered: Knowledge, Infrastructure, Tourism

In the next section we address some of the themes receiving special attention in this book in more detail.

1.3.1 Innovation and Knowledge

Innovation takes place in various ways (see Table 1.2). The most eye catching form is the introduction of revolutionary new products that may have long run effects on production and consumption patterns. However, in many cases, innovations occur in a much more modest way by means of gradual improvements of existing products that may take place during a rather long period. Another relevant distinction is between technological and non-technological innovations. Technological innovations have a high-tech character and depend strongly on large R&D processes, accordingly. In addition to these technology dominated innovations there are also many innovations that are much more of an organizational character; the R&D component is less important here (cf. Van Langen 1998).

Table 1.2 Classification of innovations

	revolutionary	gradual
high-tech	I	II
low-tech	III	IV

In the past many revolutionary innovations have taken place without a high tech character. Examples are the use of the plough in agriculture, the introduction of larger ships in sea transport, etc. In the 20th century, however, revolutionary innovations tend to have a high tech character (case I). Case III seems to be an exceptional case nowadays. The number of really revolutionary innovations is not so large however. Most R&D efforts are oriented towards gradual improvements of products (case II). In addition to high-tech innovations there are also many low tech innovations, which are often of an organizational character (production of new services based on given technologies).
Large technological institutions and universities tend to dominate the high tech activities. From this angle of the preparation of innovations we observe that there may be substantial regional differences. Present day

5

organization of production implies that R&D and production are often separated. This leads to a differentiation of economic activities that is often not captured in statistical data because these are usually based on the sectoral point of view so that distinctions between activities such as command and control, R&D, production, distribution and service provision remain invisible. Although R&D and production may be spatially separated, this does not mean to say that the economic importance of universities and large technological institutions for a region remains limited to R&D only (see Florax 1993). One of the main advantages of regions with a university is that they have a relatively high share of well qualified persons in the labour force, and also part of the graduate students will look for a job in the same region.

Given the large resources needed for R&D and the risks involved, firms will tend to protect their findings by means of patenting methods. This reduces the speed of diffusion (also in a spatial respect) once the R&D activities have led to successful results. The barriers to diffusion are much smaller in the low-tech part of the innovation field. Here copying may lead to fast adoption of new ideas. Given the low cost and high quality of communication technology nowadays the ultimate bottleneck in diffusion and adoption is no longer the availability of information about new ideas as such, but the flexibility of firms and of the environments in which they operate.

1.3.2 Infrastructure

Transport infrastructure has a very long life time compared with most other capital goods. Therefore, decisions about infrastructure supply potentially have impacts on spatial developments during a very long period. During the last two centuries technology of transport has undergone major changes leading to long run waves: after canals in the first half of the nineteenth century, the following period was dominated by rail; the period after World War II is dominated by highways (see Figure 1.2).

These waves have had clear spatial implications. An interesting aspect of successive infrastructure networks is that they were often duplicating each other. This means that once patterns of interregional trade and communication are given, new infrastructures are primarily built in such a way that existing links are reinforced. An interesting example can be given for the Netherlands. The first canal to allow barges for interurban passenger transport was built between the cities of Amsterdam and Harlem in 1632 (see De Vries 1981; Van der Ham 1989). After it proved to be successful the idea was duplicated by many other cities so that a large network of canals for intercity transport emerged. The first paved road of importance was constructed exactly parallel to the canals. The same holds true for the first railway line (1839), the first telegraph connection (1845), and the first interurban telephone connection (1888). This extreme constancy of location of major innovations in the transport and communication sectors during three centuries underlines that new infrastructure initiatives are often strongly influenced by existing infrastructure networks so that the spatial changes that might potentially be expected from new infrastructure networks is much smaller than is sometimes expected. This implies that major changes in infrastructure networks in many cases lead to a conservation of economic positions so that in this respect we may expect a positive correlation in the economic position of regions in the course of time (see Figure 1.1).

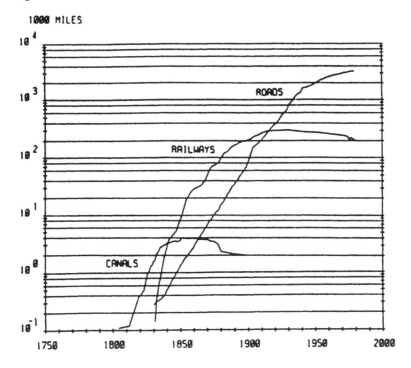

Figure 1.2   Waves in transport infrastructures in the USA

Source: Nakicenovic (1989).

This does not mean to say of course, that nothing changes in the basic form of infrastructure networks. There are examples where infrastructure initiatives have clearly changed the relative positions of cities. For example, the 'New Waterway' giving Rotterdam an adequate link with the North Sea in 1872 has clearly undermined the once dominant economic position of the port of Amsterdam.

Also with respect to the divergence-convergence debate infrastructure networks are important. Even though major changes in infrastructure networks tend to conserve existing patterns they may nevertheless change the opportunities for core and backward regions. An example is given in Chapter 8 where it appears that in the case of economies of scale in production one may expect that a reduction of transport costs leads to opportunities to exploit scale economies implying a trend of concentration of manufacturing production in core regions. However, when transport costs continue to decline one may expect that manufacturing production is shifted to peripheral regions (the lower production costs outweigh the transport costs). Thus we would arrive at a pattern of *polarization reversal*: infrastructure improvements first tend to lead to an increase of interregional inequalities; in a later stage the opposite occurs.

An important aspect of the infrastructure cycles presented in Figure 1.2 is that as infrastructure of a certain type reaches maturity the economic meaning of further expansion tends to get smaller and smaller. In a country that is already well served by a highway network, an addition highway will have limited economic impacts; thus as networks expand, their impacts on economies will become smaller (cf. Rietveld and Bruinsma 1998).

1.3.3 Tourism

One of the structural developments in the present day economies is that people have higher incomes to spend, more time for leisure, and altered attitudes towards work and leisure; in addition the costs of travel have become much smaller. These developments have strongly stimulated tourism as an economic sector (see Van den Borg 1991).

The qualities that enable locations to attract tourists relate to: natural resources, cultural resources, facilities relevant for tourists and climate. These qualities are traded off against the costs of tourist activities, accessibility and travel time.

From the viewpoint of regional inequalities tourism has some interesting features. There is a tendency that underdeveloped regions formerly specializing in agriculture suddenly become attractive as destinations for tourists. A similar point holds true for a good number of older cities that were rather stagnant in the 19th century. Because of their stagnation (no need to remove old buildings) much of their cultural beauty has been retained so that they have become interesting centres for tourism in the second half of the 20th century. Examples are cities like Venice, Bruges and Amsterdam.

Various stages can be distinguished when a region is discovered as an attractive location for tourism (see van der Borg 1991). For urban areas in the initial stage of tourist development day trippers tend to dominate the scene. Their economic impact is limited because day trippers tend to spend limited amounts of money. When sufficient resources are invested in promotion and tourist facilities in a next stage residential tourism (tourists spending more than one day in the city) may take off. This leads to substantially higher expenditures of tourists. Depending on the success of a tourist attraction, capacity constraints may become relevant and tourist activities may start to crowd out other economic activities. For example, large expansion of the tourist sector may claim land and labour that are withdrawn from other activities. This makes clear that the analysis of regional impacts of tourism should not only take into account positive effects via the multiplier chain, but also negative ones.

1.4   Aim and Outline of Book

The aim of this book is to contribute to the understanding of the spatial impacts of structural economic change. Special attention will be paid to implications on spatial equity.

The book starts with four contributions to spatial aspects of the *knowledge economy*. *Nijkamp, Kangasharju and Van Geenhuizen* address the issue of technogenesis and investigate in an exploratory way whether local factors are important for innovativeness of firms. Particular attention is given to the knowledge base of cities. The paper also models effects of relevant local factors on innovativeness of firms by means of logit analysis and a qualitative impact approach based on rough set analysis. Cities in three European countries are considered. The empirical results show that local factors are more important for product than for process innovations. Among more than 20 local factors, the interviewed firms appear to consider support measures for skills training particularly important for innovations. Skills training links with a local university contribute significantly to the propensity to innovate.

Van Geenhuizen explores an evolutionary approach to firm dynamics while using a micro-perspective. Adaptation over time is used as an explanatory background for innovative behaviour (both product and process innovations) and firm survival. The focus of analysis is on mature firms. The findings that emerge from the in-depth study among a small sample of Dutch firms are the conditioning (limiting) impacts of initial product markets and previous innovations on the adoption of new technology, and the negative impact of this path dependency on survival. The paper concludes with a short exploration of the ways in which characteristics of a region may influence path dependency in firm's behaviour.

Shefer and Frenkel discuss the endogenous character of technological change. They hypothesize that for product and process innovations different spatial patterns will be found: the further removed from the centre the lower the rate of product innovation; for process innovations regions in between the centre and the periphery are expected to have the highest rate of innovation. Their empirical research on innovation behaviour of firms in Northern Israel yields that with high tech firms the rate of innovation is indeed positively affected by the degree of urbanization. When the same approach (logit analysis) is applied to traditional firms a less pronounced result is found: even a tendency may exist that the rate of innovation of traditional firms is lower in the large agglomerations. The authors discuss the implications of these results for regional development policies.

Felsenstein examines some of the expenditure and knowledge-based (human capital) impacts associated with Ben Gurion University located in the Southern part of Israel. This university, which is located in a semi-arid and sparsely populated area, has a particular regional development mission. Expenditure impacts on regional output, income and employment are estimated concurrently based on faculty, staff and students expenditures and university procurement patterns. Human capital effects are captured through estimating the present value of future income streams accruing to university graduates who stay on the region upon completion of their studies. Both impacts point to the university as a significant factor in regional economic development.

There are two contributions to the theme of the link between *tourism and regional development*. *Fleischer* discusses the impacts of tourism in rural areas. In several rural regions in Israel depending highly on agriculture, tourist activities have given a welcome contribution to incomes of farmers who became active as suppliers of farm tourism activities. The chapter discusses policy aspects by investigating the impact of so-called tourism incubators who give training to the rural population (mainly farmers). Such schemes seem to be readily adaptable in other national contexts and may give rural regions a push needed for a takeoff of tourist activities.

Freeman and Sultan estimate the contribution of tourism to the Israeli economy and its spatial distribution. Direct, indirect and induced multipliers are computed by means of a multiregional input-output model. The conclusion is that the sum of the value added from indirect output is about 4 percent of GDP, and that from induced impacts is about 7 percent of GDP. Foreign tourism impacts tend to be focused on the central regions. The reverse holds for domestic tourism that tends to favour the peripheral regions.

Infrastructure and regional development is dealt with in two other chapters. *Rietveld and Bruinsma* discuss the impact of road infrastructure on productivity and regional inequalities in Europe. They argue that a promising way to investigate the impact of roads on regional productivity is to use accessibility indicators rather than direct indicators of the road stock in production functions. Highway construction often has clearly visible impacts on economic activity in the corridors concerned; however, the larger share of the effects seem to be relocations of firms in the same region. Impacts of infrastructure construction on accessibilities of European regions are computed; they are relatively small and tend to be dominated by the impact of non-physical border effects.

Shefer and Shefer critically review the literature on transport infrastructure in light of current policies to promote regional development. They review among others the impacts of the Channel Tunnel and of orbital motorways near large metropolitan areas. They conclude that new investments can only be assessed in a regional context, with the consideration of other economic factors, such as the local business climate, relative prices of other factors of production, and concurrent private investment, in order to predict local and regional economic impacts. The authors also point at possible adverse effects of infrastructure construction in peripheral regions: a new transportation link may actually help drain resources out of the region to a more prosperous one.

A final group of papers addresses *modelling and policy* aspects of regional and urban development. *Boomsma* presents estimates of a regional economic model of a peripheral province in the Netherlands. This FREM model has been built for labour market forecasting and simulation purposes on a medium term and aims to produce good forecasts of developments on the regional labour market, given forecasts of the national labour market. FREM simulation results appear to outperform those of a naive random walk model.

Kuiper analyses interregional disparities in the EU in the period between 1950 and 1990. He gives special attention to differences in employment shares of economic sectors in the European regions. The aggregate pattern for the period considered shows a large decrease in the share of the agricultural sector, a rise and decrease of the manufacturing sector and an increase in the service sector. The difference in the employment structure in the top and backward regions in 1950 and 1990 has declined strongly: the employment structures of regions have become more and more similar. Because of possible differences in labour productivity, this convergence of economic structure does not necessarily imply that also regional production per capita has converged. However, the paper gives indications that also differences in regional production per capita have decreased, though at a slower rate.

Atzema addresses diverging developments of Dutch cities and the role of agglomeration economies. He shows that Dutch cities have a slower than average national growth of production, productivity and employment. The main reasons for these differences are changes in the composition of local production structure and the failures of the urban production environment (congestion in road transport and lack of space for expansion). He concludes that agglomeration economies still play a role, but that they have to be considered at a broader spatial level of urban fields. He mentions as a policy implication of these findings that the concept of 'compact city' does not offer the right solution to the current urban economic problems.

References

Bertuglia, C.S., Lombardo, S. and Nijkamp, P. (eds) (1997), *Innovative Behaviour in Space and Time*, Springer, Berlin.

Borg, J. van der (1991), *Tourism and Urban Development*, Tinbergen Institute, Amsterdam.

David, P.A (1986), 'Clio and the economics of QWERTY', *American Economic Review*, vol. 75, pp. 332–37.

Florax, R. (1992), *The University: A Regional Booster*, Avebury, Aldershot.

Gifford, J.L. (1996), 'Complexity, adaptability and flexibility in infrastructure and regional development', in Batten, D.F. and Karlsson, C., *Infrastructure and the Complexity of Economic Development*, Springer, Berlin, pp. 169–86.

Ham, W. van der (1989), *Tot Gerief van de Reiziger; Vier Eeuwen Amsterdam-Haarlem*, SDU, The Hague.

Jacobs, J. (1984), *Cities and Wealth of Nations*, Random House, New York.

Janelle, D.G. (1969), 'Spatial reorganization', *Annals of the Association of American Geographers*, vol. 59, pp. 348–64.

Krugman, P. (1991), *Geography and Trade*, MIT Press, Cambridge, Mass.

Kuznets, S. (1995), 'Economic growth and income inequality', *American Economic Review*, vol 45, pp. 1-28.

Lambooy, J.G., Wever, E. and Atzema, O., *Ruimtelijke Economische Dynamiek*, Coutinho, Bussum.

Langen, P. de (1998), *Innovations in the Freight Transport Sector*, Erasmus University, Rotterdam.

Myrdal, G. (1957), *Economic Theory and Underdeveloped Regions*, Duckworth, London.

Nakicenovic, N. (1989), 'Expanding territories: transport systems past and future', in Batten, D.F. and Thord, R. (eds), *Transportation for the Future*, Springer, Berlin, pp. 113–30.

Nelson, R.R. and Winter, S.G. (1977), *An Evolutionary Theory of Economic Change*, Belnap Press, Cambridge, Mass..

Nijkamp, P. (1989), *De Regio in Het Centrum*, Geoboek, Groningen.

Nijkamp, P. and Rietveld, P. (1987), 'Technological development and regional labour markets', in Fischer, M.M. and Nijkamp, P. (eds), *Regional Labour Markets*, North Holland, Amsterdam, pp. 117–37.

OECD (1997), *Economic Globalization and the Environment*, Paris.

Ram, R. (1995), 'Economic development and income inequality, an overlooked regression constraint', *Economic Development and Cultural Change*, vol. 43, pp. 425–34.

Richardson, H.W. (1973), *Regional Growth Theory*, McMillan, London.

Rietveld, P. and Bruinsma, F. (1998), *Is Transport Infrastructure Effective?*, Springer, Berlin.

Sala-i-Martin, X.X. (1991), 'The clssical approach to convergence analysis', *Economic Journal*, vol. 106, pp. 1019–36.

Vernon, R. (1966), 'International investment and international trade', *Quarterly Journal of Economics*, vol. 80, pp. 225–67.

Vries, J. de (1981), *Barges and Capitalism*, HES, Utrecht.

Wallerstein, I. (1974), *The Modern World-system*, Academic Press, New York.

Williamson, J.G. (1965), 'Regional inequality and the process of national development: a description of the patterns', *Economic Development and Cultural Change*, vol. 13, pp. 3–45.

Part A
Spatial Aspects of Innovation and Knowledge Production

2 Local Opportunities and Innovative Behaviour: A Meta-Analytic Study of European Cities

PETER NIJKAMP, ANDAKI KANGASHARJU AND
MARINA VAN GEENHUIZEN

2.1 The Critical Role of the Urban Milieu

Science and technology are often regarded as competitive weapons of cities or regions. Consequently, the interest in dedicated science and technology initiatives which aim to stimulate urban and regional economies is increasing. The growing role of knowledge in wealth creation at the urban and regional level is more and more recognized (see Van Geenhuizen and Nijkamp 1996a and 1996b; and Gibbons et al. 1994). There is, however, also an increasing awareness that knowledge creation needs specific urban or regional breeding place conditions, and – as a consequence – presently the critical role of urban and regional milieus and cultures in knowledge development is increasingly coming to the fore (see Florax 1992; Van Geenhuizen et al. 1996a and 1996b; and Lambooy 1996).

The above breeding place hypothesis presupposes that the process of knowledge development is not uniformly distributed over space, but is contingent on specific locational and local conditions, which may concern the availability of venture capital, access to advanced communications and transportation infrastructure, presence of research facilities and so forth. Many of these conditions are met in cities (or urban areas), which explains why such areas are prominent places for technological innovation and incubation (see Charles and Howells 1992; Davelaar 1991). In addition, there is the clear tendency that modern industries are becoming, on the one hand, more science-based and knowledge-intensive and, on the other hand, increasingly oriented towards urban areas regarding their management and research function. These areas are able to influence positively their future development, as many business activities in a post-industrial era tend to become sensitive to the urban milieu and urban quality of life. At one level globalization means a levelling of access to new knowledge and technology, such as through the spread of electronic networks and databases. Accordingly, urban areas are losing their advantage of knowledge producing localities. However, on another level particular uncertainties in

15

management and research can only be reduced in specific urban regions with excellent knowledge resources and learning capacity (Amin and Thrift 1994; 'Van Geenhuizen and Van der Knaap 1997; and Kanter 1995). This capacity is based on knowledge that is created and released locally but also on connectivity with sources of knowledge somewhere else in the world. The recent shift to knowledge- based and information-oriented urban areas takes place because of the network externalities, and the abundant knowledge resource and incubation potential of these areas. Thus, knowledge, science and technology are likely to become primary forces driving development towards and orientation to the urban milieu, which is marked by creativity, synergy and innovation (see Camagni 1991).

In a recent study by Van Geenhuizen et al. (1996b) it is argued that the urban knowledge capacity is a major asset in the economic competitive power of cities. This knowledge capacity comprises essential activities in the urban space, leading to several scale and scope advantages, notably (see FAST 1992):

- new research and development (R&D) results (including product innovation)
- new research methods (hardware and software) (including process innovation)
- new dissemination and marketing channels for research products (or innovations)
- new ways of organizing and managing R&D.

In the same FAST document it is argued – and empirically demonstrated on the basis of a large sample of European cities – that the local availability of a knowledge and information pool (e.g. skilled staff and scientists) is critical for the production of new R&D results, followed by availability of land and buildings, local suppliers of equipment, and presence of local financial institutions. A more detailed analysis of the local knowledge and information pool brought to light that several local factors are important here: skilled labour, training support for researchers, presence of libraries, presence of conference facilities, availability of local cooperation partners, local subcontractors and management links with local educational facilities.

In conclusion, modern cities have the opportunity to act as major islands of science-based innovations through the use of local networks offering local economic synergy and through the connectivity with (inter)national information and communication networks. Further empirical evidence on the relevance of the 'local milieu' for future innovations activities of European companies can be found in Traseler et al. (1994). Most notable is the overwhelming importance for European firms of labour market skills and training support regarding all four types of innovation. This is followed by local synergy from suppliers, subcontractors, customers, and universities for product innovations, and connectivity advantages (through telecommunication and transport) regarding other types of innovation.

Clearly, it is also evident that several cities have major deficiencies in the supply of the above success conditions. For example, several firms mention lack of office space as a major bottleneck. Also local support (e.g. contacts with the local public sector and the attitude of local politicians towards the R&D sector) are usually regarded as major impediments (see again FAST 1992). In general, access to local and international transport and telecommunication networks appears to be a top priority urban policy concern. The FAST dossier then concludes that there is need for action.

All cities in the New Europe will have to come to grips with the fact that economic welfare will depend on the establishment of an integrated system of creation and transfer of scientific knowledge as the knowledge content of goods and services is rising. Income opportunities of citizens and the public sector will critically depend on the innovation potential of cities. Enhancing the milieu as a necessary condition for such a potential to materialize becomes a top priority task. It will require a multilevel approach as the milieu is the result of actions by many decision-making units in the private and public sector.

Although it has to be recognized that in particular modern information and communication allow in principle for a rapid diffusion of scientific knowledge, in reality many innovative activities are rather centripetal as far as their invention, development and management is concerned. Consequently, we observe concentration and deconcentration tendencies at the same time. Clearly, improvement of knowledge networks at a wider scale than the metropolitan level would be needed to cope with the problems of peripherality and of the social-geographical exclusion.

2.2 Local Dynamics and Innovativeness

Regional and local dynamics depend to a large extent on entrepreneurial innovation. Besides, intrinsic regional features may affect innovativeness of firms within a given region, in addition to the different engagement of these firms in the development of new technologies and processes. Thus, on the one hand, the region's innovative activity is determined by R&D activity, size, market power, industry, and phase of the 'industry-technology' life-cycle of firms located in the region (see Ormrod 1996 and Love et al. 1996). On the other hand, regional characteristics affect the innovative activity of firms by enhancing or inhibiting the effects of innovative inputs of firms in the region. Davelaar (1991) coins these factors as production structure and 'production milieu' components, respectively. Consequently, firms which are located in different regions, but have identical innovative inputs, may have different innovative outputs resulting in differing innovativeness of regions (see Figure 2.1). According to Camagni

(1991), the local (innovative) milieu may enhance innovativeness and thus growth of firms, if it reduces the intrinsic uncertainty of the innovation process concerned. Clearly, there is a complex array of factors determining local economic dynamics.

A fairly comprehensive analysis of spatial aspects of innovation has been given by Davelaar (1991) who distinguishes four groups of local factors which affect local innovativeness: (A) agglomeration economies which include location economies accruing from the presence of the same industry, and urban economies accruing from the presence of different industries; (B) demography and population structure which refers to local resources of human capital, local customers and size of the local market area; (C) availability of specialized information and intensive communication networks (information infrastructure) also including educational institutes; and (D) social overhead capital (physical and institutional infrastructure) which responds faster to new demand for technological systems in central areas than in the periphery and which requires various local institutions and physical infrastructure (see also Davelaar and Nijkamp 1997). These force fields are mapped out in Figure 2.1. We will translate some of the major linkages from Figure 2.1 in four testable hypotheses in an empirical setting.

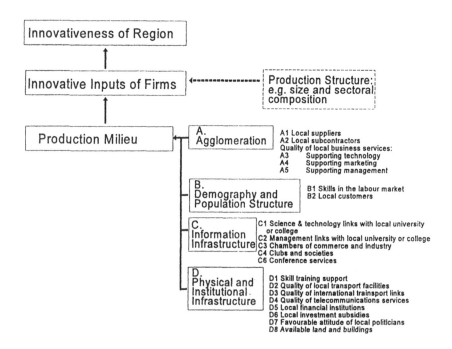

Figure 2.1   Operational variables for the four groups of explanatory local factors (A–D)

18

It needs to be mentioned that the critical role of the so-called 'production milieu' can also be interpreted in a different way. Advocates of the 'innovative milieu' school argue that, in addition to infrastructural factors, human capital, (mainly) informal linkages between firms in a region and synergy effects from a common cultural, psychological and political background are decisive (Camagni 1991). In other words, this school emphasizes more the synergy effects, which promote a collective learning process and reduce dynamic uncertainty, than Davelaar's static local factors, like infrastructure, which reduce transaction costs and produce external economies (see also Gertler 1996 and Harrison 1996).

The importance of local resources of human capital results from the fact that it tends to stimulate local collective learning processes, because labour is more mobile within a region than between regions. Boschma (1994) argues that local education and research facilities contribute to this local accumulation of skills and knowledge, because producers gain when at least part of the costs of job training as well as basic R&D are carried out by such institutions specialized in knowledge acquisition and transfer.

Furthermore, Camagni (1991) emphasizes the importance of informal linkages both between firms and within various economic actors such as firms, employees and institutions. Local formal and informal networks between firms, which are essential in the acquisition of the latest technology, will likely lead to lower information gathering costs. Local institutions are important parts of local networks, because they overcome market imperfections which inhibit innovative behaviour. The development of collective knowledge as well as formal and informal linkages between suppliers of labour, capital and institutions contribute to a regional identity and culture, which may result in a desire for cooperation. According to Camagni (1991), common cultural roots are important in the formation of tacit knowledge in order to understand and use complex messages, and in the formation of commonly accepted beliefs in new products and technologies in a given area.

Our previous observation on the role of uncertainty in innovative behaviour may lead to our first testable hypothesis. Because process innovations enhance the use of existing products, the uncertainty is lower here, and thus the role of local factors tends to be smaller. Therefore, the first hypothesis is:

H1: local factors are more important for product than for process innovations.

It should be noted that in the standard approach to the analysis of technological change, the innovation model has essentially three stages: (i) basic research produces a scientific or technological discovery; (ii) creative firms develop this invention towards a new product; (iii) and existing firms apply this product for commercial use. Through market reactions, successful commercial use has feedback effects on scientific basic research as well as on R&D efforts of firms (see e.g. Kline and Rosenberg 1987). Davelaar (1991) argues that such a change in science and technology leads to major inventions and basic innovations which, together with socio-institutional and economic forces, form a new technological system whose occurrence may be discontinuous in time. Dosi (1988) emphasizes the importance of basic research from the viewpoint that the progress in scientific knowledge widens the pool of potential technological paradigms (or technological systems) from which only a small set of paradigms is actually developed. New technological systems, which happen to emerge, give birth to new technological trajectories or sequences of innovations, along with a swarming process of (new Schumpeterian) firms producing further product and process innovations with a decreasing marginal product. A good example of such a technological regime (or system) is the microelectronics industry which has been built up around such major innovations as the transistor (Boschma 1994). These swarming processes along technological trajectories form life cycles for technologies and industries. In essence, this approach is closely related to the well known spatial product life cycle approach developed by Vernon (1966). When adjustments and innovations within existing systems become rare and marginal, new technological systems or regimes will eventually replace the old ones. Therefore, our second hypothesis is related to this life cycle approach so that economic dynamics is introduced.

At the beginning of an industrial life cycle firms produce numerous early (and often significant) innovations, which are mostly product innovations and which are encouraged by the technological push of a basic scientific invention. Products are then not yet standardized, which means that the uncertainty concerning market reactions is high. Innovations during this phase put specific demands on the surrounding business environment. Information concerning unstandardized products, market reactions and skills on the labour market in terms of producing and developing these new products are important conditions for a successful innovation. In a later stage, when main products within the new industry have been established and when they are becoming more standardized, the role of the business environment may decline. Therefore, our second hypothesis to be tested is:

H2: local factors are more important for a (more innovative) younger than for an (less innovative) older industry.

Clearly, this hypothesis is plausible, because younger industries tend to produce more product innovations than older ones. Local factors are more important for product than process innovations for the reasons mentioned above. In addition, new product innovations tend to become more marginal during the later phases of the industrial life cycle, while process innovations tend to become more wide spread. Product innovations lose importance over time, as they cannot be created endlessly within one and the same technological system. Process

20

innovations will then gradually take over, because when further product innovations are increasingly hard to create and when products become more standardized, firms try to develop better production processes to ensure or enhance their competitiveness. Thus, free market competition is a driving force.

It is of course true that local factors are not equally valuable. And therefore, we will also study more carefully the subset of local factors, which appear to act often as critical success conditions for entrepreneurial innovations. Such a more detailed analysis will be carried out in order to model the effects of this subset of local factors (production milieu) on innovativeness of firms. The impact of the 'production milieu' in empirical research is not always very significant. Davelaar (1991) argues that after controlling for the industrial structure, there is limited evidence for a positive impact of the urban 'milieu' on innovativeness of firms. This statement however, may be questioned and should at least be further investigated and tested. Therefore, the third testable hypothesis in our series is:

H3: the local 'production milieu' has a positive impact on innovativeness of firms in the area concerned.

Having specified three hypotheses to be tested in an applied context, we will now proceed by describing the data base for our empirical work.

2.3   The Data Set: Description and Exploratory Analysis

The hypotheses of our study require information on the micro level of firms. The data set used in our empirical work stems from the so-called URBINNO study[1] and has been compiled by extensively interviewing many manufacturing companies in the United Kingdom (208 firms), the Netherlands (33) and Italy (32). Interviews on a structured basis were held among firms in different manufacturing industries in different cities. For practical reasons, the empirical investigation in our study is mainly concentrated on those industries which have for the sector concerned a sufficient number of observations. These are: manufacturing of machinery and equipment (SIC 29); electrical machinery and apparatus (SIC 31); medical precision and optical instruments, watches and clocks (SIC 33); and motor vehicles, trailers and semitrailers (SIC 34). In addition to these sectors, our empirical investigation is also dealing with two other, aggregate sectors in order to have a sufficiently large data base, viz. textile, clothing and leather industries (SIC 17, 18 and 19 taken together), and basic materials and metal industries (SIC 27 and 28). This seems a plausible approach, because the latter industries are sufficiently close to one another to benefit from the same source of technological development, so that they are likely to live on the same technological trajectory. The urban background of innovative behaviour has been given due attention in the interviews, in the sense that a systematic typology of cities in all the countries concerned is made.

We have adopted the most straightforward measure of innovativeness (see Harrison et al. 1996); innovativeness of industries in a city is measured by calculating the percentage of firms that has adopted an innovation during the past few years. The frequency of these firms is given in Figure 2.2. These results indicate that 39.9 percent of the total of 273 firms mentioned an innovation in the sense defined above. At a two-digit level, industry 34 turned out to be the most innovative, as 77.3 percent of the firms in that industry mentioned an innovation. In contrast, in the industries 27-28 together only 29.0 percent mentioned an innovation, while this figure was even down to 21.1 percent for the firms in the industries 17-19. There are thus quite some variations in outcomes, and it is therefore interesting to seek a spatial bias in these outcomes.

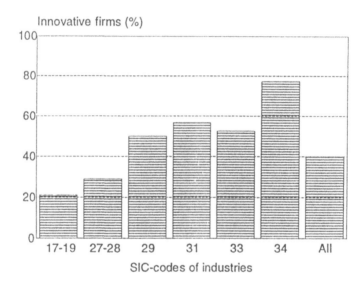

Figure 2.2   Innovativeness of firms by industry class

We will now first present some exploratory results from a descriptive analysis of our data set. To begin with, our two first hypotheses (H_1 and H_2) on the importance of the local 'milieu' will be tested by means of exploratory background variables derived from Davelaar's (1991) classification into four local factors (see for details Figure 2.1 above). The lists of specific local factors under the four headings are examples of factors whose presence will plausibly contribute to the innovativeness of firms in the region. The factors distinguished in Figure 2.1 are the ones included in above mentioned URBINNO questionnaire. Given a set of individual firm data, the importance of local factors for product and process innovations will be tested. Figure 2.3 shows the results for all

22

industries together. This figure includes only those 11 local factors which the respondents considered commonly as valuable factors in terms of either product or process innovations.

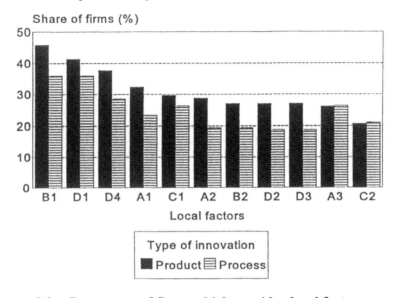

Figure 2.3   Percentage of firms which consider local factors important for innovation

According to the firms surveyed, local factors are more important for product than for process innovations. There are only two exceptions: 'Management links with local university or college' (C2) and 'Quality of local business services supporting technology' (A3) are more important from the point of view of process innovations than from that of product innovations. Hence, our overall results suggest that the firms in our sample behaved in accordance with our first hypothesis (H1). The results also indicate that local skills in the labour market (B1), and local skills training support (D1) are the most important local factors. It appears that 48.6 percent of firms consider skills in the labour market as of 'some importance' or of 'major importance' for product innovations, while 36.1 percent of firms do so for process innovations. The respective numbers concerning training support are 41.4 and 36.1 percent. From an indepth analysis among medium sized firms in the Netherlands it appeared that the strong labour market concern dealt with the following three types of attributes: (1) shortages of certain handicraft skills, (2) shortages in skills to apply modern technology in traditional fields, such as informatics in textile industry, and (3) a general shortage of practical skills of young people who complete vocational and academic training (Van Geenhuizen and Nijkamp 1996a). Clearly the latter two point to a potentially important role of local universities. The quality of telecommunications services (D4), local suppliers (A1) and science and technology links with universities (C1) are the next important factors.

The above results imply that firms can apparently benefit from cooperation with a local university, because certain links with the local university would improve those local breeding place factors which were mentioned most commonly as important among the firms surveyed (see also Van Geenhuizen and Nijkamp 1996b). For instance, the second important local factor, i.e. 'Training links (D1) with local universities', supports the most important local factor, i.e. 'Skills in the labour market' (B1); and a nearly as important factor, viz. 'Science and technology links with university' (C1) enhances knowhow. Both factors would be possible candidates to promote innovativeness of firms. The role of university links of firms for innovativeness will be further examined by using a logit and rough set analysis below in Subsections 2.4.1 and 2.4.2, respectively.

Figure 2.4 presents the results for the selected industries, for example, firms in less innovative industries, SIC 27-28, appear to consider local factors as less valuable than firms in more innovative industry classes (e.g. SIC 34). The results clearly show that the local factors are more important for the more innovative (younger) industries than for the less innovative (older) industries.

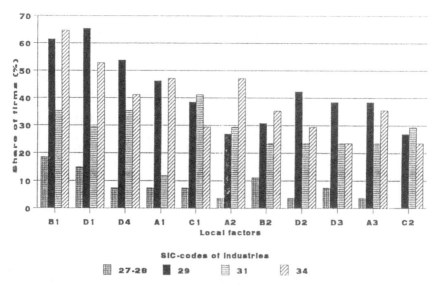

Figure 2.4 **Percentage of firms in different industries which consider a local factor as important for innovation**

Figure 2.5 presents the results for a classification of industries (this classification was made according to industrial innovative behaviour). The black bar represents highly innovative and the bar with streaks low innovative industries (57 percent of firms in the highly innovating industries mentioned an innovation in contrast to only 18 percent of firms in the low innovating industries). Local factors are clearly more often important for highly innovative than for low innovative industries. Therefore, these results indicate that – regardless of the classification used (high or low innovative industry, different industries) – there is a structural tendency that the more firms innovate the more important local factors are. Clearly, these results support our second hypothesis (H_2).

So far we have been investigating how firms in different industries value local factors in terms of innovations. The exploratory analysis did not reveal, however, whether or not local factors actually affect innovativeness of firms, i.e. so far we have not tested our third hypothesis. This is the subject of the next section.

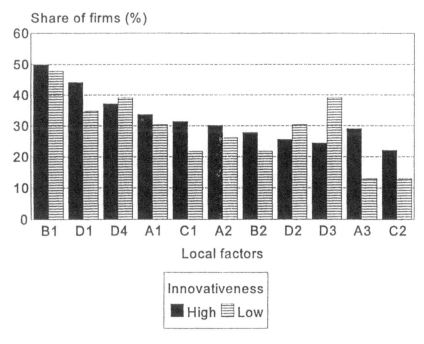

Figure 2.5   Percentage of firms in two categories which consider a local factor as important for innovation

2.4   Explanatory Analysis

2.4.1   *Logit Analysis*

We will now offer an explanatory analysis for the firm's innovative behaviour by applying a logit analysis. We will model innovativeness by industrial and production milieu variables in order to test our second and third hypotheses. Logit analysis cannot be applied to testing of our first hypothesis, because our dataset does not include separate measurable variables for product and process innovations.

In our data set on industrial attributes only 0–1 categorical variables are available. For various modelling purposes we have altogether 13 dummy variables in our data set. In the present context, the most interesting variables are of course industrial and urban 'milieu' variables. Variables which begin with IND... (e.g. IND1719DUM) are dummies for the 6 selected industries. The urban 'milieu' variables mainly represent those local factors, which were commonly found to be important among firms surveyed, viz. various links of firms with local institutions. A variable which begins with LINK... is one of the 3 dummies for the industries which have commercial (LINKCOMM), training (LINKTRAI) or recruitment (LINKRECR) links with a local university or college. The possible impact of commercial (consultancy, testing, subcontracting, joint ventures) and training links is more easily justified than that of recruitment links, because they directly correspond to two commonly and highly valued local factors, viz. 'Skills training support' and 'Science and technology links'. Nevertheless, we do not wish to exclude the dummy for recruitment links a priori. ASSTRAIN is the dummy for firms which have received training assistance from a local (or regional) public sector institution or agency.[2]

We will first model the propensity to innovate by using all 13 dummies which reflect industrial structure, location, or local factors. We will use here Theil's sequential elimination procedure, by discarding one redundant variable at a time from the equation beginning with the most insignificant variable (Theil 1971). This reduction procedure will be continued until only statistically significant regressors are left in the explanatory model.

The above described procedure leads to the statistical results shown in Table 2.1. These results imply that the relatively more innovative (younger) industries contribute significantly to the propensity of a firm to innovate. The less innovative (older) industries do not contribute to the innovation propensity. We recall here that SIC-industries 17-19 and 27-28 are less innovative and that 29, 31, 33, and 34 are more innovative industries. This result was also found in the exploratory analysis.

Training links appear to be positively related to innovativeness, but commercial or recruitment links are not (see Table 2.1). This indicates that at least such local factors as training links with a local university tend to contribute to innovations, a result which partially supports our third hypothesis (H_3). This also complies with the above obtained results that 'milieu' factors, which affect innovativeness of firms, are not equally important. In particular, this result is in line with the previous finding that firms regard skills training support more often as an important local factor inducing innovations than science and technology links (commercial links) or managerial links with the local university. It also turns out that training support from other local or regional institutions is not a statistically significant regressor either. This implies that skills training support offered by a university tends to be more important than that offered by other skills training institutions.

Table 2.1 Innovation as dependent variable in a logit analysis

-2 Log Likelihood: 367.30157 (restricted model)
-2 Log Likelihood: 323.413 (full model)

Variable	B	S.E.
IND29DUM	1.0613	.3427
IND31DUM	1.2892	.4229
IND33DUM	1.2720	.5115
IND34DUM	2.0964	.5507
LINKTRAI	.9312	.2799
Constant	-1.6011	.2635

Note: B=estimated coefficient and S.E.=standard error.

A related question is now for which industries the most important factor, viz. training links, contributes to innovativeness. Also, an important question whether is the other links (commercial and recruitment) contribute to innovativeness in any industry. In other words, we are interested in finding out a possible confirmation for our second hypothesis and further support for our third hypothesis. We can partially test these hypotheses by distinguishing the firms within each industry into two classes, viz. those with a link (LINKTRAIN, LINKCOMME and LINKRECR) and those without a link (LINKTRNO, LINKCONO and LINKRECNO). This subdivision is made for all three links, namely training, commercial and recruitment links. After the model reduction procedure described above the estimation results are given in Table 2.2. This table prompts us to make the following comments on the results.

The firms in the industries 29 and 33 with training links appear to innovate more often than the firms in the other industries with training links and the firms in the same industries without training links (see Table 2.2). This implies that training links are more important for the relatively more innovative (younger) than for less innovative (older) industries, and thus gives partial support to the second hypotheses. In addition, the firms in the industry 31 with commercial links tend to innovate more often than the firms in other industries or in the same industries without commercial links. On the one hand, firms in industry 34 with commercial links appear to be more innovative than firms in other industries with commercial links and firms in the same industry without commercial links. On the other hand, an opposite result is found: firms in industry 34 without commercial links turn out to be more innovative. These results imply that commercial links would not play a decisive role in the motor vehicle industry (34), but would certainly play a role in the electronics industry (31). Nonetheless, this implies that commercial links are also more important for the relatively younger than for older industries, which also renders partial support to the second hypothesis. Also the third hypothesis is partly supported by these results, which indicate that such local factors as training and commercial links with a local university influence the innovativeness of firms.

Table 2.2 Innovation as dependent variable in a logit analysis

–2 Log Likelihood: 367.302 (restricted)		
–2 Log Likelihood: 310.698 (full)		
Variable	B	S.E.
IND33DUM*LINKTRAIN	3.0709	1.0717
IND29DUM*LINKTRAIN	2.4603	.5762
IND34DUM*LINKCOMM	2.1981	.6776
IND34DUM*LINKCOMNO	2.2469	.8177
IND31DUM*LINKCOMM	1.6873	.5708
IND29DUM*LINKRECRU	-1.7174	.8552
Constant	-.9942	.1608

Table 2.2 also shows that firms in industry 29 with recruitment links tend to innovate less often than firms in other industries with such links and firms in the same industry without recruitment links. This does not seem to be the case for other industries. These results tend to suggest that for one of the younger industrial sectors the recruitment links would even have a negative effect on innovativeness, a finding which implies a low importance of recruitment links for innovativeness. Despite the latter observation our statistical results seem to largely confirm our two hypotheses.

2.4.2 Rough Set Analysis

A limitation of the analysis in Subsection 2.4.1 is the large number of categorical (binary) variables. Now we will seek some further evidence for the importance of the production milieu for innovativeness of firms (H_3) by applying rough set analysis. Rough set analysis is a fairly recent classification method of an 'if-then' nature (see e.g. Pawlak 1991; and Slowinski 1993).[3] The analysis classifies objects into equivalence classes using available attributes which act as equivalence relationships for the objects considered. Objects in the same equivalence class are indiscernible (indistinguishable). A class which contains only indispensable equivalence relationships (attributes) is called a core. An attribute is indispensable if the classification of the objects becomes less precise when that attribute is left out. The values of the attributes of all objects may be subdivided into condition (background) and decision (response) attributes.

The aim of rough set analysis is usually first, to classify decision attributes on the basis of condition attributes and second, to form decision rules which are implication relationships between the description of the condition attributes and that of decision attributes. Decision rules can be seen as conditional statements of an 'if-then' nature. Rough set analysis basically evaluates the importance of attributes for a classification of objects, reduces all superfluous objects and attributes, discovers most significant relationships between condition attributes and objects' assignments to decision classes, and represents these relationships e.g. in the form of decision rules (Slowinski and Stefanowski 1993). Rough set analysis is clearly very appropriate in case of qualitative or categorical statements obtained in interviews. Therefore, we will apply rough set analysis for our empirical work on the background factors of innovative behaviour.

In our rough set analysis a total of 273 firms appear to act as indiscernible objects. The decision attribute (dependent variable) here is whether or not a firm has innovated. Our investigation will focus on those condition attributes (local milieu factors) which in the above exploration turned out to be the most important. The condition attributes (explanatory variables) are the following: 1) industry (SIC industries 17–19, 27–28, 29, 31, 33, 34, and the class 'rest'); 2) training links (yes, no); 3) commercial links (yes, no); 4) recruitment links (yes, no) with a local university; and 5) assistance (investment, training, or other) given by a local or regional institution.[4] Production milieu variables (2-5) represent important local factors, i.e., various links of firms with local institutions (see Figure 2.2).

As shown in the first row in Table 2.3, the condition attributes appear to allocate 69 firms to the class 'innovation' and 126 firms to the class 'no innovation' (lower approximations). This means that out of the total of 273 firms, 71.4 percent firms can be classified to either the innovative or the non-innovative category. An interesting rough set result is that all condition attributes turn out to belong to the core. In other words, there are no redundant attributes, which means that an exclusion of one of these features would reduce the accuracy of classification. This result tends to show that both the production milieu and structure are important attributes of innovativeness. With regard to production structure, however, we need to make a restriction. The production structure is only an important attribute when the industry sectors involved are significantly overrepresented in the urban areas under study.

The relative importance of the attributes can be investigated by removing, one at a time, the attributes from the core. The lower rows in Table 2.3 show the number of classifications and the quality (percentage) of classifications when each attribute is excluded in turn. The second row indicates that when the attribute 'Industry' is excluded, the quality of classification is the lowest; then, only 30.4 percent of the firms can be classified. The quality of the classification decreases the least when the attribute 'Recruitment links' is excluded. Then, even 65.6 percent of the firms can still be classified. Although link attributes (milieu variables), namely training, commercial, recruitment and assistance attributes, tend to be less important than the others for the proper classification of the firms in terms of innovativeness, they belong to the core and are necessary for a high quality classification. In other words, the above rough set results clearly indicate that production milieu tends to affect the innovativeness of firms in a region, a finding which supports our third hypothesis (H_3). Thus, we may conclude that also rough set results tend to confirm our prior expectations laid down in three hypotheses.

Table 2.3 Lower approximations for rough set classes

N=273	Innovation	Innovation	Quality of classification
Classification with core attributes			
	69	126	0.714
Classification with a temporarily reduced condition attribute			
Industry	26	57	0.304
Training links	60	104	0.601
Assistance	56	110	0.608
Commercial links	56	112	0.615
Recruitment links	61	118	0.656

2.5   Concluding Comments

Our industrial society is increasingly moving towards a knowledge-based society, characterized by close links with R&D and educational centres. The present study has investigated the importance of local factors on innovativeness. Empirical results on the importance of local factors supported the three main hypotheses specified. The exploratory analysis produced some evidence that local factors are considered as more important for product than for process innovations and that they are more important for more innovative, younger industries than for less innovative, older industries. We also saw that a possible cooperation of firms with a university may incorporate those factors, which were most commonly mentioned as important, viz. skills of the labour force by training links, and science and technology links. The logit analysis revealed that among those links with universities, especially training links tend to promote more innovativeness than commercial or recruitment links, a result which leads to a policy recommendation on the significance of increased schooling and training expenditures. Both rough set and logit analyses produced also some evidence that the production structure of regions is not insignificant, but does certainly not entirely govern the innovativeness of regions, as in particular cases distinct local factors appear to affect innovativeness of firms. This implies that the production 'milieu' component also clearly affects innovativeness of regions. In other words, this calls for actions by local and regional governments to improve the quality of the local business environment.

This analysis had a strong focus on links of firms in European cities with local universities, based upon specific labour market needs. Two factors which also appeared to influence the innovativeness of regions, i.e. local production networks (suppliers, subcontractors and customers) and local connectivity with larger (global) networks (telecommunication and transport links) have received much less attention. It is the interaction of the three factors from a knowledge perspective, which is an interesting field for further research, because it is largely open. The question then is whether the local labour market needs and production network needs are concerned with reduction of uncertainty using locally produced and released knowledge, or – via connectivity – using globally available knowledge (potentially in a specific niche). It would be interesting to scrutinize whether there is a difference between European cities in local self-containment of knowledge production, local conditions to insert global knowledge in the local economy, and the existence of a blend of local and global knowledge, and how this relates to the need of innovative firms for fast adjustment in view of risk and uncertainty. Thus, particularly the relationship between the local and global asks for attention, in terms of mutual dependency and cross-fertilization. In addition, it is increasingly realised that knowledge networks – regarding type and geographical scale – may be different between different (young) sectors and even between product groups within sectors (Storper 1996). Dependent on different demands for local knowledge and access to global knowledge, different urban policies need to be established in European cities.

Acknowledgements

This study was part of a research project funded by the Academy of Finland. The authors wish to thank Tomaso Pompili and Peter Townroe for their assistance in collecting the data.

References

Amin, A. and Thrift, N. (1994), 'Living in the Globe', in Amin, A. and Thrift, N. (eds), *Globalization, Institutions, and Regional Development in Europe*, Oxford University Press, Oxford, pp. 1–22.

Baaijens, S. and Nijkamp, P. (1997), 'Meta-Analytic Methods for Comparative and Exploratory Policy Research', *Journal of Policy Modelling* (forthcoming).

Bergh, van den J.C.J.M, Button, K. Nijkamp, P. and Pepping, G. (1997), *Meta-Analysis for Meso Environmental Policy*, Kluwer, Dordrecht.

Camagni, R. (1991), 'Local 'Milieu', Uncertainty and Innovation Networks: Towards a New Dynamic Theory of Economic Space', in Camagni, R. (ed.), *Innovation Networks: Spatial Perspectives*, Belhaven Press, London and New York, pp. 121–44.

Camagni, R. (1991), 'Local 'Milieu', Uncertainty and Innovation Networks: Towards a New Dynamic Theory of Economic Space', in Camagni, R. (ed.), *Innovation Networks: Spatial Perspectives*, Belhaven Press, London and New York, pp. 121–44.

Charles, D. and Howells, J. (1992), *Technology Transfer in Europe*, Belhaven, London.

Davelaar, E.J. (1991), *Regional Economic Analysis of Innovation and Incubation*, Avebury, Aldershot, UK.

Davelaar, E.J. and Nijkamp, P. (1997), 'Spatial Dispersion of Technological Innovation: A Review', in Bertuglia, C.S., Lombardo, S. and Nijkamp, P. (eds), *Innovative Behaviour in Space & Time*, Springer-Verlag, Berlin.

Dosi, G. (1988), 'The Nature of the Innovative Process', in Dosi, G. et al. (eds), *Technical Change and Economic Theory*, Printer Publishers, London and New York.

FAST (1992), 'The Future of European Cities; The Role of Science and Technology', Dossier no. 4, Commission of the European Communities, DG XII, Brussels.

Florax, R. (1992), *The University: A Regional Booster*, Avebury, Aldershot, UK.

Geenhuizen, M. van, Damman, M. and Nijkamp, P. (1996a), 'The Local Environment as a Supportive Operator in Innovation Diffusion', Research Memorandum 1996-15, Dept. of Economics, Free University, Amsterdam.

Geenhuizen, M. van, and van der Knaap, G.A. (1997), 'R&D and Regional Network Dynamics in the Dutch Pharmaceutical Industry', *Journal of Economic and Social Geography*, vol. 88, no. 4, pp. 307–70.

Geenhuizen, M. and Nijkamp, P. (1996a), 'What Makes the Local Environment Important for High Tech Small Firms', in Oakey, R. (ed.), *New Technology-Based Firms in the 1990s*, vol. II, Paul Chapman, London, pp. 141–51.

Geenhuizen, M. and Nijkamp, P. (1996b), 'Technology Transfer: How to Remove Obstacles in Advancing Employment Growth', in Kuklinski A. (ed.), *Production of Knowledge and the Dignity of Science*, Euroreg, Warsaw, pp. 79–96

Geenhuizen, M. van, Nijkamp, P. and Rijckenberg, H. (1996b), 'Universities as Key Actors in Knowledge-based Economic Growth,

Reserach Memorandum 1996–14', Dept. of Economics, Free University, Amsterdam.

Gertler, M.S. (1995), 'Being There: Proximity, Organization, and Culture in the Development and Adoption of Advanced Manufacturing Technologies', *Economic Geography*, vol. 71, no. 1, pp. 1–26.

Gibbons, M., Limoge, C., Nowotny, H.,Schwartzman, S., Scott, P. and Trow, M. (1994), *The Production of Knowledge: the Dynamics of Science and Research in Contemporary Societies*, Sage, London.

Harrison, B., Kelley, M.R. and Gant, J. (1996), 'Innovative Firm Behavior and Local Milieu: Exploring the Intersection of Agglomeration, Firm Effects, and Technological Change', *Economic Geography*, vol. 72, no. 3, pp. 233–58.

Kangasharju, A. and Nijkamp, P. (1997), 'Innovation Dynamics in Space: Local Actors and Local Factors', Discussion Paper, Tinbergen Institute, Free University of Amsterdam, (forthcoming).

Kanter, R.M. (1995), *World Class: Thriving Locally in a Global Market*, Simon and Schuster, New York.

Kline, S.J. and Rosenberg, N. (1987), 'An Overview of Innovation', in Landau, R. et al. (eds), *The Positive Sum Strategy*, National Academy Press, Washington, DC.

Lambooy, J.G. (1996), 'Knowledge Production Organization and Agglomeration Economies', Research Paper, Economic-Geographical Institute, University of Amsterdam.

Love, J.H., Ashcroft, B. and Dunlop, S. (1996), 'External Ownership, Corporate Structure and Product Innovation', Paper presented at 36th Congress of the European Regional Science Association.

Ormrod, R.O. (1990), 'Local Context and Innovation Diffusion in a Well-Connected World', *Economic Geography*, vol. 66, no. 2, pp. 109–22.

Ratti, R. (1991), 'Small and Medium-sized Enterprises, Local Synergies and Spatial Cycles of Innovation', in Camagni, R. (ed.), *Innovation Networks: Spatial Perspectives*, Belhaven Press, London and New York, pp. 71–88.

Storper, M. (1996), 'Innovation as Collective Action: Conventions, Products and Technologies', *Industrial and Corporate Change*, vol. 5, no. 3, pp. 731–90.

Theil, H. (1971), *Principles of Econometrics*, John Wiley, New York.

Traseler, J., Schubert, U. and Townroe, P.M. (1994), 'R&D Activities in Companies and Universities and their Role in Urban Development, Research Paper Vienna University of Economics and Business Administration.

Vernon, R. (1966), 'International Investment and Institutional Trade in the Product Cycle', *Quarterly Journal of Economics*, vol. 80, pp. 190–207.

Notes

1. The URBINNO group ('Urban Innovation') was a network of researchers in several European countries. The objective of the group was to study innovations in several urban areas from various points of view, viz. population, urban economy, institutions and infrastructure, and from a micro-urban (i.e. firm level) perspective.

2. Due to an incomplete dataset, our logit analysis had to exclude a few indicators on production structure which may be expected to affect the propensity to innovate (such as size, market power and growth rate of a firm).

3. Formally, a rough set is characterized by the feature that it is not possible to tell a priori which objects belong to a given set, although it is in principle possible to identify all objects which may belong to that set (see for details, Van den Bergh et al. 1997, and for several applications, e.g. Baaijens and Nijkamp 1997).

4. The analysis also included variables for areal categories (central, intermediate, and periphery) and competitive edge (innovativeness; cost-effectiveness; and marketing, financing, or other). The results for those variables are given in Kangasharju and Nijkamp (1997).

3 An Evolutionary Approach to Firm Dynamics: Adaptation and Path Dependency

MARINA VAN GEENHUIZEN

3.1 Focus on Mature Firms

Factors affecting innovation and survival of firms have been investigated from a range of different viewpoints. One stream of research has focused on the firms' abilities to act adequately upon technological change as a major determinant of survival. In particular, some studies have noted the emergence of a dominant innovation as a key event affecting the probability of survival (e.g. Suarez and Utterback 1995; Utterback 1994). A different stream of research – based upon resource exchange theory - focuses attention on firms' abilities to gain access to critical resources, such as finance and technical information (e.g. Pfeffer and Salanchik 1978). A related stream of research – population ecology – suggests that varying density (carrying capacity), legitimation and competition play a major role in the survival of organizational populations (Hannan and Carrol 1992; Hannan and Freeman 1989).

While most of the above research has no particular emphasis on newly established firms, spatial research on firm survival has given strong attention to new firm formation and concomitantly, favourable spatial seedbed and growth conditions for young (small) firms (cf. Felsenstein and Schwartz 1993; Keeble and Walker 1994; Keeble and Wever 1986; Reynolds et al. 1994). Within this type of research, there is also a growing literature on the contribution of new firms to create new employment (cf. Cooper 1993; Keeble and Kelly 1986; Oakey 1993; Storey 1994).

Spatial studies have paid much less attention to *mature* firms, to the way (strategies) in which they succeed in surviving and to favourable local (regional) conditions for this survival. However, an understanding of dynamics of mature firms is of prime interest for academics and policy makers because these firms encompass a majority of the stock of firms. For example, in France the segment older than ten years has a share of almost 70 percent (Guesnier 1994). In addition, mature firms are often well-rooted in the local economy and have higher levels of employment than new small firms. Job growth in the small firm segment, on the other hand, is not very impressive and open to debate (cf. Alderman 1996; Oakey 1993).

Mature firms have overcome problems of establishment such as shortage of capital (for financing the start or through-start), shortage of management and marketing experience, and lack of organizational endurance. Thus, by focusing on mature firms 'turbulence' caused by new establishments is avoided in the analysis. Accordingly, the analysis can be confined to medium- and long-term structural dynamics linked with new technology.

While the emphasis in much research is on the level of populations of firms, studies that focus on individual firms and connect individually varying influences over time with survival, are scarce. However, the latter type of study is now increasing in popularity because it may shed a different (complementary) light on causal factors (e.g. Alderman 1996; Beyers and Lindahl 1997; van Geenhuizen 1993; Vaessen 1993). The analysis here will focus on individual firms.

3.2   Evolutionary Views on Firm Dynamics

Evolutionary approaches (Nelson and Winter 1982; Dosi and Nelson 1994; Silverberg et al. 1988) seem rather useful in the analysis of the development of firms on the individual level. These approaches seek to explain the movement of an entity (or entities) over time, and the causes of the state of an entity at a moment in time in terms of how this entity got there. In addition, the explanation includes both random elements which generate some variation in the characteristics in question and mechanisms that systematically confirm existing variation.

Thoughts on evolutionary economics have increased in popularity in the past decade. While major steps haven been taken by Nelson and Winter in the early 1980s, there is currently an increase in the pace of advancement in evolutionary thinking and its application (cf. Baaij 1996; Cimoli and Dosi 1995; Dosi and Nelson 1994; Hodgson 1995; Metcalfe 1995; Schamp 1996). The current wave of evolutionary theorizing is fostered by various converging factors (Dosi and Nelson 1994), such as the recognition of the difficulties of equilibrium theory – and the concept of perfectly rational actors – in the interpretation of wide fields of economic behaviour, the providing of useful heuristics for applied research, and the contribution of applied research to fruitful inductive generalizations from which evolutionary theory can draw behavioural assumptions. In addition, evolutionary theories of dynamic systems allow for the analysis of various forms of non-linearity.

Evolutionary economic approaches provide the following important notions, more or less in analogy with evolutionary biology (Arthur 1994; Dosi and Nelson 1994; Metcalfe and Gibbons 1986; Nelson and Winter 1982):

- *Firms* embody the units of selection (equivalents of genes) such as technologies, strategies, inherent preferences, etc. They are subject to various types of selection with the market as the single most important *selection environment*. In addition, there are selection environments such as institutions (e.g. government regulation). Competition is the major mechanism of selection, but its strength varies between economic sectors and markets over time (de Jong 1985). There is competition with regard to access to scarce resources (Pfeffer and Salanchik 1978) and market share. Threats and opportunities emerge from the activity of suppliers, customers, and new entrants, as well as the emergence of substitute products and new technologies (Porter 1985). Although evolutionary approaches are not explicit in this respect, competition leads to closure of weak performing firms through two mechanisms, i.e. failure (bankruptcy) and acquisition by stronger firms. Different from Darwinian biology, the survival of strong units does not rest on mutation by chance but on a more or less active *adaptation* to the environment.

Fitness is the extent to which firms interactively adapt themselves to the multiple selection environments. The process of adaptation to the environment is largely directed by *routines*, i.e. forms of rule-guided behaviour that are largely invariant to fine changes in the environment. Thus, routines function as stable carriers for knowledge and experience. They are based upon the learning history of the firm and pre-existing knowledge and are associated with *incremental* adjustments, i.e. close to pre-existing patterns. This means that firms' behaviour is largely *path-dependent*. Path dependency is the situation in which it is difficult to abandon once selected technologies or product markets, based upon an accumulation of experience, routines (and networks) and capital in previous times. In other words, increasing returns from a previously chosen behaviour makes withdrawal from this behaviour unlikely. In circumstances that are significantly new, however, firms are able to experiment and discover novel behaviour (including imperfect adaptation and discoveries from failure). This brings the focus of some evolutionary approaches on learning as a key capability of firms, and on the role of regional networks in learning (cf. Camagni 1991; Cimoli and Dosi 1995; Malerba 1992; Storper 1993). *Stress* arises when changes in the environment are occurring too fast for a timely adaptation, or when firms undertake too many adaptations at the same time (multiple change) (van Geenhuizen and Nijkamp 1996). Stress may be evident in uncoordinated behaviour.

Although not accepted in all strands of evolutionary thinking, some evolutionary models emphasize that particular firms look forward to anticipate future developments, while other firms do not (Silverberg et al. 1988). Accordingly, there are offensive firms (breaking new ground) and defensive firms. A similar typology is recognized in theories about innovative behaviour (Freeman 1982; Porter 1985), i.e. first innovators, and followers and non-innovators. First innovators aim to maintain a lead over innovative competitors. This strategy is costly in terms of research efforts and risky in that the technology can fail or be overruled by a superior, adapted, new technology, but profits may be high in the first periods (Olleros 1986). The point here is the recognition of *diversity* between firms in capability and preferences for various adaptation (Silverberg et al. 1988). In major strands of ecological thinking a large variety within a population is thought to be advantageous to survival compared with a small variety. A large variety, for example, makes the population less vulnerable to specific shocks in the environment.

The question to be answered in this *exploratory* analysis is how subsequent adaptations in the past have had a decisive influence on innovative behaviour and survival of firms. Two manufacturing sectors are included in this retrospective analysis, namely the textile industry and the pharmaceutical industry. The empirical results are based on 14 indepth case studies drawn from a larger sample of 100 firms (van Geenhuizen 1993). Interviews with corporate managers and desk research (company documents, branch publications) constitute the main information sources in these indepth case studies. The analysis covers the years between 1950 and 1993, in order to depict structural dynamics.

3.3   Product and Process Technology

3.3.1 Textile Industry

This section focuses on the adoption of technical textiles and the process of tufting (the latter mainly in the carpet industry). Technical textiles were introduced in the Netherlands in the late 1950s in connection with various new types of fibre. Technical textiles include transport fabrics (such as for safety belts), geo-textiles (for road-bed stabilization and banks), technical apparel resistant to specific hazards (heat, chemicals), and leisure fabrics and materials (such as for boats). Technical textiles can be regarded as relatively radical innovations because totally different markets are involved compared with traditional textiles. Tufting was introduced in the Dutch carpet industry in 1958. The process of tufting is different from weaving in that the carpet piles are stitched onto a base and then fixed with a latex backing. Since the 1960s, due to greater labour productivity compared with weaving, tufted carpets became much cheaper than similar woven qualities. As a result, tufted floor coverings came within easy reach of mass consumption. Tufting is therefore, considered as an important process innovation (Toyne 1984). Together with a growing market demand since the 1960s (increased prosperity and a massive housing construction), tufting created a tremendous growth in the carpet industry (van Geenhuizen and van der Knaap 1994).

Table 3.1 summarizes the adaptations of four companies as far as the introduction of advanced technical textiles is concerned.

Table 3.1 Previous adaptation and adoption of advanced technical textiles

Case study 1

1950	Main product: Interior textiles
From 1957	Increased market penetration for interior textiles
1969	Merger (production of cotton prints added)
1975-1984	Further growth in interior textiles (carpets, curtains)
1984	Forward integration in interior textiles (retailing)
	Occasional attention for technical textiles
1985	Persistent growth in interior textiles and high segment consumer textiles (increasingly abroad).

Case study 2

1950	Main product: Garment cloth
1957	Merger
From 1957	Development of new technical textiles
1960	Adoption and creation of new fibres, partially by joint ventures abroad
1969	Product development in advanced technical textiles
1976-1978	Withdrawal from spinning, stepwise withdrawal from weaving
1980	Persistent growth in advanced technical textiles
	Diversification beyond textiles (synthetic products)
1991	Withdrawal from consumer textiles.

Case study 3

1950	Main product: Garment cloth and interior textiles
1960	Merger (aimed at cost reduction in spinning and weaving)
1970	Growth by related activities (e.g. textile services)
	Reduction of spinning and weaving
From 1972	Product development (advanced interior textiles, i.e. sun blinds) and development of an advanced finishing process for interior textiles
1975-1976	Withdrawal from spinning
1984	Adoption of advanced technical textiles (i.e. by acquisition)
1987	Withdrawal from technical textiles and renewed focus on interior textiles

Case study 4

1950	Main product: Garment cloth and blankets
1975	Merger (aimed at cost reduction in weaving)
1978	Withdrawal from merger
1982	Management buy-out
1982	Transition to advanced technical fabrics (airplanes) and small flexible organization

The paths represent three different patterns, i.e. no strong attention for technical textiles or only a temporary attention (illustrated by Case study 1 and Case study 3), an early adoption (Case study 2), and a late adoption (Case study 4). These patterns are connected with a diverse adaptation of the firms in previous years and concomitant different pressure from competition. Since the early 1970s various firms shifted to a successful production of upgraded interior-textiles and printed and finished fabrics (Case study 1 and 3). At that time the markets were clearly growth markets, in such a way that the firms involved had no reason to move to a new direction.

By contrast, other firms were less successfully spinning and weaving for the highly competitive market of garment cloth and adopted the strategy of cost reduction, being most evident in mergers aimed at scale economies. Many of these firms, however, were forced to close down given persistently high production costs and a modest design, compared with e.g. Italian fabric (van Geenhuizen and van der Knaap 1994). Some firms made an early and successful shift to technical textiles and could survive (illustrated by Case study 2). Thus, previous activity in particular product markets largely explains the diverse adoption of technical textiles. Case study 4 is special because it represents dramatic attempts to enhance the survival of the weaving industry by merging, with strong financial support from the Dutch government. Such mergers aimed essentially at achieving economies of scale, not at product innovation, and were as such clear signs of *path dependency* of the firms involved. Most such projects failed after a couple of years leading to liquidation. In a few cases, however, a management buy-out could force them to open the road to technical textiles, mostly in niche markets (Case study 4).

In the adoption of tufting, a different access to resources has caused a differentiation in adoption time of this technology. In the small firm segment the adoption included an important shift in products, namely from hard floor covering (sisal and coir) to soft covering (wool and synthetics). This comprehensive (and radical) change reinforced a wait-and-see policy and concomitant late adoption as illustrated by Case studies 5 and 7 (Table 3.2). A further cause of late adoption was the previous introduction of product improvement and new product technology in areas outside the one of tufting. In other words, there was no pressing need for the adoption of tufting, or there were no resources available at that time due to previous innovations. By contrast, larger firms – usually better endowed with resources – tended to be early adopters of tufting (Case studies 8 and 9).

Interestingly enough, in the years following the adoption of tufting the 'small' tufters have developed strong subcontracting relationships within the region of location, in such a way that they could benefit from various externalities. In this situation they were able to increase their capability to innovate later in time.

Table 3.2 Previous adaptation and the adoption of tufting

Case study 5

1950	Main product: Mats (carpets) of coir (small scale)
1970	Major product improvement (PVC backing of coir mats)
1976	Adoption of tufting of soft floor covering (in 1973 in cooperation with another local factory)
1980	Upgrading of the product quality of tufted floor covering

Case study 6

1950	Main products: Mats (carpets) of coir and sisal (small scale)
1969	Adoption of tufting of soft floor covering
1974	Additional specialization in carpet backing and dying by contrast of other carpet manufacturers
1986	Adoption of tufting of synthetic grass

Case study 7

1950	Main products: Mats (carpets) of coir (small scale)
1967	Adoption of product technology of needle-felt
1972	Adoption of tufting of soft floor covering
1985	Product differentiation of needle-felt
1989	Upgrading of the product quality of tufted floor covering.

Case study 8

1950	Main product: High-quality woven carpets and furniture coverings (large scale)
1965	Adoption of tufting of carpets and floor covering
1972	Expansion of manufacturing and sales organization abroad
1977	Closing down of weaving department and major contraction
1982	Liquidation.

Case study 9

1950	Main product: High-quality woven carpets (large scale)
1963	Adoption of tufting of carpets and floor coverings
1965	Expansion by means of various take-overs (in Belgium)
1975/6	Adoption of new dying technology (within a joint venture)
1981	Generation of new product technology of synthetic grass (for sports grounds)

3.3.2 Pharmaceutical Industry

This section pays attention to the changing level of innovation over time, as apparent from an output indicator (number of patents granted)

(Note 1). New product technology is the single most important basis for competition in the innovative pharmaceutical industry (van Geenhuizen and van der Knaap 1997). A relatively tight *government regulation* has, however, caused various unfavourable conditions for basic innovation as a tool in competition. The market for prescription drugs is strongly regulated by patent protection and registration procedures for new drugs on the supply side, and policies for prescription and reimbursement of drugs on the demand side (van Geenhuizen and van der Knaap 1997; Howells 1992). First, the effective period of protection – in which profits are gained as return on R&D investment – has decreased significantly in the Netherlands, from about thirteen years around 1965 to five years in the late 1980s (van Geenhuizen and van der Knaap 1997). Secondly, government measures have advanced the production of generic drugs in order to reduce the costs of healthcare services. Generic drugs are relatively low priced, chemically identical copies of drugs for which the patent period has expired, often produced by other manufacturers than the basically innovative ones. Thus, the selection environment of regulation has put a high burden on the continuation of basic innovation. In addition to this, R&D expenses and risks in basic research have increased significantly since the early 1970s, due to the depletion of existing research areas and opening of (entirely) new ones, among others in biotechnology.

Figure 3.1 indicates different paths of innovative behaviour under the above unfavourable conditions. The first path – a sustained high level – is exemplified by Case study 10. The patent history of this particular case is dominated by penicillin and antibiotics, and to a smaller extent by steroids. Medium sized firms like this one could maintain a high level of innovation by advanced in-house research and various R&D networks on a global scale, as well as withdrawing from non-core activities since the early 1980s. Other medium sized firms joined a multinational in order to take risks in basic research and to generate benefits from economies of scale and scope. By contrast, a number of medium sized firms suffered from shortsightedness due to success from current products, and consequently, had difficulties in catching-up in high R&D efforts. The latter development – clearly a negative example of path dependency – can be illustrated with Case study 11. Such firms often moved to a broad diversification, sometimes leading to a weakening of the firms' coherence and knowledge base (Hill and Hansen 1991). A third path – a small number of patents clustered in time – is associated with small specialized companies, with R&D and innovation only in one narrow field (Case study 12).

Aside from the above development paths, there is one in which basic product innovation plays no role at all. Firms of this category produce mostly generic drugs, OTC-medicines, or standardized compounds.

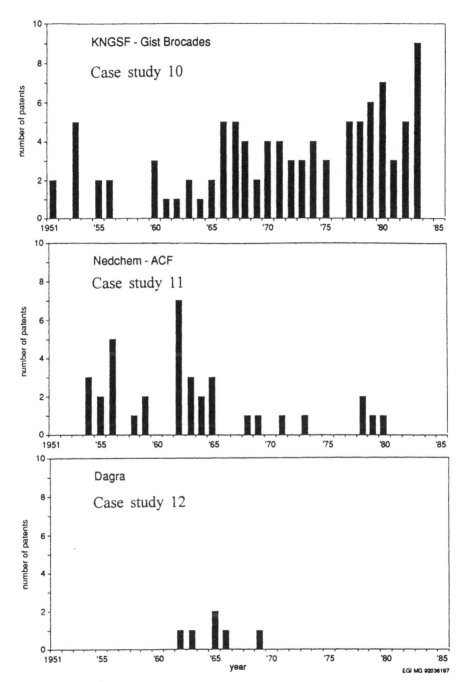

Figure 3.1   Patent histories

Source: Public Register of the Dutch Patent Office.

This pattern is often associated with the origin of the firms as trade companies in the years following the second world-war, e.g. aimed at importing American war surplus. A subsequent smooth shift to manufacturing was only possible by focusing on generics and OTC-drugs, being associated with relatively small risks. This behaviour clearly illustrates path dependency.

3.4   Firm Failure

This section first explores firm failure based on a concise survey of empirical studies. Most studies are concerned with start-up firms, but some with mature firms (Table 3.3) (see also, Alderman 1996). This part is followed by a discussion of case study evidence.

Studies indicate first of all the importance of age. The probability of failure is relatively large in the first two years, followed by a decrease (cf. Audretch 1991; Ekamper 1995; Freeman et al. 1983). However, in the small firm segment, the probability of failure tends to increase again at the age when the entrepreneur is about to end his career and needs to be succeeded (at firm ages between 20 and 35 years) (Ekamper 1995). The literature also points to exit barriers and to economic sector and ownership characteristics as important factors. For example, there seems to be a negative influence of multinational ownership on the probability of survival. With regard to individual sites of multi-sited firms, characteristics like relative size, product range, and technological level seem to affect survival. Further, the presence of R&D and design activities seems to have a positive impact. A final factor to be mentioned here is managerial choice. This seems to be a powerful influence in connection with the emergence of a new technology, particularly in fast changing industries (Christensen et al. 1996).

The previous analysis indicates that most studies have linked the probability of survival (failure) to structural characteristics of firms. Only a few have linked this to past adaptations such as innovative behaviour. The latter dynamic perspective is used in the remaining section, including case studies that represent offensive firms (early adopter of new technology), defensive firms (non-adopter of new technology), and fast growing firms with multiple adaptation (Table 3.4).

Case study 8 illustrates an early adoption of new technology, under the specific circumstance of a lack of focus on this technology. This pattern is often based on path dependency when firms are quite successful in using an old technology. In this particular case, the lack of focus on tufting is apparent in the expansion of the weaving department. Strategies like these cause a large claim on resources aside from the new technology, as well as a loss of potentially high profits from this technology. Such outcomes may then be followed by an uncoordinated search behaviour and a simultaneous adoption of different strategies. Case study 13 also illustrates the phenomenon of under-estimation of a new technology at the time of successful manufacturing based upon an older technology. In this particular case of path dependency, the firm remained producing high quality woven carpet and floor covering and refused to introduce tufting. A further cause of failure has been the late move to a market niche (air planes). Late innovation seems difficult to sustain if at the same time other circumstances grow worse, such as bad luck in the operation of a production subsidiary abroad.

Table 3.3 Factors influencing survival/failure of mature firms

Factor (authors)	Comment
Age (Ekamper 1995)	Lower propensity for survival at the age when the owner-entrepreneur ends his/her career.
Ownership (Dunne et al. 1985)	Small dependent firms have a lower probability of survival than small independent firms. Large dependent firms have a higher probability for survival than large independent firms.
Ownership (O'Farrel & Crouchley 1983)	Multinationally-owned firms have a higher propensity for closure than Irish owned firms (Ireland).
Exit barriers (Clarke & Wrigley 1995)	Among multi-plant firms high levels of sunken costs may prevent closure of less profitable plants.
Sector (O'Farrel & Crouchley 1983)	Firms in clothing and textiles have a high propensity for failure.
Size (Christensen et al. 1996)	For larger firms the probability of failure is reduced.
Size and product-range, and technological level (Fothergill & Guy 1990)	In multi-site firms decisions for closure of individual sites tend to be related to inappropriate size, less important products and less technological sophistication of these sites.
Innovative activity (Alderman 1996)	Product development processes may have a positive influence on site survival in multi-site firms.
Managerial choice and new technology (Christensen et al. 1996; Olleros 1986)	Firms that incorporate key elements of a dominant product design have a larger probability of survival than others. First innovators face a high probability of closure.

Source: Among others Alderman (1996).

As far as the adoption time of a technology is concerned, it is difficult to generalize about the right time in view of survival. It appears that an early adoption is only advantageous within a limited period, namely just prior to the emergence of a dominant design (Christensen et al. 1996). Accordingly, adoption time as a factor affecting survival needs to be considered in relation to the development of the specific technology at hand.

Table 3.4 Previous adaptation connected with failure

Case study 8 (extended version)

1960	Large scale manufacturing (weaving) of high-quality carpets and furniture covering
1965	Adoption of tufting of carpets and floor covering
1969-1971	Expansion of weaving department
1972	Acquisition of former joint venture (abroad)
	Expansion of sales organization abroad
1973-1974	Adoption of different strategies (markets)
1977	Closing down of weaving department and major contraction
1982	Liquidation.

Case study 13

1960	Medium scale manufacturing (weaving) of high quality woollen carpets, and coir and sisal floor covering
1968	Withdrawal from coir and sisal products
	Increased sales of woollen carpets abroad
From 1970	A further move to innovative manufacturing of top quality woven carpets and covering
	Increased sales in West Germany and the US
1975	Acquired by Irish carpet manufacturer as a 'bridge' towards Europe (sales channels)
1984-1989	Manufacturing abroad (acquisition in the US)
1985	Move towards market niche for high quality carpets & covering
1989	Withdrawal by mother company
1990	Liquidation.

Case study 14

1970	Manufacturing of generic (OTC) drugs and trade (wholesale and retail) activities
1977	Expansion in manufacturing of generic drugs and wholesale trade (including dental products, hardware and software)
1985	Penetration of foreign markets with manufacturing of generics and trade activities abroad (US and UK) through acquisition and alliances
1991	Withdrawal from manufacturing and trade abroad
1993	Liquidation.

Case study 14 illustrates a firm adaptation that often occurs in growth markets. Generic drugs exemplify a growth market since the Dutch government started to advance the prescription (and reimbursement) of generic drugs in the early 1980s. Various fast growing firms in this market extended different activities at the same time, such as wholesale and retail activity, and manufacturing and trade abroad. However, without a sufficient increase in resources, and organizational capability and learning to master change, such an accumulation of changes puts too heavy a burden on firms, with bankruptcy as a likely result.

3.5   Concluding Remarks

The analysis has brought to light various forms of path dependency that influence innovative behaviour, such as based upon success in previously chosen product-markets and innovations, and based upon previous mergers within a cost reduction policy. These previous developments have an impact on the pressure (need) for later innovation, the fit of new innovations (technology and markets) to the existing product range, and resources available for later innovation. The findings in this analysis underline a highly differentiated adoption of product and process innovation, with sometimes different outcomes under specific conditions (including sector, firm size and ownership), as shown by earlier empirical work (e.g. Davies 1979). Within this context, particular types of path dependency have a negative influence on survival. This appeared to be associated with an early adoption of crucial technology but lack of focus on this technology and with non-adoption of crucial technology. In addition, the phenomenon of multiple change appeared to be a danger for survival. Thus, it has been shown that particular adaptations are important in determining the subsequent development of firms.

Up to this point, the analysis has been largely qualitative. What is necessary in followup research is to derive conclusions on a *quantitative* basis for a population of firms. For example, it would be of interest to assess the probability of firm failure for non-adopters for various years after the first introduction of the innovation in the market. Clearly, such analysis needs to take into account a combination of subsequent adaptation and their time, such as (in one of the previous case studies) a non-adoption of new technology followed by a relative late move to a market niche. Analysis like this can make use of *event-history* methods, including the concepts of hazard function and conditional transition probabilities (e.g. Hannan and Tuma 1985; Hannan and Freeman 1989).

A further interesting research avenue would be to compare path dependency of firms in the same sector and technology but located in *different regions*. One may argue that in principle all regional economies growing on the basis of a specific new technology and concomitant resources, tend to develop path dependency. Such a development seems rooted in agglomeration economies, being the spatial equivalent of the phenomenon of dynamic increasing returns from an increased use of new technology (Boschma and Lambooy 1997). Spatial clustering of (dis)similar firms leads to an improved production milieu (e.g. cost savings from proximity and new infrastructure investments) and this in turn, attracts more firms connected with the specific technology and resources. However, there are enough reasons to suppose that regions may differ in conditions that shape path dependency of firms over the years, particularly when older technologies need to compete with new ones. This section will conclude with some speculative thoughts on such conditions with a particular emphasis on information flows from an organizational (institutional) perspective.

Information flows are important in the learning of firms, as is their capacity to absorb this information and translate it into adequate strategic decisions and action. The following (spatial) conditions are considered to be associated with formal and hierarchically controlled information flows: a dominance of homogeneous, vertically integrated firms, and a culture of formal contact networks (Grabher 1993; Maillat et al. 1997; Saxenian 1994). In addition, a segmented and corporatist milieu with an emphasis on the defence of individual interests, is considered relevant in this context. The resulting one-sided information and slow information circulation are seen as causes of *reinforcing* path dependency (enhancing 'lock-in'). By contrast, a dominance of small and medium sized firms operating in flexible subcontracting networks, and the presence of a collective learning process within a partnership approach are accompanied with an inherent *alertness* (producing early warning signals), as well as diversified and easy circulating information.

It would be interesting to compare adaptation paths of populations of firms in a sector with competing old and new technology, located in regions that contrast according to the above dimensions. A main hypothesis would be that path dependency – as apparent for example, from cost-oriented mergers and non-adoption – is stronger in regions with one-sided and slow information flows compared with regions with diversified and fast information flows. It is, however, needless to say that such comparative research asks for a careful selection of regions, and a high level of standardization of operationalizations and data collecting on firms' adaptations over time.

References

Alderman, N. (1996), 'Innovation and Survival Amongst Mature Establishments in the Mechanical Engineering Industry', *Geoforum*, vol. 27, no. 4, pp. 461–77.

Arthur, W.B. (1994), *Increasing Returns and Path Dependency in the Economy*, University of Michigan Press.

Audretsch, D.B. (1991), 'New Firm Survival and the Technological Regime', *Review of Economics and Statistics*, vol. 75, pp. 441–50.

Baaij, M.G. (1996), *Evolutionary Strategic Management. Firm and Environment, Performance over Time*, PhD dissertation. University Nijenrode, Eburon Publishers, Delft.

Beijers, W.B. and Lindahl, D.P. (1997), 'Strategic Behaviour and Development Sequences in Producer Service Business', *Environment and Planning A*, vol. 29, pp. 887–912.

Boschma, R. and Lambooy, J. (1997), 'New Variety and Adjustment of the Spatial Matrix of Regions', RSA Nederland Conference, Utrecht.

Camagni, R. (ed.) (1991), *Innovation Networks: Spatial Perspectives*, Belhaven Press, London.

Christensen, C.M., Suarez, F.F. and Utterback, J.M. (1996), *Strategies for Survival in Fast-Changing Industries*, MIT, Cambridge, MA.

Cimoli, M. and Dosi, G. (1995), 'Technological Paradigms, Patterns of Learning and Development: An Introductory Roadmap', *Journal of Evolutionary Economics*, vol. 5, pp. 243–68.

Cooper, A.C. (1993), 'Challenges in Predicting New Firm Performance', *Journal of Business Venturing*, vol. 8, pp. 241–53.

Davies, S. 1(979), *The Diffusion of Process Innovations*, Cambridge University Press, Cambridge.

Dosi, G. and Nelson, R.R. (1994), 'An Introduction to Evolutionary Theories in Economics', *Journal of Evolutionary Economics*, vol. 4, pp. 153–72.

Ekamper, P. (1995), 'Opheffing van Bedrijfsvestigingen: Een Sterftetafel-benadering', *Planning: Methodiek en Toepassing*.

Felsenstein, D. and Schwartz, D. (1993), 'Constraints to Small Business Development Across the Life Cycle: Some Evidence from Peripheral Areas in Israel', *Entrepreneurship & Regional Development*, vol. 5, pp. 227–45.

Freeman, C. (1982), *The Economics of Innovation*, MIT Press, Cambridge, MA.

Freeman, J., Carrol, G.R. and Hannan, M.T. (1983), 'The Liability of Newness: Age Dependency in Organisational Death Rates', *American Sociological Review*, vol. 48, pp. 692–710.

Geenhuizen, M.S. van. (1993), 'A Longitudinal Analysis of the Growth of Firms. The Case of The Netherlands', PhD Thesis, Erasmus University, Rotterdam.

Geenhuizen, M. van, and Knaap, G.A. van der (1994), 'Dutch Textile Industry in a Global Economy', *Regional Studies*, vol. 28, pp. 695–711.

Geenhuizen, M. van, and Knaap, G.A. van der (1997), 'Dynamics of R&D and Regional Networks in the Dutch Pharmaceutical Industry', *Journal of Social and Economic Geography*, vol. 88, pp. 307–20.

Geenhuizen, M. van, and Nijkamp, P. (1996), 'What makes the Local Environment Important for High Tech Small Firms?', in Oakey, R.P. (ed.), *New Technology-based Firms in the 1990s, Volume II*, Paul Chapman, London, pp. 141–51.

Grabher, G. (1993), 'Rediscovering the Social in the Economics of Interfirm Relations', in Grabher, G. (ed.), *The Embedded Firm. On the Socioeconomics of Industrial Networks*, Routledge, London, pp. 1–31.

Guesnier, B. (1994), 'Regional Variations in New Firm Formation in France', *Regional Studies*, vol. 28, pp. 347–58.

Hannan, M.T. and Freeman, J. (1989), *Organizational Ecology*, Harvard University Press, Cambridge, MA.

Hannan, M.T. and Tuma. N.B. (1985), 'Dynamic Analysis of Qualitative Variables: Applications to Organizational Demography', in Nijkamp, P., Leitner, H. and Wrigley, N. (eds), *Measuring the Unmeasurable*, Dordrecht: Kluwer, Dordrecht, pp. 629–61.

Hannan, M.T. and Carroll, G.R. (1992), *Dynamics of Organizational Populations: Density, Legitimation and Competition*, Oxford University Press, New York.

Hill, C.W.L. and Hansen, G.S. (1991), 'A Longitudinal Study of the Cause and Consequences of Changes in Diversification in the US Pharmaceutical Industry 1977–1986, *Strategic Management Journal*, vol. 12, pp. 187–99.

Hodgson, G.M. (1995), *Economics and Biology*, Edward Elgar Publishers, Aldershot.

Howells, J. (1992), 'Pharmaceuticals and Europe 1992: The Dynamics of Industrial Change', *Environment and Planning A*, vol. 24, pp. 33–48.

Jong, H.W. de, (1985), *Dynamische Markttheorie*, Stenfert Kroese, Leiden.

Keeble, D. and Kelly, T. (1986), 'New Firms and High Technology Industry in the United Kingdom: The Case of the Computer Electronics', in Keeble, D. and Wever, E. (eds), *New Firms and Regional Development in Europe*, Croom Helm, London, pp. 75–104.

Keeble, D. and Walker, S. (1994), 'New Firms, Small Firms and Dead Firms: Spatial Patterns and Determinants in the United Kingdom', *Regional Studies*, vol. 28, pp. 411–27.

Keeble, D. and Wever, E. (eds) (1986), *New Firms and Regional Development in Europe*, Croom Helm, London.

Maillat, D., Lechot, G., Lecoq, B. and Pfister, M. (1997), 'Comparative Analysis of the Structural Development of Milieux: The Watch Industry in the Swiss and French Jura Arc', in Ratti, R., Bramanti, A. and Gordon, R. (eds), *The Dynamics of Innovative Regions*, Ashgate, Alderhot, pp. 109–37.

Malerba, F. (1992), 'Learning by Firms and Incremental Technical Change', *The Economic Journal*, vol. 102, pp. 845–59.

Metcalfe, J.S. and Gibbons, M. (1986), 'Technological Variety and the Process of Competition', *Economie Applique XXXIV*, vol. 3, pp. 493–520.

Nelson, R.R. and Winter, S.G. (1982), *An Evolutionary Theory of Economic Changes*, Harvard University Press, Cambridge, MA.

Oakey, R. (1993), 'High Technology Small Firms: A More Realistic Evaluation of Their Growth Potential', in Karlsson, C., Johannisson, B.

and Storey, D. (eds), *Small Business Dynamics: International, National and Regional Perspectives*, Routledge, London, pp. 224–42.

Olleros, F.J. (1986), 'Emerging Industries and the Burnout of Pioneers', *Journal of Product Innovation Management*, vol. 3, pp. 5–18.

Pfeffer, J. and Salanchik, G.R. (1978), *The External Control of Organizations: A Resource Dependence Perspective*, Harper & Row, New York.

Porter, M.E. (1985), *Competitive Advantage: Creating and Sustaining Superior Performance*, The Free Press, New York.

Reynolds, P., Storey, D.J. and Westhead, P. (1994), 'Cross-national Comparisons of the Variation in New Firm Formation Rates', *Regional Studies*, vol. 28, pp. 443–56.

Saxenian, A. (1994), *Regional Advantage. Culture and Competition in Silicon Valley and Route 128*, Harvard University Press, Cambridge, MA.

Schamp, E. W. (1996), 'Some Reflections on Evolutionary Theory in Economics and Economic Geography', 5th Dutch-German Seminar on Economic Geography, Mulheim/Ruhr Germany.

Silverberg, G;. Dosi, G. and Orsenigo, L. (1988), 'Innovation, Diversity and Diffusion: A Self-organisation Model', *Economic Journal*, vol. 98, pp. 1032–54.

Storey, D.J. (1994), *Understanding the Small Business Sector*, Routledge, London.

Storper, M. (1993), 'Regional "Worlds" of Production: Learning and Innovation in the Technology Districts of France, Italy and the USA', *Regional Studies*, vol. 27, pp. 433–55.

Suarez, F.F. and Utterback, J.M. (1995), 'Dominant Designs and the Survival of Firms', *Strategic Management Journal*, vol. 16, pp. 415–30.

Toyne, B. (1984), *The Global Textile Industry*, Allen & Unwin, London.

Utterback, J.M. (1994), *Mastering the Dynamics of Innovation*, Harvard Business School Press, Boston.

Vaessen. P. (1993), *Small Business Growth in Contrasting Environments*, PhD Thesis, Catholic University, Dept. of Economic Geography, Nijmegen.

Note

It needs to be emphasized that patents as an innovation indicator suffer from various general shortcomings (van Geenhuizen 1993). In the pharmaceutical industry, multiple and related innovations are quite common, in such a way that various related patents represent only one innovation. For this reason, the interpretation needs to focus on broad patterns and trends.

4 Agglomeration and Industrial Innovation in Space: An Empirical Analysis

DANIEL SHEFER AND AMNON FRENKEL

4.1 Introduction

This chapter reports the results of a study concerned with the effect of extended factors, clustered under the term agglomeration economies, on the rate of industrial innovation.

In recent years, industrial innovation has been recognized as a major source fostering economic growth. The resurrection of interest in economic growth models, prompted by the seminal work of Romer (1986) and Lucas (1988), brought to the fore the importance of endogenous technological progress. This new development was contrary to the neoclassical model of growth theory espoused by Solow (1956 and 1970), in which technological progress was assumed to be exogenous. Furthermore, Solow focused his attention primarily on the process of capital accumulation and its relationship to a steady state, not on the process of generating technological progress. Thus, under the assumptions of constant returns to scale and fixed technology, as capital per worker rises, diminishing marginal productivity of capital sets in, and capital investment will be made at a rate sufficient only to replace depreciation and provide capital for new workers.

The restrictive assumptions embedded in the neoclassical model – exogenous technology, constant returns to scale, and diminishing marginal productivity of capital in a perfect competition situation – do not provide good explanations for the observed process of continuous growth in per capita income.

The endogenous economic growth models that emerged in the 1980s suggest that firms may invest in new technology through expenditure on research and development if they perceive an opportunity to make a profit (Stokey 1995). Thus, technological progress could explain the persistent growth of income and consequently of income per capita or 'standard of living' (Romer 1994; Grossman and Helpman 1991a, 1991b, 1994; Pack 1994). Since economic growth is driven to a large extent by technological progress, it is essential for effective public policy to identify the group of industries whose rate of innovation is the largest (Schmookler 1966; Grossman and Helpman 1991b; Segerstrom 1991).

There is ample evidence supporting the hypothesis that innovation activities are more prevalent among the fastest-growing industries. Thus, it would be promising to investigate the phenomenon of innovation activities among firms belonging to this specific group – industries that most often provide the engine of economic growth (Suarez-Villa and Walrod 1997).

Industries that are heavily engaged in technological innovation usually possess a high market value resulting in a competitive advantage, at least during the first stage of the diffusion process. Thus, these activities provide new and, at times, unique opportunities for the development of firms, the expansion of their market share, profitability and employment growth.

Open economies can take advantage of an expanded market and through increasing returns to scale, enjoy greater production efficiency and a higher rate of economic growth. Greater production efficiency enables industries to expand their domestic market share through import substitution and increases in local consumption and, at the same time, to penetrate new foreign markets and increase their export share (Grossman and Helpman 1990a, 1990b; Porter 1990; Noponen et al. 1993; Krugman 1979, 1990, 1991, 1995).

4.2 Innovation and Regional Growth

The contribution of innovation to regional growth has been widely discussed in the literature (Davelaar 1991; Feldman 1994; Feldman and Kutay 1997; Davelaar and Nijkamp 1997; Frenkel and Shefer 1997). Regional development, as a location where technological innovation takes place, is usually accompanied by new economic activities, market expansion, and technological adaptation. Regions with a high level of innovation have become a destination for highly skilled labour and an impetus for improved social and physical infrastructures (Lucas 1988). From a technological point of view, advanced economic activities improve competitive advantage and increase market share at least during the first stage of the innovation diffusion process. Therefore, we hypothesize that regions characterized by a high level of technological innovation will show a greater acceleration of economic growth compared to other regions (Grossman and Helpman 1990a, 1991b, 1994; Krugman 1979, 1991, 1995; Stokey 1995).

The ability of a firm to innovate is contingent upon two major groups of variables. The first group is internal, and the second external to the firm, or location specific (Davelaar and Nijkamp 1989; Harrison et al. 1996; Shefer and Frenkel 1998).

The following variables can be identified in the first group: size, age, ownership type, branch of industry to which the firm belongs and the extent of R&D activities taking place in the firm. R & D activities can be measured either by the number of employees engaged in that activity or by the total expenditure allocated to it (Jaffe 1989; Andretsch and

Feldman 1996). The second group of variables, those that are external to the firm, creates the *local innovative milieu* or the economic environment conducive to innovation. These variables include the degree of cooperation and collaboration among firms and the degree of economies of localization and agglomeration as depicted by the spatial concentration of either similar (competitive) or complementary firms or by the size of the regional population (Shefer and Frenkel 1998).

This *local innovative milieu* is perceived as enhancing the innovative capability of firms. It is considered a cost-reducing factor that diminishes uncertainty and increases production efficiencies (Dieperink and Nijkamp 1988, 1990; Camagni 1991, 1995; Kleinknecht and Poot 1992; Shefer and Frenkel 1998; Frenkel et al. 1998).

This chapter concentrates on the effect of the external variables on the firm's rate of innovation. These external variables, which in this chapter are subsumed under the term agglomeration economies, create the *local innovative milieu* or the economic environment conducive to innovation.

4.3   Spatial Diffusion of Product and Process Innovation

Technology diffusion is a complex process, involving changes in the behaviour of economic agents. Several studies have emphasized the great importance of the technology diffusion process for market development; nevertheless, it is surprising to find that only a few policies are designed to foster this process. The expected societal return on new technology without the diffusion process will be insignificant.

The diffusion process may be understood by integrating three basic elements: companies, environment and technology (Camagni 1991). The integration of these three elements helps to create the prerequisite conditions for adopting innovation.

A common distinction made in studies of technological innovation diffusion relates to the division between *product innovation* and *process innovation* in the regional context (Davelaar 1991; Dosi 1988). Development regions are able to adopt new technologies associated with production processes; however, they may face severe difficulties in engaging in product innovation. Process innovation usually can be bought 'off the shelf' on the open market. Product innovation, on the other hand, is not as readily available. The reason is that innovation is the means by which a firm can maintain its competitive edge over its rivals. Therefore, in the short run, product innovation is less transferable in terms of diffusion (Oakey 1984; Oakey et al. 1980; Thwaites, et al. 1981; Alderman 1990; Alderman and Fischer 1992; Alderman, et al. 1988).

Innovation transfer involves a component of risk or uncertainty. The importance of information is shown, among other ways, by its ability to reduce uncertainty. Greater importance must be placed on the uncertainty component as it pertains to innovation activity than is presently afforded it by popular economic models. Uncertainty is concerned not only with the lack of information regarding the exact income and expenditures associated with the various alternatives, but most often with the limited knowledge of the nature of the alternatives (Freeman et al. 1982; Nelson and Winter 1982).

Dosi (1988) believes that a distinction should be made between uncertainty expressed in terms of partial information about the occurrence of known events and what is termed 'strong uncertainty'. The latter exists when a set of possible events is unknown, and therefore it is impossible to determine the results of the specific activities of each given occurrence. Innovation is characterized in most cases by strong uncertainty.

We can presume that a greater amount of uncertainty and limited bits of information are being transmitted to locations at a distance from the concentration of people and economic activities – the metropolis. There are two major processes that may be distinguished: the first is the movement from the centre to the boundaries, or the outer ring (suburbs), of the metropolitan area; the second is the strong connection, in spite of the distance separating them, between centres of activities – metropolitan areas. This affinity between centres skips intermediate areas, which could be considered peripheral to the metropolis. Given these diffusion processes, we would expect that the rate of innovation will follow similar spatial patterns; that is, a gradual decline in the rate of innovation as one proceeds from the centre toward the periphery.

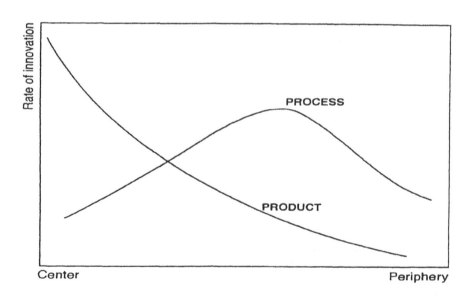

Figure 4.1   Hypothetical spatial distribution of product and process innovation

56

As for the difference in spatial variation that may exist between product and process innovation, we hypothesized that the spatial pattern would vary as depicted in Figure 4.1. The following empirical analysis will focus specifically on the phenomenon of spatial product innovation and the effect of agglomeration economies on the rate of innovation.

4.4   Agglomeration Economies

Agglomeration economies are perceived as enhancing the innovative capacity of firms. They are cost-reducing factors that diminish uncertainty and increase production efficiencies (Camagni 1991; Kleinknecht and Poot 1992; Shefer and Frenkel 1998).

There are ample theoretical and empirical studies that demonstrate the effect of agglomeration economies on production efficiency (see, for example, Shefer 1973; Richardson 1974, 1995; Sveikauskas 1975; Segal 1976; Carlino 1979, 1982; Nakamura 1985; Sveikauskas et al. 1988; Henderson 1986, 1988; Jaffe et al. 1973; Giersch 1995; Harrison et al. 1996; Matellato 1997).

Indeed, modern location theory posits the significant role that agglomeration, localization and scale economies play in explaining the growth of cities. These form the hubs which generate new ideas and technological progress. Agglomeration economies, localization and the economies of scale of the single firm are the principle forces that foster the continuous concentration of people and economic activities in some selected points in space. Agglomeration economies, though, is not a very tangible concept, since it encompasses several loosely defined factors. It can be measured by the number of employees in a particular industry (localization economies) or by the total number of employees in all manufacturing industries and/or the business service industry (see Moomaw 1988, 1998; and Sveikauskas et al. 1988). A good surrogate for urban agglomeration could also be the total number of people residing in a given locality (Moomaw 1983; see also Moomaw 1981; Shefer 1987; and Dieperink and Nijkamp 1988a and 1988b).

4.5   Data Source

The data collected on the structure of regional innovation was concerned with industrial firms, in a selected number of fast-growing industrial branches (Shefer et al. 1998). These included the following three major branches of industry: electronics (including optics and precision instruments), plastics and metal products.

Identification of the fast-growing industries was based on the analysis of the rate of growth in output, employment and export in each of the industrial branches. Industrial rates of growth serve as an indicator for defining the regional economic employment potential. The assumption is that firms belonging to the fast growing industrial branches have a significant growth potential, and their impact on the region's economy will therefore be greater than that of firms belonging to the declining industrial branches. Industries demonstrating significant export potential – in which the export component comprises a significant proportion of the branch's output – are more likely to grow compared to industries which rely mainly on local markets (Shefer et al. 1998).

The northern region of Israel was selected for the current study. The northern region is one of the most fascinating regions in Israel in terms of the composition of its residents (Jews and non-Jews, veteran settlers as well as new immigrants), its settlements (type and pattern), and its landscape. In 1995, some 1.4 million people, constituting about 26 percent of the population of Israel, resided in the region, which extends 5,000 sq. km., or 23 percent of the total land area of the state (see Map 4.1).

The northern region of Israel was divided into three sub-regions: 1) Haifa Metropolitan Area – central zone. 2) Central Galilee – intermediate zone, the areas that surround the Core zone, on the fringe of the metropolitan area, and are within acceptable commuting distance. Although this zone was considered peripheral until not too long ago, the recent tide of population expansion in the Core zone 'spilled over' into the surrounding areas, bringing about a change in their rate of growth and regional functionality. 3) Eastern Galilee - peripheral zone, an area removed from the metropolitan influence, and is not within acceptable commuting distance. It exhibits most of the classical characteristics of a peripheral zone, including fewer employment opportunities, as well as fewer social, commercial and infrastructure services. This area consists of the Upper and Eastern Galilee and all along the Jordan Valley, from Metula and Kiryat Shemona in the north to Bet She'an in the south-east (see Map 4.1).

The fundamental research question is linked to the spatial rate of product innovations by the industrial firms in the various sub-regions. For this reason, the region chosen encompasses the three types of sub-regions: metropolitan area, intermediate zone and peripheral zone.

Table 4.1 depicts comparative data on the research region. The data indicate that the Haifa metropolitan area provides a large percentage of employment opportunities. The percentage of employees drops sharply and significantly when moving out of the metropolitan area toward the intermediate zone, and from there on to the peripheral area. A more equitable distribution of employment can be seen in the manufacturing industries (see Table 4.1). This is due to the fact that in recent years the intermediate zone in Israel has been undergoing a transformation, attracting new industrial plants. This trend is reflected in the high proportion of young firms which have been set up in this sub-region. This phenomenon is linked to the availability of land for the development and expansion of firms, the development of needed infrastructures, road and communications networks, and the relative proximity to a large pool of highly skilled labour residing on the outskirts of the metropolitan area.

58

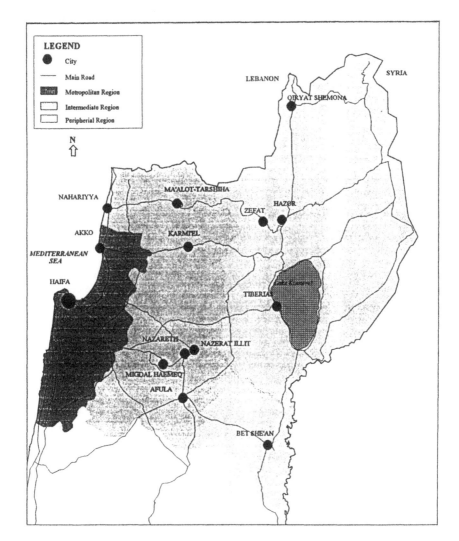

Map 4.1   Major areal division of Israeli northern region

The data was collected via field surveys, from a carefully selected sample of firms. In order to conduct the survey, questionnaires were constructed for gathering the data on the firm's level. Data concerning innovation activity, as well as information concerning firm's characteristics (such as ownership type, size, age, R&D activities, etc.) was included in the questionnaires.

Personal interviews were held with senior managers in each of the firms included in the sample. In total, 211 industrial firms, from the three selected industrial branches, were personally interviewed. This sample comprised approximately 72 percent of the firms in the surveyed region, associated with these three industrial branches (see Table 4.2). The distribution of the firms in the sample, by geographical location and industry type, are depicted in Tables 4.2a, 4.2b and 4.2c.

Table 4.1 Distribution of population and employment among sub-regions of the northern region in 1995 * (in 000')

Type of Zone	Population size number %	% of Employees	% of Manufacturing Employees
Metropolitan area (Haifa)	575.3 40.0	62.3	46.3
Intermediate Zone	628.4 43.7	26.8	40.5
Peripheral Zone	235.0 16.3	10.9	13.2
Total	1,438.7 100.0	100.0	100.0

* The data is an estimation based on analysis from the C.B.S manpower survey of urban settlements with more than 10,000 residents (it consists of more than 70 percent of the total employees in the area).

Sources: Statistical Abstract of Israel 1995.

Table 4.2a   Sample distribution by location

Sub-region	Total number of firms in the region		Number of firms in the sample		Sample of total firms (in %)
	N	%	N	%	
Core (metropolitan)	85	28.8	66	31.3	77.6
Intermediate	142	48.1	82	38.9	57.7
Peripheral	68	23.1	63	29.9	92.6
Total	295	100.0	211	100.0	71.5

Table 4.2b   Sample distribution by industrial branch

Industrial branch	Total number of firms in the industry		Number of firms in the sample		Sample of total firms (in %)
	N	%	N	%	
Electronics/optics	119	40.3	86	40.8	72.2
Plastics	105	35.6	80	37.9	76.2
Metal products	71	24.1	45	21.3	63.3
Total	295	100.0	211	100.0	71.5

Table 4.2c   Sample distribution by industrial branch and location

Industrial branch	Metropolitan	Intermediate	Peripheral	Total
Electronics/optics	36	34	16	86
Plastics	15	29	36	80
Metal products	15	19	11	45
Total	66	82	63	211

Table 4.3 depicts the percentage distribution of industrial firms, according to sub-region and industrial branch. The data indicate that, in addition to the variations in the overall distribution of the industrial firms in space, there are also differences in the sectoral distribution of the industries located in the study areas. The electronics industries dominate the sample in the Haifa metropolitan area (54.4 percent), as well as the intermediate zones (41.5 percent). The peripheral zone, on the other hand, is distinguished by the predominance of the plastics industry (57.1 percent); this phenomenon is linked to the concentration of kibbutzim in the peripheral zone and to the high prevalence of plastics firms in the kibbutz industry.

Table 4.3 Distribution of firms by industrial branch and location (in percent)

Industrial Branch	Northern region	Sub-regions		
		Metropolitan	Intermediate	Periphery
Electronics	40.8	54.4	41.5	25.4
Plastics	37.9	22.7	35.4	57.1
Metals	21.3	22.7	23.2	17.5
Total	100.0	100.0	100.0	100.0
N	211	66	82	63

4.6 Results of the Empirical Analysis

Our principal objectives in this study are to empirically test the hypothesis stating that agglomeration economies positively and significantly affect the rate of innovation. However, before we conduct that analysis, we would like to present the results of the analysis carried out on the rate of industrial innovation by geographical location and industrial branch.

4.7 Analysing the Rate of Innovation

In the present study we defined innovative firms as those firms that have created product innovation during the past three years. Included in this definition are activities leading to the development of new products, the adoption of products which are new to the market, and the substantial improvement of existing products (development of the next generation of products). These activities emanate from in-house investments in R&D, or the purchase of knowhow through outsourced R&D services. Firms that dealt exclusively with developing or adopting innovative processes, or with adopting new products not requiring R&D investment, were not classified as innovative firms.

The regional variation of the innovation pattern is reflected in the frequency of innovation among the firms located in each of the defined sub-regions. Analysis of the sample demonstrated the different locational patterns of firms with respect to innovation, considering their industrial branches. The results suggest that it would be appropriate to examine the impact of the industrial branch on the rate of regional innovation, while categorizing firms into two basic industrial groups on the basis of technological character. The first group represents the hi-tech industries, and it includes the electronics industry, electro-optics, optics, and precision instruments. The second group represents the more traditional industries, and it includes the plastics and metal products industrial branches.

The reasons for this division are also connected to the fact that the number of plants affiliated to the metal products industry are relatively small. The similarity in behaviour among the traditional industrial branches (plastics and metal products) on the one hand, and the difference between these industries and the hi-tech industries on the other hand, both lend justification to this grouping. Furthermore, numerous variations have been found in the innovative properties characterizing these two industrial groups. This divergence is reflected in the high expenditure on R&D made by the hi-tech industries compared with those made by the traditional industries. Innovation development is a prerequisite activity for hi-tech firms. These firms must therefore invest in R&D, including basic research, and are obliged to engage highly skilled labour in order to handle the complex technological problems. By contrast, for the firms in the traditional industries innovation is not as essential, and is linked chiefly to process innovation, aimed at improving and/or adopting new products.

Table 4.4 depicts the results of the null hypothesis which states that there is no difference in the rate of innovation between hi-tech and more 'traditional' firms. As can be easily discerned from the statistical results, a statistically significant difference exists between these two groups of firms. The rate of innovation in the hi-tech firms was found to be statistically and significantly higher than that found in the 'traditional' firms.

Table 4.4 Comparison of rate of innovation between firms belonging to the hi-tech and traditional groups of industries (in percent)

Innovation	Hi-tech	Traditional
Innovative firms	74.4	49.6
Non-Innovative firms	25.6	50.4
Total	100.0	100.0
N	86	125
χ^2	13.05	
p	0.000	

These findings corroborate our hypothesis that firms belonging to the group of hi-tech industries have a greater probability of engaging in innovation. This is a significant finding that could assist us in designing effective public policies aimed at inducing regional innovation.

The distribution of innovative firms, when categorized into the two aforementioned industrial groups, demonstrates that significant differences exit between the three sub-regions, and more so within the hi-tech industrial group. As depicted in Tables 4.5 and 4.6, a significantly high rate of innovation exists in the hi-tech industries (74.4 percent). By contrast, firms representing the traditional industries show a lower rate of innovation, only 49.6 percent. The rates of innovation of firms affiliated to the traditional industries is progressively increasing as one moves from the metropolitan area toward the intermediate zone and the periphery (36.7 percent, 45.8 percent and 61.7 percent respectively), see Table 4.6.

Table 4.5 Distribution of hi-tech firms by innovation and location (in percent)

Innovation	Total	Metropolitan	Intermediate	Peripheral
Innovative firms	74.4	88.9	67.6	56.3
Non-Innovative firms	25.6	11.1	32.4	43.8
Total	100.0	100.0	100.0	100.0
N	86	36	34	16

$\chi^2 = 7.553$; p= 0.023

An examination of the inter-area variations, as depicted in Tables 4.5 and 4.6, points to the existence of a trend in regional behaviour, with regard to innovation, in the two industrial groups. A significant decrease in the rate of innovation in hi-tech firms can be observed as one progresses from the metropolitan area to the intermediate zone, and from there, to the periphery. These inter-area differences are statistically significant. A reverse regional trend has been observed in the traditional industries, where the rate of innovation increases with the movement from the metropolitan area toward the intermediate zone, and from there, to the periphery. These regional differences are of moderate statistical significance.

Table 4.6 Distribution of traditional firms by innovation and location (in percent)

Innovation	Total	Metropolitan	Intermediate	Peripheral
Innovative firms	49.6	36.7	45.8	61.7
Non-innovative firms	50.4	63.3	54.2	38.3
Total	100.0	100.0	100.0	100.0
N	125	30	48	47

$\chi^2 = 5.033$; p= 0.079

4.8 Multivariate Analysis

4.8.1 The Logit Models

The logit model is a discrete choice model which assumes that a firm must choose between two alternatives: either to engage in innovation or not. Thus, the dependent variable in these models is the firm's decision either to engage in innovation or not. This choice is influenced by the firm's internal attributes such as: expenditure on R&D, percent of skilled labour force employed, size and age of the firm as well as its location and the *local production milieu* – agglomeration economies (Shefer and Frenkel 1998). Three models were used independently to explain the rate of innovation in each of the two groups of firms: hi-tech and 'traditional'.

The independent variables introduced in the models that explain the probability of a firm engaging in innovation are categorized into two types:

a. Firms' Attributes:
Firm R&D activity – the assumption is that product innovation is dependent on the firm's annual expenditure on R&D and the number of employees engaged in R&D.
Skilled labour force – the assumption is that product innovation is positively related to the rate of highly skilled labour employed by the firm.
Firm age – it is hypothesized that younger firms are more innovative compared with older firms. The age of a firm is a continuous variable, i.e. number of years.

Firm size – it is hypothesized that larger firms are more innovative compared with small firms. Firm size is measured according to the number of employees (the sample was divided into three groups: small firms up to 20 employees; medium sized firms, with 20–99 employees; and large firms, employing more than 100 workers).

The impact of the *local production milieu* on the rate of innovation is examined by means of three alternative agglomeration indices calculated for each of the three identified sub-regions.

b. Agglomeration economies:
Agglomeration I – is measured by the total number of employees in the business services.
Agglomeration II – is measured by the total number of employees in the industry concerned (also termed localization economies).
Agglomeration III – is measured by the population density in each of the three sub-regions.

Since the geographical size of the sub-regions are not identical, the absolute size of the population does not constitute an index of the relative concentration of economic activities. We therefore decided to use population density as a surrogate measure of concentration, thereby cancelling-out the differences which exist in the geographical size of each sub-region (see also Moomaw 1983; Carlino and Voith 1992; and Ciccone and Hall 1996).

We assumed that the agglomeration effect follows an exponential function, therefore the agglomeration index was calculated by squaring the population density parameter in each of the sub-regions (Shefer 1987, also used this method).

The logit model was applied separately to the two defined industrial groups – the hi-tech industries and the 'traditional' industries. These models enabled an examination of the impact of each of the above mentioned variables on the rate of product innovation.

As can be seen in the results presented in Table 4.7 for the three models, both internal R&D and a skilled labour force affect the rate of innovation in all firms positively and significantly. Young firms are more likely to innovate in the hi-tech industry. This variable, though, has a negative effect on the group of firms belonging to the traditional industries. Size of firms, on the other hand, has a positive and significant effect on the rate of innovation in the traditional industries. In the hi-tech industries, size of firm has less significant effect on the rate of innovation.

As for the agglomeration economies variables, all of the three alternative indices used appear to affect the rate of innovation in the hi-tech industries positively and significantly. In the traditional industries the effect is less pronounced; furthermore, the direction is negative (although it is not always statistically very significant).

Table 4.7 LOGIT Model results – evaluation of the probability of product innovation in the hi-tech and traditional industries (t-value in parentheses)

Independent Variable	A. Hi-tech Industries			B. Traditional Industries		
	Model A1	Model A2	Model A3	Model B2	Model B2	Model B3
Constant	-4.929	-4.787	-5.014	-4.580	-4.434	-4.459
	(-3.14)*	(-3.15)*	(-3.13)*	(-4.16)*	(-3.99)*	(-4.02)*
Internal R&D	3.156	3.028	3.099	4.231	4.271	4.246
(yes = 1)	(3.36)*	(3.39)*	(3.35)*	(3.95)*	(3.99)*	(3.97)*
Skill of Labour Force	2.953	2.850	2.909	1.630	1.652	1.666
(High = 1)	(2.79)*	(2.79)*	(2.77)*	(3.01)*	(3.03)*	(3.03)*
Age of Firms	2.549	2.303	2.359	-1.850	-1.891	-1.795
(Young = 1)	(2.11)*	(2.00)*	(2.02)*	(-2.27)*	(-2.29)*	(-2.20)*
Size of Firms	1.947	1.803	1.856	1.225	1.245	1.257
(Large = 1)	(1.84)**	(1.77)**	(1.78)**	(2.10)*	(2.12)*	(2.13)*
Agglomeration I: Business Services	1.72E-03 (2.25)*	_____	_____	-0.91E-03 (-1.70)**	_____	_____
Agglomeration II: Labour Force	_____	0.84E-07 (2.09)*	_____	_____	-0.21E-07 (−1.87)**	_____
Agglomeration III: (Population Density)	_____	_____	0.24E-05 (2.24)*			-0.16E-05 (−2.05)*
N	82	82	82	122	122	122
Initial Likelihood	-56.84	-56.84	-56.84	-84.56	-84.56	-84.56
Final Likelihood	-25.86	-26.47	-26.47	-46.58	-46.24	-45.87
p^2	0.55	0.53	0.53	0.45	0.45	0.46
$\bar{p}^2$	0.48	0.47	0.47	0.43	0.44	0.44

* Significance at $p < 0.05$

** Significance at $p < 0.10$

(1) Dummy variable, reference group in parentheses

4.9 Conclusion

Our analyses revealed that significant variations exist between the effect of agglomeration economies, however defined, on the rate of innovation in the two groups of industries: hi-tech and traditional.

The hi-tech industry is positively and significantly influenced by the high concentration of people and economic activities. The rate of innovation in this industry is positively increasing with the prevalence of agglomeration. Agglomeration economies, on the other hand, negatively effect the rate of innovation in traditional industries.

One obvious conclusion that we can draw from this analysis is that it would be counter productive to push hi-tech firms away from the core toward the periphery. Such a policy would concomitantly diminish the rate of innovation in those firms. On the other hand, the rate of innovation in firms belonging to the plastics and metals industries will not be affected by a move from the core toward the intermediate and peripheral zones.

These conclusions suggest that public policies designed to promote regional growth and development should be location and *industry-specific*.

Acknowledgement

This research was partially supported by the fund for the promotion of research at the Technion.

References

Alderman, N. (1990), 'New Patterns of Technological Change in British Manufacturing Industry', *Sistemi Urbani*, vol. 3, pp. 287–99.

Alderman, N. and Fischer, M.M. (1992), 'Innovation and Technological Change; An Austrian Comparison', *Environment and Planning A*, vol. 24, pp. 273–88.

Alderman, N., Davis, S. and Thwaites, A.T. (1988), 'Patterns of Innovation Diffusion', Technical Report CURDS, University of Newcastle upon Tyne, Newcastle upon Tyne.

Andretsch, D.B. and Feldman, M.P. (1996), 'R&D Spillovers and the Geography of Innovation and Production', *American Economic Review*, vol. 86, no. 3, pp. 630–40.

Camagni, R.P. (1984), 'Spatial Diffusion of Pervasive Process Innovation', paper presented at the 24th European Congress of the Regional Science Association, Milan, Italy, August 23–31.

Camagni, R.P. (ed.) (1991), Innovation Networks: Spatial Perspectives, Belhaven Press, London.

Camagni, R.P. (1995), 'The Concept of Innovative Milieu and Its Relevance for Public Policies in European Lagging Regions', *Papers in Regional Science*, vol. 74, no. 4, pp. 317–40.

Carlino, G. (1979), 'Increasing Returns to Scale in Metropolitan Manufacturing', *Journal of Regional Science*, vol. 19, pp. 363–73.

Carlino, G. (1982), 'Manufacturing Agglomeration Economies as Returns to Scale: A Production Function Approach', *Papers of the Regional Science Association*, vol. 50, pp. 95–111.

Carlino, G. and Voith, R. (1992), 'Accounting for Differences in Aggregate State Productivity', *Regional Science and Urban Economics*, vol. 22, no. 4, pp. 597–617.

Ciccone, A. and Hall, H.E. (1996), 'Productivity and the Density of Economic Activity', *American Economic Review*, vol. 86, no. 1, pp. 54–70.

Davelaar, E.J. (1991), *Regional Economic Analysis of Innovation and Incubation*, Avebury, UK.

Davelaar, E.J. and Nijkamp, P. (1989), 'The Role of Metropolitan Milieu as an Incubation Centre for Technological Innovation: A Dutch Case Study', *Urban Studies*, vol. 26, pp. 517–25.

Davelaar, E.J. and Nijkamp, P. (1997), 'Spatial Dispersion of Technological Innovation: A Review', in Bertuglia, C.S., Lombardo, S. and Nijkamp, P. (eds), *Innovative Behaviour in Space and Time*, Springer, Berlin.

Dieperink, H. and Nijkamp, P. (1988), 'Innovative Behaviour, Agglomeration Economies and R&D Infrastructure', *Empec*, vol. 13, pp. 35–57.

Dieperink, H. and Nijkamp, P. (1990), 'The Agglomeration Index', *Geography Research Forum*, vol. 10, pp. 20–8.

Dosi, G. (1988), 'Sources, Procedures and Microeconomic Effect of Innovation', *Journal of Economic Literature*, vol. 26, pp. 1120–71.

Feldman, M.P. (1994), *The Geography of Innovation*, Kluwer Academic Publishers, Dordrecht.

Feldman, M.P. and Kutay, A.S. (1997), 'Innovation and Strategy in Space: Towards a New Location Theory of the Firm', in Bertuglia, C.S., Lombardo, S. and Nijkamp, P. (eds), Springer, Berlin, pp. 239–50.

Freeman, C., Clark, J. and Soete, L. (1982), *Unemployment and Technical Innovation: A Study of Long Waves and Economic Development*, Frances Pinter, London.

Frenkel, A. and Shefer, D. (1997), 'Technological Innovation and Diffusion Models: A Review', in Bertuglia, C.S., Lombardo, S. and Nijkamp, P. (eds), *Innovative Behaviour in Space and Time*, Springer, Berlin.

Giersch, H. (ed.) (1995), *Urban Agglomeration and Economic Growth*, Springer, Berlin.

Grossman, G.M. and Helpman, E. (1990a), 'Trade, Innovation and Growth', *American Economic Review*, vol. 80, no. 2, pp. 86–91.

Grossman, G.M. and Helpman, E. (1990b), 'Comparative Advantage and Long-Run Growth', *American Economic Review*, vol. 80, no. 4, pp. 796–815.

Grossman, G.M. and Helpman, E. (1991a), 'Endogenous Product Cycles', *Economic Journal*, vol. 101, pp. 1214–29.

Grossman, G.M. and Helpman, E. (1991b), *Innovation and Growth in the Global Economy*, MIT Press, Cambridge.

Grossman, G.M. and Helpman, E. (1994), 'Endogenous Innovation in the Theory of Growth', *Journal of Economic Perspectives*, vol. 8, no. 1, p. 23–44.

Harrison, B., Kelley, M.R. and Gant, J. (1996), 'Innovative Firm Behaviour and Local Milieu: Exploring the Intersection of Agglomeration, Firm Effects and Technological Change', *Economic Geography*, vol. 79, no. 3, pp. 233–58.

Henderson, J.V. (1986), 'Efficiency of Resource Usage and City Size', *Journal of Urban Economics*, vol. 19, pp. 47–60.

Henderson, J.V. (1988), *Urban Development: Theory, Fact and Illusion*, Oxford University Press, New York.

Jaffe, A.B. (1989), 'Real Effects of Academic Research', *American Economic Review*, vol. 79, no. 5, pp. 957–70.

Jaffe, A.B., Trajtenberg, M. and Henderson, R. (1993), 'Geographic Localization of Knowledge Spillovers as Evidenced by Patent Citations', *Quarterly Journal of Economics*, vol. 63, no. 3, pp. 577–98.

Kleinknecht, A. and Poot, T.P. (1992), 'Do Regions Matter for R&D?', *Regional Studies*, vol. 26, no. 3, pp. 221–32.

Krugman, P. (1991), *Geography and Trade*, MIT Press, Cambridge.

Krugman, P. (1995), *Development, Geography and Economic Theory*, MIT Press, Cambridge.

Krugman, P. (1979), 'A Model of Innovation, Technology Transfer, and Trade', *Journal of Political Economy*, vol. 83, pp. 253–66.

Lucas, R.E. Jr. (1988), 'On the Mechanics of Economic Development', *Journal of Monetary Economics*, vol. 22, no. 1, pp 3–42.

Matellato, D. (1997), 'Innovation and Spatial Agglomeration', in Bertuglia, C.S., Lombardo, S. and Nijkamp, P. (eds.), *Innovative Behaviour in Space and Time*, Springer, Berlin.

Moomaw, R.L. (1981), 'Productivity and City Size: A Critique of the Evidence', *Quarterly Journal of Economics*, vol. 95, pp. 82–8.

Moomaw, R.L. (1983), 'Is Population Scale a Worthless Surrogate for Business Agglomeration Economies', *Regional Science and Urban Economics*, vol. 13, pp. 525–45.

Moomaw, R.L. (1988), 'Agglomeration Economies: Urbanization or Localization', *Urban Studies*, vol. 25, pp. 150–61.

Moomaw, R.L. (1998), 'Agglomeration Economies: Are They Exaggerated by Industrial Aggregation', *Regional Science and Urban Economics*, vol. 28, pp. 199–211.

Nakamura, R. (1985), 'Agglomeration Economies in Urban Manufacturing Industries: A Case of Japanese Cities', *Journal of Urban Economics*, vol. 17, pp. 108–24.

Nelson, R.R. and Winter, S.G. (1982), *An Evolutionary Theory of Economic Change*, Bleknap Press, Harvard University, Cambridge, MA.

Noponen, H., Graham, J. and Marjusen, A.R. (1993), *Trading Industries, Trading Regions*, Guilford Press, New York.

Oakey, R.P. (1984), 'Innovation and Regional Growth in Small High Technology Firms: Evidence from Britain and the USA', *Regional Studies*, vol. 18, pp. 237–51.

Oakey, R.P., Thwaites, A.T. and Nash, P.A. (1980), 'The Regional Distribution of Innovative Manufacturing Establishments in Britain', *Regional Studies*, vol. 14, pp. 235–53.

Pack, H. (1994), 'Endogenous Growth Theory: Intellectual Appeal and Empirical Shortcomings', *Journal of Economic Perspectives*, vol. 8, no. 1, pp. 5–72.

Porter, M.E. (1990), *The Competitive Advantage of Nations*, The Free Press, New York.

Richardson, H.W. (1974), 'Agglomeration Potential: A Generalization of the Income Potential Concept', *Journal of Regional Science*, vol. 14, pp. 325–36.

Richardson, H.W. (1995), 'Urbanization, Industrial Dynamics and Spatial Development: A Company Life History Approach', in Giersch, H. (ed.), *Urban Agglomeration and Economic Growth*, Berlin.

Romer, P.M. (1986), 'Increasing Returns and Long-Run Growth', *Journal of Political Economy*, vol. 94, no. 5, pp. 1002–37.

Schmookler, J. (1966), *Invention and Economic Growth*, Harvard University Press, Cambridge, MA.

Segal, D. (1976), 'Are There Returns to Scale in City Size', *Review of Economics and Statistics*, vol. 58, pp. 339–50.

Segerstrom, P.S. (1991), 'Innovation, Imitation and Economic growth', *Journal of Political Economy*, vol. 99, no. 4, pp. 807–27.

Shefer, D. (1973), 'Localization Economies in SMSs: A Production Function Analysis', *Journal of Regional Science*, vol. 13, no. 1, pp. 55–64.

Shefer, D. (1987), 'The Effect of Agricultural Price-support Policies on Interregional and Rural-to-Urban Migration in Korea: 1976–1980', *Regional Science and Urban Economics*, vol. 17, pp. 333–44.

Shefer, D. and Frenkel, A. (1998), 'Local Milieu and Innovativeness: Some Empirical Results', *The Annals of Regional Science*, vol. 32, pp. 185–200.

Shefer, D., Frenkel, A., Koschatzky, K. and Walter, G.H. (1998), *Targeting Industries for Regional Development in Israel and in Germany – A Comparative Study*, Working Paper, Technion, The S. Neaman Institute for Advanced Studies in Science and Technology, Haifa, Israel.

Solow, R.M. (1956), 'A Contribution to the Theory of Economic Growth', *Quarterly Journal of Economics*, vol. 70, pp. 65–94.

Stokey, N.L. (1995), 'R&D and Economic Growth', *Review of Economic Studies*, vol. 62, pp. 469–89.

Suarez-Villa, L. and Walrod, W. (1997), 'Operational Strategy, R&D and Intra-metropolitan Clustering in a Polycentric Structure: The Advanced Electronics Industries of the Los Angeles Basin', *Urban Studies*, vol. 34, no. 9, pp. 1343–80.

Sveikauskas, L. (1975), 'The Productivity of Cities', *Quarterly Journal of Economics*, vol. 89, pp. 391–413.

Sveikauskas, L., Cowdy, J. and Funk, M. (1988), 'Urban Productivity: City Size or Industry Size?', *Journal of Regional Science*, vol. 28, no. 2, pp. 185–202.

Thwaites, A.T., Oakey, R.P. and Nash, P.A. (1981), 'Industrial Innovation and Regional Development', final report to the Department of the Environment, CURDS, University of Newcastle upon Tyne, Newcastle upon Tyne.

5 Expenditure and Knowledge based Regional Impacts Associated with a University: Some Empirical Evidence

DANIEL FELSENSTEIN

5.1   Introduction

This chapter investigates some of the local and regional economic development impacts associated with Ben-Gurion University of the Negev (BGU). Amongst Israel universities, BGU is unique in that it has a particular regional development mission. The establishment of the university in 1969 was seen as an important step in improving the quality of life of a semi-arid region distant from the economic and cultural centre of the country, 'seeding' the local economy with new ideas and technologies, boosting the desert-capital city of Beer Sheva, attracting skilled graduates, faculty and staff to the area and generally acting as an instrument of regional development.

This chapter presents an assessment of this mission in two respects. First, it examines the expenditure impacts associated with the university. These relate to the income, output and employment impacts related to the university. In contrast to other studies, these impacts are examined from a welfare perspective. For example, a university-induced increase in income, can only be accredited to the university if it improves local welfare. If much of the income gain could have been achieved in alternative employment, then personal welfare is not really improved. The mechanisms examined that generate these changes are university procurement and the spending and consumption patterns of staff, faculty and students.

Second, the chapter looks at the knowledge-based impacts generated by the university. This is an area that has received scant attention in the literature and is more problematic to estimate. A university is rather different to other local large scale employment and income-generating institutions, such as a local manufacturing firm, shopping mall or office complex. It is expected to have a 'seeding' effect on the local economy. This is accomplished by attracting and retaining students, staff and faculty in the area, improving local attractiveness and image and subsequently upgrading the local cultural and educational infrastructure. In addition, it is expected to generate knowledge that will attract new firms and be of use to existing economic agents.

While a comprehensive assessment of all these missions is beyond the scope of this chapter, one related issue that is addressed in this chapter is the university impact on local human capital. This is a particularly important policy issue in that if BGU functions as an 'entrepot' or conduit for students who receive an education locally and then disperse to other parts of the country, an important regional development opportunity has been missed. This chapter attempts to measure the future earnings of a cohort of BGU graduates locally over the life cycle of their employment careers. This provides an indication of the contribution that they make to the local economy as a result of their education at BGU. This contribution will of course multiply itself many times over when considering all the graduating cohorts over a longer time period, such as a decade.

5.2   Expenditure and Knowledge-Based Impacts; the Issues

Following Florax (1992), university impacts are classified as expenditure-induced and knowledge-induced. The former represent the backward linkages of the university with the local and regional economy. They impact on the main components of the local economy, namely local business, government and households. University-related expenditure linkages are concerned with buying inputs from these sectors in the local economy. Knowledge-based impacts reflect the forward linkages of the university. They impact in three main and interdependent areas. First, they affect regional human capital formation. Second, they influence the creation and dissemination of knowledge locally. Finally, these forward linkages impact on the attractiveness and place-value of a given location. If the university has seeded the local human capital base and generated knowledge that has improved local welfare, then the location in which all this takes place is likely to become a more attractive place and a cumulative growth dynamic will have been set in place.

A common approach to estimating expenditure effects has been to concurrently estimate the output and income impacts of the university and then convert these income effects into units of employment (Haywood 1993; LEPU 1995). This is usually achieved through the calculation of Keynesian (or Keynesian-type) regional multipliers (Sinclair and Sutcliffe 1988) on a case-by-case basis (see for example Lewis 1988; Bleaney et al. 1992; Armstrong 1993). In these analyses, the impacts of the 'induced migrants' are not often considered. These migrants are those faculty, staff and students attracted to the area as a result of the available of the university and in whose absence are likely leave the area. An assessment of the impact of the university on the local economy has to take account of the counter-factual situation in which the university did not exist and these migrants would not stay in the area. The welfare question also needs to be addressed here. While the spending of the induced migrants undoubtedly has an economic impact locally, the question arises as to whether their level of welfare has in fact changed. If they are indifferent to their present place of employment (ie could have attained a similar level of welfare at another university elsewhere) then a case can be made for not attributing their income impacts to the university (Bleaney et al. 1992). Empirical estimates of university impacts that compare the 'with' and 'without' induced migrants income effect show differential behaviour across the multipliers calculated. Income multipliers have been found to be volatile to changes in parameter magnitudes while the output multipliers resulting are more robust (Felsenstein 1995).

The approach towards estimating knowledge and human capital formation has involved taking a specific growth process, such as labour market formation, new firm formation or innovation diffusion as the focus and looking at the relative growth induced by the institution of higher education (see for example Beeson and Montgomery 1993, Bania et al. 1993; Florax 1992).

An explicit focus on regional human capital formation has been much less common. Human capital formation effect over the long term is heavily contingent on the continued residence of faculty and students in the region. It can be argued that by raising the average level of general human capital in the area, the institution of higher education increases productivity of all labour in the area. This is because the skill composition of the labour force will affect the technology used thereby indirectly upgrading all labour. In addition on-the-job training over the course of a working lifetime will also contribute specific, and not just general, human capital (Becker 1975).

The regional effect will be most strongly felt if some of the students stay on in the area after completion of studies. It is true that the presence of the university means that a continually renewing body of students is present in the area the whole time. However, the fact that the university plays a 'conduit' or 'entrepot' role in the local economy with local and non-local students flowing in and out of the area, means that an opportunity cost occurs which is equal to the income foregone over the period in which local students were studying. Conversely, by attracting migrants from outside the area (students who later stay on in the area) or by stabilizing the rate of out-migration of skilled labour previously attracted, the university is instrumental in increasing local value added in terms of the prior education that these migrants bring with them.

The empirical estimation of the human capital contribution of the university to a particular geographic area, has attracted less attention than the expenditure issues (Bluestone 1993; Berger and Black 1993; Brown and Heaney 1997). These studies deal with estimating the extra earnings of university graduates attributable to their university education, the rate of return to higher education in the area by projecting the future earnings capacity of university graduates who stay on to live in the area, the added local incomes and taxes generated by these more educated graduates who opt to live locally after completing their studies and so on. In very few studies however has the university role as a regional 'anchor' or regional 'conduit' been specifically addressed. It is to these issues that we now turn.

5.3   Context and Data

At the outset it should be noted that the sheer magnitude of the BGU in a relatively small local and regional economy cannot fail to have economic development implications. As a large scale consumer of inputs (labour, goods, services) and generator of outputs (skills, knowhow, attractiveness), BGU is most likely to be a major factor in local and regional economic development. Even without a proactive, explicit role in promoting local economic activity, the presence of an institution that employs close to 1,500 employees, attracts over 10,000 students and generates annual payroll and purchasing expenditures of close to $120 million, must impact heavily on the local economy.

BGU operates in the city of Beer Sheva whose population is slightly over 160,000 and whose metropolitan catchment area encompasses a population of close to 400,000. At the institutional level, the employment magnitude of BGU is similar to that of the two single largest industrial plants in the region. The context therefore is one of a large scale labour-intensive organization providing hard-to-quantify outputs largely for non-local (i.e. export) demand.

The data for this analysis have been culled from a variety of sources. Institutional data were provided by various BGU administrative departments such as the Finance, Computer and Accounting, Employment and Wages, Student Admissions and Purchasing departments. These figures refer to 1995/6 and relate only to the BGU site at Beer Sheva and not to the other smaller university facilities such as the Desert Research Institute at Sde Boker, the Ben Gurion Heritage Centre and various applied research units.[1]

Detailed data on faculty, staff and student place of residence and expenditure patterns were survey generated. These figures were collected over the period April–June 1996 from a sample of 74 faculty, 61 staff, 790 BA students and 290 MA students. The faculty and staff samples were self-generating with survey questionnaires distributed to all university faculty and staff at the Beer Sheva location. The student samples were stratified by year of study and faculty with extra weighting given to students in their graduation year. This was necessary for the analysis of human capital effects that follows. In general, the survey achieved slightly over 10 percent coverage of faculty, staff and students (over 1400 respondents) which is a figure that is higher both relatively and absolutely, than generally attained in surveys of this kind (see Elliot et al 1988; Beck et al 1993).

Detailed data were collected on residential patterns of faculty, staff and students. This was necessary in order to estimate the propensity to consume locally that forms a vital component of the local expenditure effect. The 'induced migrant' effect amongst staff and faculty was discounted from this impact. As for students, the main adjustment related to those students who would have remained in the area even in the absence of the university. Including their expenditures would serve to inflate the university impact. Detailed description of these necessary adjustments and assumptions can be found elsewhere (Felsenstein 1997).

Detailed survey data were also collected on faculty, staff and students expenditure patterns and direct university procurement. Again, the accurate assessment of these impacts needs to consider a plausible specification of the counter-factual situation. In the absence of BGU, there would not have been not any direct procurement impacts, all those students with permanent addresses outside the region would not be spending locally; local students would have gone elsewhere to study, many of the staff would have continued to reside locally, sought alternative employment or been unemployed while much of the faculty would have not have come to Beer Sheva and would have been employed elsewhere.

Survey data relating to a wide range of consumption products show a heavy local orientation (see Felsenstein 1997 for survey details). However, these figures, while revealing, are by no means the final word in estimating the extent of local spending induced by BGU. As averages, they gloss over the different propensities to consume locally by faculty, staff and students residing in different places. They are therefore upwardly-biased and need to be adjusted to account for these variations. In addition, assuming that these propensities to spend locally are a major factor in estimating the expenditure impacts of BGU, we need to be able to specify a range of propensities and estimate the impact of BGU across this range. This will show us how volatile or robust these parameter values really are.

5.4   Expenditure Impacts

5.4.1   Method

The notion of 'induced migrants' is operationalized by estimating expenditure impacts for two segments in the local population: those who would be living in the area irrespective of the university presence (non-migrants) and those whose presence is attributable to the university ('induced' migrants). The assumption is that university faculty and academic-related staff (high-level executive, management and professional staff) are part of a national labour market. In the absence of the university it is assumed that they would hold identical employment at different locations outside the Southern region. Assuming a competitive market, their incomes would remain the same while their geographic distribution would differ. In contrast, other staff (secretarial, clerical, technical, service and maintenance) are all assumed to be non-migrants. In the absence of the university they would be unemployed or employed at lower levels in view of the above average unemployment levels that are a feature of the Southern region economy. Those who are Beer Sheva residents would continue to reside in the city while those who commute-in from the small towns outside would be considered unemployed at their place of residence.

In the analysis that follows, the impact of BGU is estimated twice: once including the impacts of 'induced migrants' and once excluding them. We count as induced migrants all faculty and top level management. In payroll terms, this adds up to $36.6 million. In addition, the wage bill of the university has been adjusted downwards to include only 5 percent of all expenditures of faculty and staff who live outside the Southern region. Finally, faculty wages have also been further adjusted (upwards) to include an assumed average of additional income of 30 percent above their university wages generated by private consultancy, lecturing and so on.[2]

With respect to students a further set of assumptions are necessary. To account for the discrepancy between local (term-time) and permanent addresses on expenditure impacts and in order not to overstate the university impacts in the case of local students who would be spending locally even in the absence of BGU, we adjusted the local monthly expenditures of BGU students over a 10 month (school year) period as follows;

5.4.1.1 Undergraduates Those with a temporary address in Beer Sheva were assumed to spend 82 percent of total expenditure locally, those with a temporary address in the Southern region were credited with 50 percent local spending and those with a Tel Aviv/Central region address were assumed to spend 15 percent in Beer Sheva. Half of the proportional value of student expenditure for those students with permanent Beer Sheva or Southern region addresses (over 3000 students) was then discounted from the total. Prior work on student expenditures based on permanent and temporary addresses has suggested the use of similar proportions (Rosen et al 1985).[3]

5.4.1.2 Graduates Those with temporary addresses in Beer Sheva were assumed to spend 58 percent of their total expenditures locally, those with a Southern region temporary address were credited with 20 percent and those with a temporary address elsewhere were assumed to spend 5 percent in Beer Sheva. Again, allowance was made for graduates with permanent Beer Sheva or Southern region addresses (1500 students). This time however, only 15 percent of the value of their expenditures was discounted. This was because many of the graduates are married students whose permanent and temporary addresses are the same but have still been attracted to the area because of BGU.

The estimation method follows Bleaney et al. (1992). The gross output and disposable income impacts of BGU on the local economy (including the Southern region) are measured. These are marginal (and growth-generating) effects induced by the university, over and above what would have happened in its absence. Keynesian-type multipliers are constructed that measure the ratio of initial-round to total (final) round impacts for both disposable income and output. On the basis of these income measures an employment multiplier associated with BGU is also calculated.

This procedure is detailed in the Appendix. The multiplicand for the gross output effect of the university is expressed as university payroll expenditure and any additional income of university employees components, the proportion of student expenditure that is local, the change in local expenditure induced by the university for non-migrants (i.e. those whose disposable incomes are expected to change as a result of the university presence) and the change in local expenditure attributable to the university for induced migrants (whose spending in the area increases local incomes). Thus, the effect of two sets of migrants are included in the calculation. First, student expenditure is included as an output effect. Second, the additional local spending by induced migrants (faculty and staff) is also included due to its contribution to the local economy raising the level of the disposable income of the non-migrants. The income effect is simply the output effect taxed at the appropriate rate.

The above multiplicand (i.e. initial injection into the local economy that is then multiplied by the multiplier to yield the impact estimate), ripples through the local economy via successive rounds of spending and responding with ever-decreasing multiples of the initial injection until the stage of final convergence is reached. At this stage there is no further local impact attributable to the university. The multiplier effect of the university is simply calculated as the ratio of this final round to second round effects. Finally, the employment impacts are calculated on the basis of the income impacts. In this estimation, units of income are converted to units of employment on the basis of the ratio of wages in the universities sector to average wages in the general education sector.

5.4.2 Results

Table 5.1 presents the final outcome of the round-by-round circulation of university-generated expenditure in the regional economy and reports the results of both excluding the income effects of 'induced migrants' and including them. As a result, the estimate of total gross output and disposable income generated locally by BGU, is greater in the latter case than the former. When 'induced migrants' income effects are included, total gross output and disposable income attributable to BGU are estimated as $221.8 and $111.2 million respectively. Excluding induced migrants incomes results in a correspondingly lower figure of $206.9 million for gross output and $83.1 million for disposable income.

The resultant income multiplier is larger when induced migrants incomes are attributed to the university. The output multiplier in this case is smaller because, while gross output is slightly larger than in the 'excluded' case, the multiplicand is considerably larger and therefore the multiplier is smaller.

We assume that the results of this estimation procedure are particularly susceptible to the parameter values relating to propensities to consume locally of staff and faculty on the one hand and students on the other. The results presented in the top line of Table 5.1 relate to staff and faculty local expenditure (le) of 0.60 and student local expenditure (ls) of 0.70.

Table 5.1 Expenditure impacts: sensitivity tests for values of impact coefficients

	Including 'Induced Migrants' Income Effect				Excluding 'Induced Migrants' Income Effect			
	Gross Output[1]	Total Disp. Inc.[1]	K_O	K_I	Gross Output[1]	Total Disp. Inc.[1]	K_O	K_I
Estimated Impacts[2]	221.8	111.2	2.19	2.37	206.9	83.1	2.30	1.99
Expanded Effects[3] I	250.9	124.7	2.15	2.31	232.5	94.9	2.25	1.98
II	266.7	343.4	2.15	2.29	246.5	101.4	2.24	1.98
III	283.5	139.8	2.15	2.29	261.3	108.3	2.24	2.00
Con-tracted Effects[4] I	195.6	99.1	2.28	2.48	183.9	72.4	2.40	2.04
II	183.6	93.5	2.35	2.57	173.3	67.4	2.48	2.08
III	172.1	88.1	2.44	2.69	163.2	62.7	2.58	2.14

1. All Figs $ million; current prices 1996.
2. Local Staff Faculty expenditure (le) = 0.60; local student expenditure (ls) = 0.70.
3. I le = 0.70; ls = 0.80; II le = 0.75; ls = 0.85; III le = 0.80; ls = 0.90
4. I le = 0.50; ls = 0.60; II le = 0.45; ls = 0.55; III le = 0.40; ls = 0.50

In order to test the volatility of the two most important parameters in this estimation exercise (the propensity of faculty and staff to spend locally (*le*) and the same propensity for students (*ls*)), sensitivity tests were conducted. The parameter estimates of *le* = 0.60 and ls = 0.70 were expanded and contracted by 10, 15 and 20 percent. The resultant total output, total income and respective multipliers, are also presented in Table 5.1.

Again, the results are presented both including and excluding 'induced migrants' income effect. As expected, including 'induced migrants' incomes results in consistently larger gross output, total income and income multiplier impacts. The output multiplier is consistently smaller due to the relatively large increase in the size of the multiplicand vis-a-vis the total gross output figure.

Prior work has suggested that the propensity to spend locally of faculty/staff and students is a particularly sensitive parameter (Bleaney et al. 1992; Armstrong 1993). The results in Table 5.1 seem to suggest that while the income multipliers are volatile to changes in parameter magnitudes, the output multipliers are more robust. In fact expanding the le and ls values by 10, 15 and 20 percent results in virtually no change in the output multipliers and a negligible change in the income multipliers. On the other hand, contracting these propensities to consume locally by the above magnitudes elicits a larger response in the size of the multipliers. It would seem that including the incomes of 'induced migrants' in the calculations results in slightly more volatile multipliers especially when the parameters are adjusted downwards (contracted). The case could therefore be made that including 'induced migrants' incomes, aside from overstating university impacts also results in less consistent and more volatile results. This observation has been found more consistently in previous research (Felsenstein 1995).

Finally, an employment multiplier (K_E) can be derived from the income multiplier. This procedure is based on estimating the increase in income needed to generate an additional unit of employment (see Felsenstein 1995). National data on average monthly wages in the university and general education sectors respectively shows the former to be 17 percent higher than the latter (Central Bureau of Statistics, 1996, Table 12.27). Using the income multipliers from Table 5.1 ($le = 0.60$ and $ls = 0.70$), we estimate the employment multiplier to be 2.37 when 'induced migrants' income are attributed to BGU and 2.16 when they are excluded from the calculation. In view of the relative robustness of the income multipliers, these employment multipliers are not likely to change very much when the le and ls parameters are expanded or contracted.

5.5   Knowledge-Based (Human Capital) Impacts

As noted above, long-term (human capital) impacts are a much acknowledged but often overlooked component of a university's impact on the local and regional economy. One way of approaching this issue is to look at the future income stream generated in the region by BGU graduates who continue to reside locally after completing their studies. Over the course of their working careers these graduates, with their added earning power as a result of their BGU education, will generate incomes and expenditure in the region. This is an additional, net impact created by BGU that would not have occurred had the university not existed. In addition, this kind of analysis allows us to examine the question of BGU acting as an 'entrepot' or channel for students who flow into the region and then flow out again once having graduated. A real long term regional impact is created if BGU acts as an 'anchor' rather than a stepping stone. The analysis that follows allows us to shed some light on this important regional development issue.

5.5.1 Method and Data

The approach adopted here is based on estimating the additional income generated by BGU graduates who continue to reside in the Southern region on completion of their studies. The methodology uses a multi-step process that analyses the Central Bureau of Statistics *Survey of Incomes 1994*. This is a national survey of over 14,000 respondents that has been conducted at annual or bi-annual intervals ever since 1965. This portion of this data pertaining to respondents from the Southern region is used here and is augmented with data generated from the survey of students at BGU reported above.

The first step involves creating 'earnings profiles' for different educational sub-groups amongst the population of the Southern region. Three educational sub-groups are defined for both men and women (6 groupings in all). These refer to wage earners with high school education, BA degree (graduates) and MA or Ph.D. degree (post graduates). These groupings were defined on the basis of years of schooling: high school was defined as up to 12 years schooling (inclusive), graduates as 13 to 16 years and post-graduates as 17 years schooling and up.

For each of these sub-groups, monthly income was regressed on age and age squared.[4] The regression parameters were used to build the earnings profiles for all six educational sub-groups.

Data for the above estimations was generated by identifying all the Southern region observations from the national *Survey of Incomes 1994* conducted by the Central Bureau of Statistics (Central Bureau of Statistics 1995). This resulted in a data set of nearly 2,000 observations (out an original survey of over 14,000) and this subset was further reduced to include only those individual observations whose ages were within the range of 25 to 65 years. This reduced the number of observations to 1626 (before missing values). Monthly incomes were converted into annual incomes and these figures were also augmented to account for projected annual real wage rate changes, estimated as 2 percent per annum over the last decade (see Central Bureau of Statistics 1996, Table 12.24).

5.5.2 Results

Earnings profiles for each of the educational sub-groupings across the earnings life cycle (ages 25 to 65) are presented graphically in Figures 5.1 and 5.2 where projected annual earnings (adjusted to include a real annual wage increase of 2 percent) for each age from 25 to 65 are displayed.

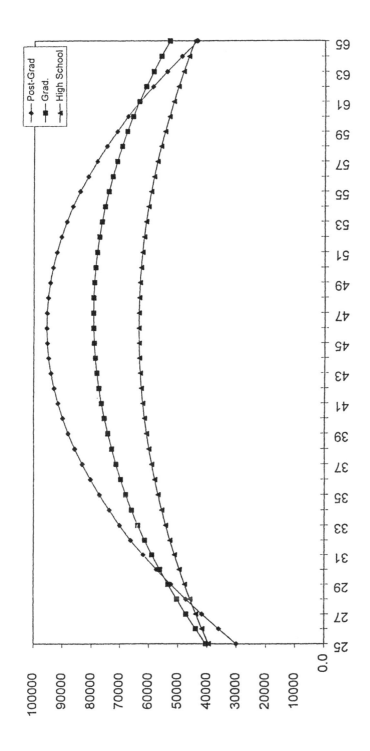

Figure 5.1   Annual earnings profiles, men by educational grouping – Southern region

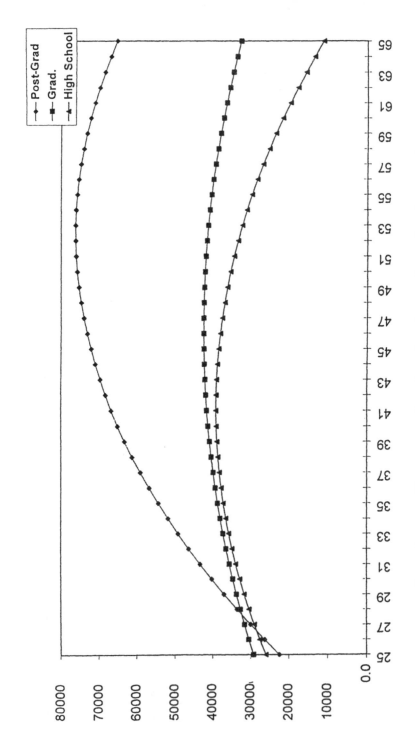

Figure 5.2   Annual earnings profiles, women by educational grouping – Southern region

Figure 5.1 seems to show a negative selection bias for the highest male educational grouping (post-graduates) at the end of the earnings life cycle. This could be indicative of a depreciation effect in human capital at this stage or simply due to the fact that this group works less hours. The annual earnings profiles for women (Figure 5.2) could also be slightly distorted as incomes have not been standardized by hours of work. In addition it should be noted that this data relates to the earnings of residents of the Southern region rather than earnings of those employed in the Southern region and this may be a further source of bias. These reservations notwithstanding, the profiles are instructive in that they allow us to estimate the increment in earnings arising from a university education.

The second major step in the analysis involves calculating the extra earnings arising from a university education. These income differentials can be calculated for each year across the earnings life cycle (i.e. from age 25 to 65). Differences in earnings across educational groupings are calculated for three pairs; the differences in earnings between i) high school and graduates, ii) high school and post-graduates and iii) graduates and post-graduates. These differences can be calculated for the three educational sub-groupings and for both men and women (i.e. six differences in all).

The results of these earnings differentials can be seen in Figures 5.1 and 5.2. For example, a man in the Southern region who has a BA degree can expect to earn over the course of his lifetime, over $150,000 more than a man who simply graduated high school. A woman from the Southern region with a post-graduate degree (MA or Ph.D.) can expect to earn during the course of her earnings career over $380,000 more than a woman with no university degree and over $300,000 more than a woman with a BA degree. The net present value of these future income streams are presented in Table 5.2.

Table 5.2 Net present value of income differentials over working lifetime by educational groupings, Southern region, 1994 ($)[1]

	PG-Grad.	PG-High Sch.	Grad-H. Sch.	Total
Men	82,592	406,777	140,189	629,558
Women	281,771	362,962	81,190	725,923

1. Incomes discounted at 5 percent rate.

The third and final step in the analysis involves trying to translate the incremental incomes earned in the Southern region due to a university education, into a figure that relates to the amount of BGU graduates that stay on in the Southern region after completing their studies. On the basis of the above calculations, how much extra income does a cohort of graduates inject into the Southern region over their earnings life cycle as a result of their education at BGU?

In 1995/6, BGU graduated over 2100 students in 1995/6 of which 48 percent were women. Taking this proportion as representative of all graduating classes, we now need to know how many BGU graduates out of the above cohort are likely to remain in the city or region upon graduating. The survey of student expenditures included a question directed at graduating students (BA and MA). They were requested to detail if they intended to remain in Beer Sheva the following year and if not, to indicate where they would be.[5] Table 5.3 outlines the results of this survey. Amongst graduating students, 31.8 percent intended to remain in Beer Sheva or the Southern region upon graduating while amongst post graduates this proportion was 63.5 percent. Applying these proportions to the graduating class of 1995/6, we can state that 548 of the 1722 graduating BA students were likely to remain in the region and 222 of the 350 MA graduates (or 245 of the 385 MA and PhD graduates combined). Of the 548 BA graduates staying in the Southern region, 51 percent (279) are likely to be women while of the MA graduates, 37 percent (82) are likely to be women.

Table 5.3 Students intending to remain in Beer Sheva and Southern region after graduation (percentages in parentheses)

Graduating Students:	Intending to Remain: Beer Sheva	Elsewhere in Southern Region	Intending to move to: Tel Aviv & Central Region	Elsewhere	Total
BA	52	16	121	25	214
	(24.3)	(7.5)	(56.5)	(11.7)	(100.0)
MA	34	6	17	6	63
	(54.0)	(9.5)	(27.0)	(9.5)	(100.0)

1. Based on survey of 214 graduating BA students and 63 graduating MA students.

If we now multiply the net present values of the income differentials (discounted at 5 percent) that appear in Table 5.2 by the estimated number of graduates and post-graduate students likely to remain in the region, we can arrive at an estimate of the total additional income generated in the region by a single cohort of graduates as a result of a BGU education. These figures are outlined in Table 5.4 for both men and women. We use the figures for incremental incomes resulting from a BA degree (Grad. – High School) and the incremental income derived from completing an MA (Post. Graduate–Graduate).

It should be noted that in these estimates, the additional income for the 35 BGU PhD graduates in 1995/6 has not been included as we did not have information on willingness to remain in the area for PhD graduates. As such, these figures are an under-estimate. In addition, by counting the additional income of post-graduates as the increment over the graduates income, we are knowingly excluding the income increment of those post graduate students that also did their BA degrees at BGU. Again this will result in an underestimate. Furthermore, in line with the view of income as a welfare measure taken in this study, the estimates only refer to the incremental earnings (return to labour) arising from a BGU education. However, these more educated graduates are also likely to cause a productivity rise and efficiency gain in the region (return to capital) that is not directly estimated here. This is a further reason for considering these figures as underestimates.

The foregoing reservations notwithstanding, Table 5.4 shows that the estimated additional income generated in the region by the 1995/6 graduating class of BGU over the course of their earnings lifetime is over $96 million. Assuming that this return to labour represents less than 70 percent of the overall effect in a 'well behaved' production function and that the other 30 percent is attributable to greater productivity (return to capital) (Bregman and Marom 1995), then the overall increment attributable to the BGU over the long term rises to over $142 million.

Table 5.4 Net present values of incremental incomes for BGU Graduating Class, 1995/6[1]

	Income Differentials		
	Post. Grad - Grad	Grad. - High School	Total
Men	11.7	38.4	50.1
Women	23.5	23.1	46.6
Total	35.2	61.5	96.7

1. Incomes discounted at 5 percent rate. Figures in $ Millions.

This represents the incremental impact for one year's cohort. Over a longer period such as a decade, the impact of BGU would be multiplied many times over. Close to half of the earnings impact is generated by women graduates, despite the fact that on average they comprise less then half (48 percent) of all BGU graduates and less than half (47 percent) of all those graduates likely to stay on in the region. The income differential figures from Table 5.2 seem to suggest that the real payoffs from a university education are felt by women with post-graduate degrees. Finally, it should also be noted that the incremental income impact attributed to BGU, does not include any multiplier effect. This additional income will of course expand in ever-decreasing increments as it trickles through the local economy. A regional income multiplier in the range of 2.0 would double this longer term income impact and this point should not be over-looked.

5.7   Conclusions

This chapter reports an initial attempt at quantifying an inherently complex issue. Estimating the expenditure impacts from a welfare perspective is important as it stresses that additional regional output and income do not automatically raise local welfare. It all depends on who are the beneficiaries of this extra economic activity. While the expenditure linkages of the highly skilled faculty attracted to the Southern region contribute to the local economy and towards raising the disposable incomes of the non-migrants, the question is whether the personal welfare of the induced migrants has really changed.

In view of BGU's regional development mission, it is necessary however to go beyond estimating the expenditure impacts associated with the university. One of the major outputs produced by a university is human capital formation. Aside from its intangible nature, the estimation of the value of this output is problematic as it generates a stream of returns into the future. The analysis above has shown that particularly large payoffs to higher education in the study area exist for women with advanced degrees. The policy implications of this finding with respect to the regional impacts of higher education for women would seem to be clear. Policies that directly or indirectly encourage women to acquire a higher education such as flexible study programs and teaching hours at institutions of higher education, longer school day, subsidized child care and so on, would seem to generate large returns in the Southern region over the long run.

A further policy issue refers to the regional business environment. This study has shown that local expenditure linkages of the magnitude of $200 million are generated annually by BGU and that each cohort of graduates that remain in the region generates a further $100 million in incremental incomes over the course of their working careers. These are significant injections into the regional economy. The question then arises as to the extent to which they boost regional growth and the public policy that can facilitate this. In order to complement the university's role as a regional anchor, a suitable regional business infrastructure has to develop. Without this, short term expenditure linkages cannot be fully exploited and the long term human potential will not be fully realized. While the Southern region has been the recipient of regional policy assistance over the last 40 years, it could be that the supply side instruments such as direct capital subsidies, physical infrastructure provision and the like, subsidy of capital investment have missed the mark.

Without a sufficiently broad regional employment and business base to absorb graduating students, the university cannot act a regional development anchor. Graduating students are a source of skilled and relatively inexpensive labour. They are a university output that creates a regional comparative advantage. On the supply side, public policy could be directed at making the region attractive to these graduates through the supply of suitable housing and quality-of-life facilities. The

88

causality here is of course circular. A more attractive environment will retain more graduates in the region and more graduates make for greater place attractiveness. On the demand side, any policy that stimulates local demand (export assistance, marketing centres, business consultancy and so on), will impact on the employment opportunities for graduates. Improving the business environment of the region and increasing the flow of information locally are likely to result in a more efficient use of underutilized resources amongst which university graduates can be counted.

Finally, looking at the knowledge-based effects also serves to remind us that the human capital effect of the university extends way beyond the incremental incomes generated by BGU graduates as a result of their schooling. It includes upgrading local social and technological capital, generating place attractiveness and a wealth of other spillover effects in the social and cultural areas that are even harder to estimate. These represent the challenge for future research in this area. Rigorous and plausible approaches for dealing with these important issues are needed for a variety of reasons. First, the issues are serious and real. Much public funding goes into higher education and there is a need to be able to measure the return on this investment in all its facets. Second, competition in the area of provision of higher education is growing. For many institutions, the ability to survive in this new competitive environment is contingent on being able to show that their mission extends beyond the traditional areas of education and research. Finally, more serious attempts to accurately measure the human capital and social infrastructure impacts of the university will prevent the latter from peddling unfounded and intuitive claims in this area.

Appendix: Procedure for Calculating Multipliers

Following Bleaney et al. (1992), the output and income multipliers are estimated concurrently. While the former is a measure of economic activity and the latter is a welfare measure, their derivation is interconnected. University expenditure activity (E) is comprised of two components as follows:

$$E = P + V \tag{5A.1}$$

where P represents payroll expenditure and V is expenditure to external vendors for purchases and services. On the basis of (5.1), the additional local gross output attributable to the university will be the above equation modified to account for other additional income earned by university employees (e.g. external consultancy and property income) and discounting purchases and services that are imported from outside. This will yield first-round gross output (O_1) as follows:

$$0_1 = P + A + bV \tag{5A.2}$$

where A is additional income and b is the proportion of purchases and services (V) that are supplied locally.

On the basis of the first-round output expression we can estimate the first round impacts on the disposable income of the non-migrants (0_1). This is simply first round gross output (O_1) minus the income attributable to the induced migrants (M) (if this factor is not being attributed to the university) and the value of local purchases and services (bV) taxed at the rate of indirect taxation (n). This is all taxed at an appropriate tax rate for the non-migrants (t) and can be expressed as:

$$I_1 = (1 - t)(0_1 - M - bnV) \tag{5A.3}$$

In order to assess the university impact we need to formulate the mutiplicand (that expression of initial injection into the local economy which is then multiplied by the multiplier to give the impact estimate) in terms of three major components; (1) the proportion of student expenditure that is local, (2) the change in local expenditure induced by the university for non-migrants (ie those whose disposable incomes are expected to change as a result of the university presence) and (3) the change in local expenditure attributable to the university for induced migrants (whose spending in the area increases local incomes). This latter component is taxed at a rate t". This is expressed as:

$$0_2 = lS + ec\, I_1 + ec(1 - t'')M \tag{5A.4}$$

where S is student expenditure and l that proportion spent locally, e, is the proportion of university staff and faculty expenditure that is local and, c, is the marginal propensity to consume. This multiplicand also represents the second-round gross output (O_2) generated by the university. Applying a direct tax rate, t, and indirect tax rate, n, yields the second round change in the disposable income of non-migrants (I_2). This also assumes that no further induced migration occurs with no new injections of income. All injections into the local economy have taken place and we are now just tracing the diminishing round-by-round effects of the initial injection:

$$I_2 = (1 - t)(1 - n)\, 0_2 \tag{5A.5}$$

The third-round output effect of a further round of local re-spending (O_3) is simply that amount of the mutiplicand (O_2) spent locally and taxed at the appropriate rate:

$$0_3 = ec(1 - t)(1 - n)\, 0_2 \tag{5A.6}$$

Similarly, the third-round impact on the disposable income of non-migrants (I_3) is a decreasing multiple of the second-round impact (I_2):

$$I_3 = ec(1 - t)(1 - n) I_2 \qquad (5A.7)$$

This process continues in ever-decreasing multiples of the initial injection as a smaller and smaller local impact is registered with each successive round of spending. At final convergence (O_Z and I_Z), the output and income multipliers are defined as the ratio of final round to second round (multiplicand) effects. The output multiplier, K_O, is defined as:

$$K_0 = (0_1 + 0_2 + 0_3 + \ldots + 0_z) / 0_2 \qquad (5A.8)$$

while the income multiplier, K_I, is defined as:

$$K_0 = (0_1 + 0_2 + 0_3 + \ldots + 0_z) / 0_2 \qquad (5A.9)$$

The employment multiplier (K_E) associated with the university can be calculated from the income multiplier. This is based on estimating the increase in income needed to generate an additional unit of employment. The main assumption underlying this approach is that the expenditure patterns of employees in the sector where the injection takes place and those of employees in other sectors of the local economy, are broadly similar. Total employment created locally as a result of each direct university job is calculated as follows:

$$K_E = (K_1 - 1)[w_u)/(w_E)] + 1 \qquad (5A.10)$$

where, K_I is the income multiplier and w_U and w_S are the average wages in the higher education and general education sectors, respectively.

Parameter Definitions

Expenditure activity generated by BGU (Beer Sheva facility only) (E)
Payroll of BGU (Beer Sheva facility only) (P)
Expenditure to external vendors and services (V)
Proportion of V that is local (bV)
Additional income of faculty and staff (A)
Direct tax rate for induced migrants (t")
Direct tax rate for non-migrants (t)
Indirect tax rate (n)
Proportion of faculty/staff expenditure that is local (e)
Marginal propensity to consume (c)
Total gross student expenditure (S)

Proportion of gross student expenditure that is local (lS)
Expenditure attributable to induced migrants (M)

References

Armstrong, H.W. (1993), 'The Local Income and Employment Impact of Lancaster University', *Urban Studies*, vol. 30, no. 10, pp. 1653–68.
Bania, N., Eberts, R.W. and Fogarty, M.S. (1993), 'Universities and the Startup of New Companies: Can we Generalize from Route 128 and Silicon Valley?', *Review of Economics and Statistics*, vol. 75, no. 4, pp. 761–66.
Beck, R., Curry, P., Levin, E.D., Leisel, J., Vinson, R. and Wagner, M. (1993), *The Economic Impact of Southern Illinois Univerity*, Revised Internal Report, Department of Economics, Southern Illinois University, Edwardsvill, Il.
Becker, G.S. *Human Capital*, 2nd Edition, University of Chicago Press, Chicago, Il.
Beeson, P. and Montgomery, E. (1990), 'The Effects of Colleges and Universities on Local Labor Markets', *Review of Economics and Statistics*, vol. 75, no. 4, pp. 753–61.
Berger, M.C. and Black, D.A. (1993), *The Long Run Economic Impact of Kentucky Public Institutions of Higher Education*, Department of Economics, University of Kentucky, Lexington, KKY (mimeo).
Bleaney, M.F., Binks, M.R., Greenaway, D., Reed, G.V. and Whynes, D.K. (1992), 'What does a University Add to its Local Economy?', *Applied Economics*, vol. 24, no. 3, pp. 305–11.
Bluestone, B. (1993), *UMASS/Boston; An Economic Impact Analysis*, Institute of Public Affairs, University of Massachusetts at Boston (mimeo).
Bregman, A. and Marom, A. (1993), *Growth Factors in the Business Sector in Israel (1958–1988)*, Discussion Paper No. 93.02, Research Department, Bank of Israel, Jerusalem (in Hebrew).
Brown, K.H. and Keaney, M.T. (1997), 'A Note on Measuring the Economic Impact of Institutions of Higher Education', *Research in Higher Education*, vol. 38, no. 2, pp. 229–40.
Central Bureau of Statistics (1995), *Survey of Incomes 1994*, Jerusalem.
Central Bureau of Statistics (1996), *Statistical Abstract of Israel 1996*, no. 47, Jerusalem.
Elliot, D.S., Levin, S.L. and Meisel, J.B. (1988), 'Measuring the Economic Impact of Institutions of Higher Education', *Research in Higher Education*, vol. 28, no. 1, pp. 17–33.
Felsenstein, D. (1995), 'Dealing with "Induced Migration" in University Impact Studies', *Research in Higher Education*, vol. 36, no. 4, pp. 457–72.
Felsenstein, D. (1997), *Estimating Some of the Impacts on Local and Regional Economic Development Associated with Ben Gurion*

University, Negev Center for Regional Development, Ben Gurion University of the Negev, Beer Sheva.

Florax, R. (1992), *The University: A Regional Booster? Economic Impacts of Academic Knowledge Infrastructure*, Avebury, Aldershot.

Haywood, C.F. (1993), *Analysis of the Annual Economic Impacts in Kentucky of the State's Public Institutions of Higher Education*, College of Business and Economics, University of Kentucky, Lexington, KY (Mimeo).

LEPU (1995), *Impact Study of South Bank University*, Local Economic Policy Unit, South Bank University, London.

Lewis, J.A. (1988), 'Assessing the Effect of the Polytechnic, Wolverhampton on the Local Community', *Urban Studies*, vol. 25, no. 1, pp. 53–61.

Rosen, M.I., Strang, W.A. and Kramer, J. (1985), *The University of Wisconsin-Madison and the Local and State Economies: A Second Look*, Monograph no. 2, Bureau of Business Research, Graduate School of Business, University of Wisconsin-Madison, WI.

Sinclair, M.T. and Sutcliffe, C. (1988), 'The Estimation of Keynesian Income Multipliers at the Sub-National Level, *Applied Economics*, vol. 20, pp. 1435–44.

Statistical Yearbook of the Negev 1995 (1996), Negev Development Authority and Negev Center for Regional Development, Ben Gurion University, Beer Sheva (Hebrew and English).

Notes

1. These are small ancillary operations that have been excluded due to their distant location from the main Beer Sheva campus. They are likely to introduce a distortive element into the regional patterns of expenditure linkages of BGU. In addition, the scale of their expenditures is very different to the main campus. Their total procurement expenditure (1995/6) summed to just over 3 percent of that of BGU and their wage bill to less than 10 percent.

2. This increase is the result of the differential between the average wage and average salary out of total income for scientific and academic workers in the higher education sector (Survey of Incomes 1994, Central Bureau of Statistics, Jerusalem).

3. While there is no prior work in Israel to guide the choice of these proportions, consultations with representatives of the local students union also suggest that these adjustments are well-founded and necessary. In addition, the resultant multipliers that are calculated below are subjected to a sensitivity analysis in order to test for any bias that might have been created through using these proportions.

4. Following Bluestone (1993), the exact formulation of the regression is as follows;

    $$\text{MONTHLY INCOME} = \alpha_0 + \beta_1 \text{AGE} + \beta_2 (\text{AGE})^2 + \varepsilon$$

    For complete regression results see Felsenstein (1997). It should be noted however that the above specification yielded regressions models with rather weak overall explanatory power but of similar magnitude to other studies (see Bluestone 1993). These models are probably under-specified. However, the point here is not to estimate the most parsimonious model but simply to specify the functional form between age and income in order to estimate income levels across the working life-cycle. Adding further variables such as position at work and years of schooling would have improved the overall explanatory power of the model, but that was not the objective.

5. It should be noted that intention to stay in the Southern region does not necessarily point to that decision being taken in the end. However, as the survey was conducted towards the end of the second semester of the 1966 academic year, it is reasonable to assume that most of the graduating students already had a pretty good idea of their place of residence in the following year. Ideally, a time-series of migration behaviour in the Southern region is really needed to capture this effect.

Part B
Tourism, Infrastructure and Regional Development

6 Incentive Programs for Rural Tourism in Israel: A Tool for Promoting Rural Development

ALIZA FLEISCHER

6.1 Development of Rural Tourism in Industrialized Countries

The decline in the ability of farm agriculture to generate sufficient income in Israel and other industrial countries has caused many farmers to seek new sources of income and to diversify the agricultural base (Commission of the European Communities 1992; Swinnerton 1982). Rural tourism businesses play an important role in diversifying the income of the farm and thus strengthening and stabilizing the economic base of rural regions especially where employment in agriculture is declining (Rickard 1983). A national survey conducted in Britain by McInerney and Turner (1991) shows that a large proportion of farmers prefer tourism and contracting as a means to diversify their farm activities.

Many studies show that rural tourism makes an important contribution to the local economy at both the level of the individual farmer and the entire region. A survey conducted by the University of Exeter, England (Rickard 1983) found that most farmers entered the tourism business to increase their income and that tourism does not compete with agriculture in the use of farm resources and labour.

In some parts of Western Europe, such as France and the Alps, the contribution of tourism to farm income has been substantial (Kariel and Kariel 1982; Vincent 1980). Also in Scotland, Getz (1994) documented a rural area in which rural tourism is the mainstay of the economy. In other parts of Europe, farm tourism is only an auxiliary source of income for the rural family. In northern England where about 20 percent of the farmers generate income from tourism, it accounts for only 10 percent of their net income. (Davies 1983; Evans and Ilbery 1989). Oppermann (1996) concluded in his study of farm tourism in Germany that 'although tourism is frequently suggested to farmers as a panacea, this study indicates that farm tourism provides only a small side-income...'. Similar conclusions have been drawn by Hjalager (1996), who evaluated the European Union's Objective 5b Program for the Expansion of Rural Tourism. Her study shows that 'the financial returns most often do not measure up to either the expectations of the politicians or that of the farmers'. Butler and Clark (1992) also claim that rural tourism is not always the solution to rural development. They stated that, 'The least favoured circumstance in which to promote tourism is when the rural economy is already weak, since tourism will create highly unbalanced income and employment distribution. It is a better supplement for a thriving and diverse economy than a mainstay of rural development' (Butler and Clark 1992).

The Organization for Economic Cooperation and Development (OECD) which includes most industrialized countries recognized in the Report on the Future of the Countryside (OECD 1993), the fact that employment opportunities in rural areas are declining in primary and secondary sectors. However, most rural employment growth in recent decades has come from other industries including tourism and recreation.

Rural tourism includes a variety of businesses. Vacationers not only sleep and eat in the rural areas, but they also engage in recreational activities and shop in local stores. If the multiplier effect is taken into consideration then the contribution of rural tourism to the local economy extends far beyond the farm household. A survey of four regions in England (Countryside Working Group 1991) found that on the average 44 percent of the visitors' expenditures will stay in the local region. This contribution increases with the size of the locally owned rural tourism sector. It was also found that in some areas the output multiplier (the ratio between direct and indirect expenditures) reaches 2.3 and that for each employee in rural tourism an additional 0.26 jobs were created.

Based on case studies in Canada and Germany, Page and Getz (1997) concluded that farm tourism has unique needs for financing, training and marketing. Farmers are expected to diversify into providing visitors services even though they have little or no training. Some studies found that a lack of training was the reason for a high incidence of failure in rural tourism enterprises (OECD 1994). Obtaining finance for tourism and hospitality projects can be difficult, especially in rural areas due to the absence of wealthy residents, inadequate infrastructure, availability of capital, and other reasons. That is why in many countries capital incentives have been applied exclusively to rural areas and tourism has been frequently a major recipient (Page and Getz 1997). Since rural tourism enterprises are small and in many cases located in remote areas and thus lack the expertise in marketing there is a need for cooperation in marketing (Gilbert 1989) and purchasing of supplies (OECD 1994). Rural areas are neither always ready nor willing to participate in organization.

These attributes of rural areas call for the need to develop special policy measures and incentive programs for this sector.

6.2 Incentive Programs for Rural Tourism in Industrialized Countries

In some countries, the initiative for developing rural tourism was taken by the government. The French government, for example, initiated the 'Gites Ruraux' project in the 1950s to slow down migration of the rural population to urban centres. Support was given to farmers to renovate their unutilized farm buildings into bed and breakfast (B&B) units. In the rural regions of England the government invested in the development of parks and castles as an infrastructure for rural tourism and gave financial support to farmers to develop tourism units (Robinson 1990). Other countries such as Germany, Austria and Norway underwent a bottom-up type of development with both government and non-government organizations providing support in different ways. The increase, therefore, in rural tourism was in many cases supported by national and local organizations (Pearce 1990; Stevens 1990; Kieselbach and Long 1990; Johnstone et al. 1990).

In recent years the European Union has identified tourism as one potential source of new income for rural regions, especially regions which have suffered a decline in agricultural activities. Rural tourism is being encouraged and is receiving support through various EU programs (Bates and Wacker 1996). Slee et al.(1996) claim that in the UK, on one hand, the level of public institutional support for tourism is modest compared to agricultural support policies while, on the other hand, tourism has always been seen as an effective industry for job creation and with an ability to employ displaced workers.

In the USA, as far back as 1980, the federal government (US Department of Agriculture) encouraged farmers to consider farm tourism as a means of supplementing their income and assisted them with the establishment of vacation farm cooperatives. Eleven years later, in a 1991 survey of state-sponsored rural tourism programs, Luloff et al. found that 30 US states had tourism programs specifically targeted for rural areas (Luloff et al. 1994).

Frater (1983) has compared various government assistance projects available to farm tourism as shown in Table 6.1.

In the rural regions in OECD countries local development efforts 'now often stress measures to encourage local entrepreneurship and the expansion of existing, community based enterprises as a more stable and inherently beneficial form of development' (OECD 1993). Echtner (1994), recognizing the important role of the private entrepreneur in the tourism industry states that there is a need to provide tailored business and management training tools for local tourism entrepreneurs. Lerner and Saaty (1997) in research done on small tourism businesses in Israel have shown that these management skills are an important prerequisite for successfully running tourism ventures. They also found that lack of such managerial skills is one of the main barriers to the success of the tourism venture. This indicates that policies aimed to revitalize rural economies by supporting rural tourism should include provisions for training the individual entrepreneur.

Table 6.1 Various government assistance programs to farm tourism

Country	Aids to Farm Tourism	Agency Support
Austria	Government Subsidies Discounted Interest Subsidy, Training	Provincial Level Chamber of Agriculture
Canada	Marketing Support	Provincial Level
Denmark	Marketing Support VAT Concession	Regional Level
England	Limited Capital Grants Training	ADAS
France	Capital Grants Interest Relief Grants Loans Reduced VAT Income Tax Relief Marketing	Regional and Community Levels Gites Ruraux
West Germany	Low Interest Loans 40% Capital Grants Low VAT Income Tax Relief	National Level
Holland	Marketing and Training	Tourist Agency
Switzerland	Grants in Less Developed Areas	
United States	Economic Development Administration Loans	

Source: Frater (1983).

6.3   The Development of Rural Tourism in Israel

This chapter describes and analyses the Israeli experience in supporting rural regions in the transition from an agricultural base to one grounded in small tourism enterprise development. This is part of the national strategy to support rural peripheral areas. The chapter further shows that the support schemes were designed specifically to the needs of the farmers to make the needed adjustments.

Rural tourism activities have only recently reached Israel. The rural areas of Israel are based mainly on agricultural cooperative settlements that stem from the turn of the century socialist movement. The two major types of cooperative settlements are the kibbutz and the moshav.

100

The kibbutz is a rural settlement based on the principles of collective ownership and allocation of resources, total cooperation and communal activities. The moshav is a rural settlement based on individual family farming with self-employment, mutual guarantees for capital loans and cooperative marketing. The residents of both types of settlements were engaged mainly in agricultural activities aimed at the production of food in accordance to the ideology of 'the importance of working the land' (Aharoni 1991). However, due to farmer's advances in technology and productive effectiveness, prices and real income in agriculture declined and many cooperative settlements went bankrupt. By 1985, many kibbutzim (plural of kibbutz) and moshavim (plural of moshav) were tottering or collapsing. As a result many farmers began looking for alternative sources of income. The ideology and the need to work the land no longer played a crucial role. The need to look for a new source of income brought many rural settlements to turn to other types of activities including tourism.

The takeoff point of Israeli rural tourism was 1986. This is known as the crisis year in Israeli agriculture. Since then rural tourism has been growing rapidly (Fleischer and Pizam 1997). B&B units alone have increased at the rate of 25 percent a year (Table 6.2).

Table 6.2 Profile of B&B operations

Establishment Year	Number of Businesses	Number of Units	Number of Beds	Number of Employees
1986	64	566	1900	176
1987	74	653	2183	198
1988	90	811	2746	231
1989	114	1112	3820	310
1990	145	1545	5364	396
1991	191	2031	7159	490
1992	255	2552	9066	623
1993	351	3074	11,450	781
1994	444	3507	12,572	966

Source: Fleischer et al.(1994).

Today, rural tourism in Israel is based on nature activities and rooted in the rural way of life. Tourist accommodation is generally B&B operations in kibbutzim, moshavim, and other private types of rural settlements. Local restaurants offer a range of cuisines from vegetarian food to ethnic homestyle cooking. Popular activities in rural vacations include water activities, nature walks, visiting national parks and tours of the rural settlements (Fleischer and Pizam 1997). In a short time rural tourism has consequently become an integral part of the social and economic life of many rural regions in Israel.

6.4   Economic Impact of Tourism on Rural Regions in Israel

An expenditure survey of visitors at B&B accommodation in the 1993 season (Fleischer et al 1994) reported the average amount spent by the individual visitor to be about US $45 per day. Of this, $27.40 (61 percent) was spent within the community in which the B&B establishment is located, and the remaining amount outside the community. Approximately 49 percent of the expenditures were on lodging, 16.5 percent on food in restaurants, 10 percent on food bought in grocery stores and supermarkets, 9.0 percent on gasoline, and the remaining 15 percent on attractions, entertainment and souvenirs. The majority of the non-lodging expenses (77 percent) occurred outside the B&B community (US$17.60 out of $23). The largest 'outside of the community' beneficiaries were the restaurant, food store and service station sectors, which as a group earned an average of US$11.63 per visitor per day or 26 percent of the daily expenditures.

The total revenue of the B&B's was estimated to be US$18 million in 1993 (Fleischer, Nitzav and Biran 1994). A Multi Regional Input - Output (MRIO) model developed for the Israeli economy (Freeman et al. 1990; Fleischer et al. 1988) was used in order to estimate the economic impact of rural tourism on rural regions of Israel. The open model multiplier (excluding household demand) was estimated to be 1.75 (Fleischer and Freeman 1997). Adding the multiplier effect to the direct impact generated an additional US$13.5 million for a total of US$31.5 million. It should be noted that all the indirect effects occur in non-tourism firms which supply the tourism enterprises with goods and services (Fletcher 1989). This reinforces the argument that B&B establishments are only one of the elements in the total rural tourism sector, which enhance the entire regional economy. It also shows that although rural tourism is mainly an auxiliary source of income for rural residents it has a much broader role in the regional perspective.

6.5   Support Schemes for Rural Tourism in Israel

During the period of rapid growth of rural tourism in Israel in the early 1990s four development bottlenecks were identified by the Israel Ministry of Tourism (Fleischer and Engel 1996). The most significant one was lack of know-how and professional and managerial skills of the farmers to operate a tourism business. The second was lack of suitable infrastructure in the rural settlement. The third was lack of proper planning of the settlements for tourism – the infrastructure in the rural settlements is suitable to accommodate the families living in them but not to host a large number of guests. The fourth was lack of funds to invest in the new business. Two things should be noted from this list of barriers to rural tourism development. One is that the first three barriers for entry are a result from the transition from an agricultural based economy to tourism based activities. Also, as already noted, a central feature in ensuring a successful transition from agriculture to tourism is the capacity to upgrade human capital of the individual entrepreneurs.

Responding to these needs the Israel Ministry of Tourism in cooperation with other national, local and non-governmental organizations established 'Tourism Incubators' or Centres for Tourism Training and Counselling (Fleischer and Engel 1996). The objective was to provide existing and potential entrepreneurs with a range of counselling services to help them start or expand their businesses, or to prevent their closure. The counselling centres serve two purposes. The first is supplying the entrepreneur with the tools they lack at present for running a tourism business. The second relates to the need for comprehensive in-service training to provide the necessary skills for the long term success of an ongoing enterprise.

6.6   Centres for Tourism Training and Counselling (Tourism Incubators)

There are 14 tourism incubators in Israel located in 14 different rural regions. Each one supplies its services to entrepreneurs living or operating in its region. This is because most of the entrepreneurs are in their midlife, pursuing a second career, and so training at the local level is the most convenient and efficient way of running the program. Services and assistance are supplied through individual counselling and training (one-on-one), or group training (Fleischer and Engel 1996).

The following services and assistance are provided:
- Assessing the feasibility of a new idea or project
- Preparing a business plan
- Case studies of existing tourism businesses
- Advising and guidance of small businesses on a one-to-one basis at varying stages of business development
- Participation in funding courses on the subjects of small business management and rural tourism for the individual entrepreneur within the framework of regional colleges
- Marketing counselling on a group basis. A small group of entrepreneurs from the same area receives guidance and prepares a marketing plan with a marketing expert
- Rural settlements receiving recognition as tourism villages from the government are entitled to guidance, training and advice to help them during the transformation from agricultural to tourism villages.

6.7   Tourism Incubator Activities

Since 1992 the incubators have provided services to some 800 entrepreneurs. Detailed data are available for 1994 and 1995 as seen in Tables 6.2 and 6.3. In 1994 and 1995, 503 projects were processed by incubators. 13,700 subsidized counselling hours were used out of the 27,000 hours approved. About half of the projects (54 percent) used the incubators for help in the first stages of transferring the idea into a business, including diagnosis, economic analysis and program preparation. About 37 percent of these project ideas materialized with the help of the incubators into established tourism businesses. The rest of the projects were existing businesses; about one third of them needed one-to-one guidance at different stages of the business life cycle while the rest were marketing and tourism village projects (see Table 6.3). In terms of counselling hours, the majority was allocated to one-to-one counselling for businesses that had already received approval and had started to operate (see Table 6.3).

Table 6.3 Distribution of projects and hours according to counselling field

1994–1995

Item	Projects (%)	Hours & Budget (%)
Diagnosis	25	19
Economic Analysis	14	10
Program preparation	15	10
Counselling	31	48
Marketing	11	8
Other	4	5
Total	100	100
Absolute value	503 projects	13,700 hrs ($ 822,000)

Source: Meler (1996).

Table 6.4 Distribution of projects and hours according to types of projects

1994–1995

Enterprise	Projects (%)	Hours & Budget (%)
B&B	36	38
Restaurants	10	8
Commerce	8	7
Tours	12	14
Festivals	10	10
Attractions	11	12
Tourism villages	3	3
Other	10	8
Total	100	100
Absolute value	503 projects	13,700 hrs ($ 822,000)

Source: Meler (1996).

Tourism businesses served by incubators include Bed and Breakfast, restaurants, commerce (small specialty stores), tours (jeeps, camels etc.), festivals, attractions and tourism villages (Table 6.4). B&B projects are the largest group (181 businesses). This substantiates the claim that the motor for the development of rural tourism in Israel is the B&B operation. All the other activities have developed in response to the demand created by B&B tourists for ancillary rural tourism facilities beyond the B&B operations. This has lead to the creation of additional new tourism operations (Fleischer et al. 1993).

6.8   Economic Impact of the Tourism Incubators

Since the objective of the incubators was to support tourism as an alternative source of income and employment to agriculture, it was important to assess their contribution to the economy of the rural regions. Data for this type of analysis were available only for the B&B sector from the rural accommodation census (Fleischer et al. 1994). Thus the economic impact analysis was done only for the 181 B&B business that participated in the tourism incubators program in 1994 and 1995. It should be kept in mind that they represent only one third of the total number of projects.

Two major indices were estimated in the analysis: the cost of creating a job and the ratio of the tax revenue generated by program assisted businesses and the cost of the program.

6.8.1   Cost per Job

To estimate the employment generated by the program it was first necessary to assess the cost of creating a job. Table 6.5 below demonstrates the different stages in the employment estimation. The initial number of jobs created in the 181 B&B projects was estimated from the 1994 census data. It was found that there was an average of 2.1 jobs created per B&B or some 380 jobs for the entire sector. However, it should be considered that part of this employment would have occurred even in the absence of the incubator program (the deadweight effect). This effect was determined to be about 24 percent based on an evaluation of Israeli small business loan fund program (Felsenstein et al. 1998). Taking this factor into account the total number of jobs generated by the incubator program is approximately 289.

It was found that each job created directly by the program creates an additional 0.7 jobs indirectly in businesses supplying goods and services to the B&B business (Fleischer and Freeman, 1997). Thus, the total number of jobs created by the program in 1994–95 was about 491 jobs. Since the B&B market at this stage of its development was characterized by excess demand there was no substitution effect. That is, the businesses in the program did not displace existing firms.

The total budget for the B&B enterprises in the tourism incubator program for 1994–95 was $312,360 (NIS equivalent). Therefore the subsidy-value-per-job-created attributable to the program is calculated to be $636. This is a relatively low cost and is less than other small business support programs in Israel where subsidy per job has been estimated as ranging from $836 to $1,290. (Felsenstein, et al. 1998). In comparison, the estimated cost of creating a job in a Small Business Development Center program in the USA is substantially greater at $1,750 (Chrisman and Katrishen 1995). All these figures are still very low compared to large scale regional assistance programs in Israel such as the Law for the Encouragement of Capital Investments. Albeit, it should be noted that the subsidy-per-job is for the marginal cost in creating a job not the cost-per-job.

Table 6.5 Employment estimation of B&B projects

Stages of Analysis	Number of Employees
Initial estimation (181x2.1)	380
Deadweight employment (-24%)	289
Multiplier effect (1.7)	491

6.8.2 Tax Revenues

Estimated average revenues per B&B enterprise in 1994 prices are $40,000 a year (based on the 1994 B&B census). This estimate includes 17 percent value added tax, i.e. each firm pays on the average $5,840 a year VAT. Accordingly, the 181 new firms that received tourism incubator services paid over $1 million a year in VAT besides income tax. The cost of the incubator project for the B&B firms was around $300,000 (see Table 6.3). That means that this support system generates approximately $3 in tax revenues, from VAT only, for every $1 spent on the program. In a similar analysis done in the USA on Small Businesses Development Center counselling activities it was determined that the counselling activity generated a similar $2.61 in tax revenue for every $1 spent on the program (Chrisman and Katrishen 1994).

6.9   Summary and Conclusions

In Israel, rural tourism activities are growing very fast and are projected to continue growing in the future. Rural settlements that were based on agriculture have turned to tourism due to the general decline in the agriculture sector. Most Israeli operators, as rural tourism operators in other parts of the world, have entered into business in order to supplement their income and enable them to maintain their agricultural holdings. The very nature of the rural tourism vacation creates considerable impact on the rural region for all types of businesses including non-tourism businesses. Though rural tourism in Israel is not the major source of family income (as in most other countries where this form of tourism is highly developed) it does enable farmers to diversify and retain their traditional agricultural activities. Thus, many national and local governments support tourism in rural regions as an alternative economic activity to agriculture.(Oppermann 1995; Staudacher 1984).

Tourism incubators in Israel were established as one specific means of supporting rural regions to make the necessary adjustments in infrastructure and human capital from agricultural to tourism activities. This tourism incubators program removes the most important stumbling block for the development of rural tourism, i.e. lack of professional and managerial skills of the farmers. It was also found to be justifiable from a public policy perspective since the cost of creating a job is relatively low and more importantly, the tax revenue generated from the program is higher than the cost of operating the program. From this it can be concluded that programs such as the Israeli tourism incubators are efficient in that they are aimed directly at the major bottlenecks and are low cost. They are readily adaptable in other national contexts and can give rural regions the push needed for their economic development in the process of structural economic change they are undergoing.

References

Aharoni, Y. (1991), *The Israeli Economy: Dreams and Realities.* Routledge, London and New York.

Bates and Wacker S.C. (1996), 'Tourism and the European Union: A Practical Guide', EU Funding, Other Support, EU Policy and Tourism. *European Commission, Directorate-General XXIII Tourism Unit.* Luxembourg.

Butler, R. and Clark, G. (1992), 'Tourism in Rural Areas Canada and the United Kingdom', in Bowler, I.R., Bryant, C.R. and Nellis, M.D. (eds), *Contemporary Rural Systems in Transition, vol. 2: Economy and Society,* CAB International, Wallingford, Oxon.

Chrisman J.J. and Katrishen, F.(1994), 'The Economic Impact of Small Business Development Center Counseling Activities in the United States: 1990-1991', *Journal of Business Venturing,* vol. 9, pp. 271–80.

Chrisman J.J. and Katrishen, F. (1995), 'The Small Businesses Development Center Program in the USA: A Statistical Analysis of its Impact on Economic Development', *Entrepreneurship & Regional Development,* vol. 7, pp. 143–55.

Commission of the European Communities (1992), *Farm Household Adjustment in Western Europe 1987-1991,* Luxembourg: Office for Official Publications of the European Communities.

Countryside Working Group (1991), *Tourism and the Environment – Maintaining the Balance*. Report of the Countryside Working Group, to the Tourism & Environment Task Force, English Tourist Board.

Davies, E.T. (1983), *The Role of Farm Tourism in the Less Favoured Areas of England and Wales,* Agricultural Economics Unit, University of Exeter, Exeter.

Echtner, C.M. (1994), 'Entrepreneurial Training in Developing Countries', *Annals of Tourism Research,* vol. 22, no. 2, pp. 119–33.

Evans. N.J. and Ilbery, B.W. (1989), 'A Conceptual Framework for Investigating Farm-Based Accommodation and Tourism in Britain', *Journal of Rural Studies,* vol. 5, pp. 257–66.

Felsenstein, D. Fleischer, A. and Sidi, A. (1998), 'Measuring the Employment Impacts of Regional Small Business Program', *Public Administration Quarterly.*(forthcoming).

Fleischer A., Rotem A and Banin T., (1993), *New Directions in Recreation and Tourism Activities in the Rural Sector in Israel – Demand and Supply Factors,* Research Report,(Hebrew) Development Study Center.

Fleischer, A. Biran, A. and Nitzav, Y. (1994), *A Census of Rural Accommodations in Israel,* (Hebrew) Israel Ministry of Tourism, Jerusalem.

Fleischer, A. and Engel J.(1996), 'Tourism Incubators – A Support scheme for Rural Tourism in Israel', *Proceeding of WTO CEU-ETC Joint Seminar on Rural Tourism: A Solution for Employment, Local Development and Tourism,* WTO, Madrid.

Fleischer, A., Talpaz, H. and Freeman, D. (1988), 'A General Equilibrium Model with Multiregional Input Output Tables', Socio-Economic Planning Sciences, vol. 22, no. 5, pp. 195–200.

Fleischer, A. and Freeman, D. (1997), 'Multiregional-Input-Output Analysis – A Tool for Measuring the Economic Impact of Tourism', *Annals of Tourism,* vol. 24, no. 4, pp. 998–1001.

Fleischer, A., and Pizam, A. (1997), 'Rural Tourism in Israel', *Tourism Management,* vol. 18, no. 6, pp. 367–72.

Fletcher, J.E.(1989), 'Input-Output Analysis and Tourism Impact Studies', *Annals of Tourism Research,* vol. 16, no. 4, pp. 514–29.

Freeman, D., Talpaz, H. Fleischer, A.and Laufman, O. (1990), 'A Multi Regional Input-Output Model for Israel and Extensions: Methodology and Experience', in Boyce, D.E., Nijkamp, P. and Shefer, D. (eds), *Regional Science Retrospect and Prospect,* Springer-Verlag.

Getz, D. (1994), 'Residents' Attitudes Towards Tourism: A Longitudinal Study in Spey Valley, Scotland, *Tourism Management,* vol. 15, no. 4, pp. 248–58.

Gilbert, D. (1989), 'Rural Tourism and Marketing: Synthesis and New Ways of Working,' *Tourism Management,* vol. 10, no. 1, pp. 3–50.

Hjalager, A.M. (1996), 'Agricultural Diversification Into Tourism: Evidence of a European Community Development Programme', *Tourism Management,* vol. 17, no. 2, pp. 103–11.

Johnstone, W.D., Nicholson, C. Stone, M.K. and Taylor, R.E. (1990), 'Country Work: A New Review of Rural Economic Training and Employment Initiatives', Cirencester, UK; Action with Communities in Rural England (ACRE), The Planning Exchange, Glasgow, pp. 92–106.

Kariel, H.G. and Kariel, P.E. (1982), 'Socio-Economic Impacts of Tourism: An Example from the Austrian Alps', *Geografiska Annaler,* vol. 64B, pp. 1–16.

Kieselbach, S.R. and Long, P.T.(1990), 'Tourism and the Rural Revitalization Movement', *Parks and Recreation,* vol. 25, no. 3, pp. 62–6.

Lerner, M. and Saaty, S. (1997), 'Entrepreneurship in Tourism: Performance factors of Small Tourism Ventures', *Paper submitted to the Entrepreneurship Division of the Academy of Management for the Annual Meeting in Boston.*

Luloff, A.E., Bridger, J.C., Graefe, A.R., Saylor, M. (1994), 'Assessing Rural Tourism Efforts in the United States', *Annals of Tourism Research,* vol. 21, no. 1, pp. 46–64.

McInerney, J. and Turner, M. (1991), *Patterns Performance and Prospects in Farm Diversification,* University of Exeter, Exeter.

Meler, K. (1996), *Tourism Incubators – Summary of 1994 and 1995,* Ministry of Tourism, Israel.

OECD (1993), *What Future for Our Countryside? – A Rural Development Policy,* OECD, Paris.

OECD (1994), *Tourism Policy and International Tourism in OECD Countries, 1991-1992, Special Feature: Tourism Strategies and Rural Development,* OECD, Paris.

Oppermann, M. (1995), 'Holidays on the Farm', *Journal of Travel Research,* vol. 34, no.1, pp. 63–7.

Oppermann, M. (1996), 'Rural Tourism in Southern Germany', *Annals of Tourism Research,* vol. 23, no. 1, pp. 86–102.

Page, S.J. and Getz (1997), *The Business of Rural Tourism International Perspective,* International Thomson Business Press, London.

Pearce, P.L. (1990), 'Farm Tourism in New Zealand – A Social Situation Analysis', *Annals of Tourism Research,* vol. 17, no. 3, pp. 337–52.

Rickard, R.C. (1983), *The Role of Farm Tourism in the Less Favored Areas of England and Wales,* Exeter: University of Exeter – Agricultural Economics Unit, Report No. 218.

Staudacher, C. (1984), 'Invention, Diffusion und Adoption der Betriebsinnvation Urlaub auf dem Bauernhof', *Zeitschrift fuer Agrarogeographie,* vol. 2, pp. 14–35.

Stevens, T. (1990), 'Greener than Green', *Leisure Management,* vol. 10, no. 9, pp. 64–6.

Swinnerton, G.S. (1982), *Recreation on the Agricultural Land in Alberta,* Environment Council of Alberta, Edmonton.

Vincent, J.A. (1980), 'The Political Economy of the Alpine Development: Tourism or Agriculture in St Maurice', *Sociologia Ruralis,* vol. 20, pp. 250–71.

7 The Economic Impact of Tourism in Israel: A Multiregional Input-Output Analysis

DANIEL FREEMAN AND ESTHER SULTAN

7.1 Introduction

The number of incoming tourists had been increasing at an annual rate of 15 percent over the period 1990–1995. Their expenditures in 1995 accounted for 30 percent of the export of services and approximately 11 percent of total exports. The number and the expenditures of domestic tourists had also been increasing, reflecting the continuing increase in their personal income.

The development of tourism as a means to widen the export base and generate more employment is of primary importance. Policy makers in the government need to know the magnitude of the impact of international and domestic tourist expenditures on the Israeli economy in order to make decisions about budget allocations for the development of tourist facilities.

In response to this need, the Ministry of Tourism has conducted several studies on the volume of direct purchases of incoming and domestic tourists in various economic sectors and their regional distribution. The objective of this chapter is to assess and estimate the extent of the contribution to GDP of the impacts of intra and interregional tourist expenditures. This analysis will allow the government to establish policy objectives for the development of tourist facilities in the different regions of Israel, especially in the North and South. The policy analyst might be interested in responding to such questions as: how much additional income is to be generated? How many jobs will be created? What will be the magnitude of the addition to GDP? What is the impact of direct demand in one region on the output in other regions, and what is the extent of the feedback mechanism whereby increased production in the originating region is met by successive rounds of re-imports in order to satisfy this demand.

The outcome of the analysis will enable policy makers to make decisions about the allocation of resources. Estimation of tourism's economic impact is complex because it entails an analysis of the direct purchases from several branches simultaneously.

Archer[1] (developed regional multipliers as a tool for analysing the economic impact of tourism at the single region level. These regional multipliers were based on the Keynsian model and thus were highly aggregated. Liu and Var[2] have reformulated Archer's model by disaggregation of the accommodation sector. Briguglio[3] claimed that the Keynsian Model and an Input Output (IO) model yield the same results at an aggregate level. The IO model was chosen here due to three advantages. First, IO models have the ability to evaluate the impact on each branch separately. Second, they can disaggregate the impact by contribution of each region. And third, they are able to measure the impact on contributing regions in response to the demand from the originating region and the successive rounds of repercussions between them.

Fletcher[4] and other researchers[5] propose the use of single table IO analysis as a tool whose results respond to the foregoing questions due to its capability to evaluate the simultaneous impacts of sectoral interdependencies. They have applied single table IO models to both the national and the regional levels. In the following analysis we compare our results with those found by Fletcher.[6]

As described by Blaine[7] the single-table modellers at the regional level assumed that all the leakages from the region did not re-enter it. However it can very well be that the 'imports' from other regions into the region and 'export' leaks from that region to other regions in order that they can produce to fulfil its demand, are not accounted for in the multiplier impact. Also, more importantly, the indirect and induced impacts created in other regions are ignored as part of the multiplier. This leads to a downward bias in the estimation of regional multipliers.

The Multi-regional Input-Output Model (MRIO) used in this research adds to the IO framework the capability to evaluate the impacts of tourist expenditures on interregional interdependencies simultaneously with sectoral impacts. A MRIO model was used in Israel previously in evaluating national level and regional projects, but this is the first time that it is used to evaluate the impacts of tourism.[8] The estimates of the magnitude of the economic impacts of the expenditures are then expressed both in monetary terms and in terms of the number of employees. The results are then expressed as multiregional input-output multipliers. Thus, this model takes into account the possible returns of the leakages and the impacts in other regions since it includes a multiregion trade flow matrix, thus evaluating the full impact.

7.2 Definitions

The definitions are as defined by the Israeli Central Bureau of Statistics:

International tourism includes entries of foreign nationals on a tourist visa, (and excludes: immigrant, immigrant citizens, potential immigrants or temporary residents). It includes cruise passengers as visitors. Some of the tourists stay more than one year, and some do not stay overnight.

These data do not include Israelis who live overseas and visit Israel presenting an Israeli passport.

Domestic tourism includes any Israeli resident on a trip inside Israel out of his/her usual residence environment, except for immigrant or work purposes. Two types of domestic tourism are distinguished: day trippers and travellers who stay away from home more than one night.

Income from International tourism includes foreign tourists' expenditures in Israel on goods and services. It also includes income of Israeli shipping companies and airlines catering for International passengers.

Income from domestic tourism includes all expenses of the population relating to tourism within the country.

7.3   Methodology: The MRIO Model

The classical definitions of national level or single region IO multipliers are brought forth by authors such as Miernyk,[9] and the multiregional ones by Polenske[10] and with Dipasquale.[11] They have defined three levels of impacts: direct, indirect, and induced.

While the principal objective of the national IO model is to identify and analyse the intersectoral structure of the economy, the objective of the MRIO model is to give content to spatial elements in order to study the structures and linkages of individual branches within a region and the interrelationships with other branches in the region and in other regions.

As such, MRIO models are most useful for analysing and assessing different investment strategies and their direct and indirect impacts on the economy of the investigated region and simultaneously on other regions. A further advantage is the flexibility of the model to suit the objective at hand. Thus, branches which are important to the study of tourism were highly disaggregated while the remaining sectors were aggregated to keep the size of the model manageable.

The model is composed of two multiregional direct column coefficient matrices: (1) an IO matrix, (2) a Trade Flow (TF) matrix. The services' column of the IO matrix is disaggregated into ten branches that are prominent in tourist expenditures: International air transport, air transport authority, three classes of hotels, two classes of restaurants, car rentals, sightseeing tour buses and domestic flights. The other sectors of the economy are highly aggregated, such as to make the size of 24*24 branches in each of six regions more manageable.

Two types of multipliers are shown here: Type I is the ratio of indirect + direct impacts to direct impacts[12] Type II is the ratio of induced + indirect +direct impacts to direct impacts.

The magnitude of Type I (open model) output multiplier of any sector is defined as the sum of the direct plus the indirect output divided into the final direct demand from that branch, while in Type II (Partially closed model, hereinafter referred to as: closed model) the induced impacts are added to the numerator. The model yields various multipliers of both types (output, income, employment etc.) that are all calculated on the basis of the above ratios.

7.3.1 The Technological Matrix

The structure of the matrix is based on the assumption that the intermediate uses of sector j from sectors i are constant ratios of the output of sector j. The model has a certain weakness, since it does not contain a mechanism that responds to substitution between intermediate resources due to price changes. Yet, its use is justified because the rate of change over time of the direct coefficients is very slow. Thus, the error in measurement of the impacts of intersectoral dependencies, using a model from former years in a current one, is relatively slight.

The regional I/O technological matrices ($A^n = A^n_{ij}$) are arranged along the diagonal of the matrix in a NM*NM multiregional matrix (N regions and M branches), where off-diagonal parts of the table are zeroes.

The matrix expression of intersectoral relationships, and between them and the end uses ('final uses' in IO terms, i.e: Private and Government Consumption, Investment and Exports) and the gross output in an I/O table is given in equation 7.1:

$$X = AX + Y \tag{7.1}$$

where
X= Gross Output
A= direct coefficients
Y= final Uses (hereinafter : end uses)

It is obvious that equation 7.1 does not show a regional breakdown.

7.3.2 The Integration of Interregional Trade Flows

The Technological Matrix of intermediate uses that describes inter-branch relationships in the production process is combined with a Trade Flow Matrix where $C = C_m^{gh}$ is the flow of a good in branch m from region g to region h, that has the foregoing dimensions NM*NM and includes N*N sub-matrices of trade, and in each the trade flows are along its diagonal.

Equation 7.2 combines the two matrices through multiplication:

$$X = CAX + CY \tag{7.2}$$

where C is the trade flow matrix. It can be rewritten as follows:

$$(I - CA)X = CY \tag{7.2a}$$

Equation 7.2a is inverted in order to show the dependency of gross output on the final uses (end uses), as shown in equation 7.3:

$$X = (I - CA)^{-1} CY \qquad (7.3)$$

The output multiplier B is derived from equation 7.3 as shown in equation 7.4:

$$B = (I - CA)^{-1} C \qquad (7.4)$$

7.4   Data Sources

A well known problem in constructing an IO model for analysis is the reliability and sufficiency of the data. The data that were used in this research were from the following sources.

7.4.1 Data sources of International Tourists

Statistics on incoming international tourists to Israel are collected and published by using the following methods.

7.4.1.1 Frontier control points Every foreigner who enters the country is requested to fill out a form with the following personal details: name, surname, passport number, place of residence, nationality, type of transportation used and arrival and departure dates. The data are typed into the computer system and its copy transmitted to the Central Bureau of Statistics (CBS) who processes, evaluates and publishes the data.[13]

7.4.1.2 Statistics by type of accommodation[14] All the tourist hotels report monthly on the number of available rooms and beds, numbers of guests and person nights of International and Domestic tourists. About 50 percent of them (180) report every three months on the revenue, persons employed and wages. In case that some hotels fail to report, the data are adjusted to account for the missing data according to the averages of all those that reported.

7.4.1.3 Survey of tourist expenditures[15] The Ministry of tourism conducted a survey with the objective of studying and evaluating of the pattern of expenditures by incoming tourists.[16] The procedure involved the following methods:
- A questionnaire was handed to 40,000 tourists upon their departure. It contained questions concerning the purpose of visit, type of visit, demographic profile and the amount and components of the expenditure. The response rate was about 40 percent.

- A questionnaire in a format of a diary was handed to 10,000 tourists on their arrival in Israel by air (70 percent arrived here by air). They were asked to fill it out day by day and return it on departure. They were encouraged to do it by a promise to include them in a prize draw. The response rate was only 6 percent.
- Analysis of Package Tours: A sample of 30 packages was analysed. The basic approach was to separate the costs of airfare and agent fees abroad by deducting them from the total cost of the package. The expenditures were then separated into the appropriate economic categories.

The expenditure data from the two questionnaires concerning accommodation and food did not differ by much, but the data on shopping and transportation differed significantly. The reported amounts in the diaries were much higher than the ones in the questionnaires. A possible explanation for this disparity is that small daily expenses that were noted daily in the diaries, which added up to a significant sum, were forgotten by the respondents to the questionnaires. A correction factor was applied to adjust the gap and the outcome was compared with the results of the analysis of the package tours.

7.4.1.4 Tourist hotels – income, expenditures and product The CBS has been conducting since 1981 surveys of the 'Income, expenditure and product' for the Ministry of Tourism.[17] These surveys present data of the economic accounts of the hotels by level, size, number of rooms and annual occupancy.

Two kinds of income are presented: (1) Operating income at factor prices (i.e. subsidies are included and the taxes are excluded): (2) Non-operating income which was received but was not related to the operation of the hotels. (Its sources are profits from the sale of properties, receipts from former years, profits from the sale of tradeable securities, etc.).

Purchased Inputs include operating purchased inputs (the purchase cost of goods and services, such as food, bedding, kitchen utensils, personnel uniforms, electricity, water, fuel, maintenance and repair, communication services, as well as expenditure related to the management of the hotel – (management fees, accounting, professional services, municipal taxes, fees and insurance, bad and written-off debts, etc.).

Labour Costs include all the expenditure on wages and other expenses on employees such as service workers, management and clerical employees (inclusive of kibbutz members), housing for personnel, their meals, service fees, etc.

Profit and Capital Returns include profits before deduction of depreciation on obsolescence of assets and net financing expenditures.

7.4.2 Domestic Tourism

The data of domestic tourism were taken from the following sources.

7.4.2.1 Statistics by type of accommodation

7.4.2.1 Statistics by type of accommodation Israeli person nights in hotels, youth hostels and other accommodation from the foregoing sources of tourist hotels.[18]

7.4.2.2 Household survey A telephone sample survey of 1,000 households (92 percent of Israeli households have a telephone) was conducted by the Ministry of Tourism in 1991[19] and 1994.[20] The questions encompass expenditures on all tourist activities in the country and abroad. It is planned that such surveys will be conducted every 2–3 years.

7.4.2.3 Leisure activities of persons aged 14 and over[21] A time budgeting survey was conducted by CBS from November 1991 to April 1992. The data were collected using both a diary and a questionnaire. The diaries were used to gather information on the allocation of time of people aged 14 years and over for various activities, such as work, studies, home and family involvement, entertainment and others. The questionnaires were used to provide information on the frequency of participation in specific activities such as use of free time, patterns of recreation, participation in sports activities, excursions within the country, community centre activities etc.

The investigative method was that enumerators filled out the questionnaires and assisted in filling up the diaries which were filled out for every person aged 14 and over.

Two types of questionnaires were used: (1) A family questionnaire was filled up with data about the household in general (number of rooms, home equipment, etc.): (2) A personal questionnaire about each member of the household (age, sex, etc.). Information on less frequent activities which take longer periods of time were recorded, such as education, employment, level of religiousness, personal position and satisfaction in different areas. Other questions pertained to day trips and longer vacations with overnight stays.

Two types of diaries were used: (1) A recollection of yesterday through an interview by the enumerator; (2) A diary filled out by the interviewee on a specific day after the interview. Each diary was designed for recordings of one day (24 hours), but some interviewees were asked to fill up diaries for 2–3 days. The main activity was recorded for each time block.

7.4.2.4 A supplementary survey of other tourist services[22] A supplementary survey on income, expenditure and product of restaurants, domestic flights, excursion buses and car rental was conducted in 1993. one objective was to find out the share of incoming tourists in their output. The second objective was to find out the

117

expenditure pattern of the different businesses. the third objective was to find out the multiregional distribution of the output and the costs. The sampled populations that were surveyed were relatively small: one domestic flight air line (100 percent), 6 car rental companies (80 percent), 17 companies operating as tour operators and 15 restaurants. The data were cross-checked with other sources, such as CBS and the Income Tax authorities.

When comparing the results from different sources, we found some inconsistency between the reports of the supplier sector (for example: Hotels, Tour Operators, Restaurants etc.) and the results from the Consumers' surveys. We were aware that generally, quantitative and monetary data from tourists' surveys about their expenses differed from the reports of the suppliers of the goods and the services. These are due to the difference between the reports of the suppliers' price versus the consumers' price, and the tendencies of the consumers to classify expenses into some branches more than the others, as well as the recall problems that cause to forgotten items. Nordstrom[23] indicated the same problem in his research in Sweden. Thus adjustments were made in order to align the final uses from the above two types of sources.

7.4.2.5 The sources of technical and trade flow data The IO direct coefficients of Israel for 1988[24] were adjusted to the 1994 price level in two-steps: (1) A multiplication of the table rows by wholesale price indices of the branches: (2) The sum of the intermediate uses in each column was adjusted back to its sum before the multiplication of the rows by the indices. The national level coefficients were applied in all the regions.

7.4.3 The Sources of Trade Flows

The trade flows of the agricultural and industrial sectors were derived from a truck transportation survey.[25] The trade flows of the services were derived by the difference between demand and supply in each region.

7.5   The Tourism Multipliers

The model which is used here has been constructed especially for the present study. The database is the above sources. The values are expressed in NIS in 1994 prices. The values of goods and services purchased by tourists are introduced into the end use column and then multiplied by the MRIO inverse-matrix. The multipliers are presented later on as both open-model (type I) and closed model (type II) multipliers.

Type I multipliers are the Derived Output (which includes the direct + indirect output) and its derivatives as a division by the end uses. Type II are multipliers in which the household sector is endogenized into the 'sector to sector' transaction quadrant which induces output due to the end uses of the employed directly and indirectly. These multipliers are the Compound Derived Output (direct + indirect + induced outputs; hereinafter: compound output) and its derivatives as a division by the final uses.

This chapter presents the results of a study of the Impacts of incoming and domestic tourist expenditures on the Israeli Economy.[26] The distributed impacts of twenty four branches among the six districts major regions of Israel are presented.

7.5.1 Levels of Analysis

First, at the level of the national economy: tourist expenditures (Final Uses) and their impacts on the economic branches and their recursive impacts on the branches of the direct demand. Second, at the Intraregional and interregional level: final uses from branches in each region and its impact on the branches within the region, inter-branch and interregional impacts and their returning repercussions on the final-use branches in the originating region. Third, at the level of the tourist segments: the differences between the impacts of the direct demand of the two tourist segments. And Fourth, at the sectoral level: hotels, restaurants, car rental, excursion buses and domestic flights. The tourist expenditures in these branches generate production in the whole economy.

7.5.2 Multipliers of two Segments of Tourism

In addition multipliers are collected for two segments:
• The first is a multiplier representing a weighted average of two segments of domestic tourists: Lodging tourists and day trippers.
• The second is a multiplier representing a weighted average of five segments of international tourists: tourists visiting Israel for all purposes and cruise passengers.

7.6 Major Empirical Findings

The findings are presented in three sections: section 7.6.1 the national level multipliers, section 7.6.2 the comparison with other economic branches multipliers and section 7.6.3 the regional level of tourism multipliers.

7.6.1 National Level Multipliers

National level impacts are presented in Table 7.1 part a in two separate subtotals. First, the sum of the final uses of the two segments from the economic branches in 1994 was 10.9 billion NIS, the derived output was 19.1 billion NIS and the compounded derived output was 37.6 billion NIS.

119

Table 7.1 National-level multipliers

Economic/ tourist segments	End uses & Output (million NIS, 1994, prices)			Miernyk type multipliers		Polenske type multipliers	
	End uses	Derived output	Compound derived output	Derived output	Compound drived output	Derived output	Compound derived output
End uses and Output							
Domestic	3,861	6,827	13,078	1.77	3.39	–	–
International	7,021	12,309	24,521	1.76	3.50	–	–
Subtotal from sectors	10,873	19,136	37,599	1.76	3.46	–	–
Rent from apartments	693	693	693	1.00	1.00	–	–
TOTAL	11,566	19,829	38,292 *(part a)*	1.71	3.31	–	–
Labour costs							
Domestic	1,025	1,922	2,945	1.88	2.87	0.50	0.76
International	1,940	3,768	5,762	1.94	2.97	0.54	0.82
TOTAL	2,965	5,690	8,707 *(part b)*	1.92	2.94	0.52	0.80
Other value added							
Domestic	422	896	2,099	2.12	4.97	0.23	0.54
International	873	1,704	4,062	1.95	4.65	0.24	0.58
Rent from apartments	693	693	693	1.00	1.00	0.06	0.06
TOTAL	1,988	3,293	6,843 *(part c)*	1.66	3.45	0.28	0.59
Value added							
Domestic	1,447	2,818	5,044	1.95	3.49	0.73	1.31
International	2,813	5,472	9,824	1.95	3.49	0.78	1.40
Rent from apartments	693	693	693	1.00	1.0	0.06	0.06
TOTAL	4,953	8,983	15,561 *(part d)*	1.81	3.14	0.83	1.43
No. of employees							
Domestic	20,593	33,638	46,610	1.63	2.41	–	–
International	35,613	60,208	91,357	1.69	2.57	–	–
TOTAL	56,206	93,846	140,967 *(part e)*	1.67	2.51	–	–

Second, the rent from apartments rented to international tourists which adds to the output 693 million NIS. The weighted average of 1 NIS of the end uses and output from the economic sectors of international and domestic tourists generated a derived output multiplier of 1.76 NIS at the national level, inclusive of the direct expenditure; i.e. each 1 NIS of direct expenditure generates an addition of 0.76 NIS of indirect expenditure. The rent paid by international tourists for apartments adds to the output and to the value added, but the multiplier declines slightly to 1.71 because the rent did not generate indirect impacts.

The compound output multiplier from the economic sectors was 3.46, which indicates that 1 NIS of direct demand generated an extra 2.46 NIS. The multiplier declined slightly with the addition of the rent to 3.31. Table 7.1 (part b) presents the shares of labour costs in the end uses, in the derived output and in the induced output. Two versions of multipliers are presented. Multipliers entitled Miernyk Type[27] are as follows:

- The outcome of the division of the derived labour cost from the derived output by the labour cost in the end uses. The weighted average of the two segments was 1.92, which means that each one NIS of direct labour cost generated an extra 0.92 NIS of indirect labour costs.
- The outcome of the division of labour cost in the compound output by the labour cost in the end uses. The weighted average of the two segments was 2.94, which means that each one NIS of direct labour cost generated an extra 1.94 NIS of indirect labour costs. Part c presents the magnitude of the Other Value Added (OVA) which includes the returns to capital and the indirect taxes in the derived outputs. The magnitude of the Miernyk Multiplier was 1.66 and it means that each NIS of OVA in the end uses generated an extra 0.66 NIS in the derived output. The average of the multiplier in the closed model is 3.45 which indicates that an extra 2.45 NIS is generated in the compound output by 1 NIS of OVA in the end uses.

The Multipliers entitled Polenske Type[28] are the ones that other authors[29] (see Fletcher 1989) call income multipliers and comprise the following:

- The outcome of the division of labour cost in the derived output by the end uses; it means that each one NIS of end uses generates 0.52 NIS of returns to labour.
- The outcome of the division of labour cost in the compound output by the end uses. The weighted average of the two segments was 0.80, which means that each one NIS of end uses generated 0.80 returns to labour.

Part C presents the magnitude of the OVA multiplier: the magnitude of the Polenske Multiplier is 0.24 and it means that each NIS of the end uses generates a 0.24 NIS in the derived output. The average of the multiplier in the closed model is 0.59 which indicates that 0.59 NIS is generated in the compound output by 1 NIS end uses. Table 7.1 (part d) presents the Value Added (from now on: VA) as a sum of the components of the labour costs and OVA.

- The Miernyk multiplier of the economic sectors of the open model was 1.95, and the one of the closed model was 3.49; but the addition of rent from apartments reduced them to 1.81 and 3.14.
- The Polenske multiplier of the open model was between 0.73 and 0.78 NIS, and the one of the closed model was between 1.35 and 1.40; but the addition of rent from apartments reduced them to 0.83 and 1.43 respectively.

The three levels of VA in percentage terms in the GDP of Israel of 223 billion NIS were as follows:
- Share in the end uses – 2.2 percent
- Share in the derived output – 4 percent
- Share in the compound output – 7 percent.

These data indicate that the contribution of tourism to the economy is greater than the direct impact only.

Table 7.1 (part e) demonstrates that 56,206 were employed in 1994 in the direct supply of end uses, while the ones in the derived output (including those in end uses) were 93,845, and those employed in the compound output were 140,967, which was 7.5 percent of the 1,871,000 employed in Israel. These results indicate that the employment impact of the tourist industry is much greater than the direct impact itself.

7.6.2 Comparison with Other Sectors' Multipliers

The weighted averages of the 24 economic sectors' output multipliers contribution to the tourist end uses is presented in Table 7.2 along with the multipliers of each separate sector.

It is shown that the derived output multipliers of restaurants (2.26), the hotels (1.84–1.87), the food industry (1.94) and agriculture (1.90), each has greater multiplier than the average multiplier of tourism. The lower average of the tourism multiplier is due to the fact that car rentals, air transport and tour buses have lower multipliers. Yet the average multipliers of tourism are larger than the industrial sectors (1.44 and 1.45), transport and communications (1.43 and 1.07) because their intermediate uses have a greater share of imports. This conclusion is supported by the data in Table 7.3. The table presents the proportional shares of the primary resources in the derived output multiplier.

The compound output multipliers in Table 7.2 are, of course, much larger, and illustrate the significant contribution of the induced demand of the employed in the direct and derived output.

The average tourism multiplier generates one NIS of end uses of the tourists from each of the sectors. The value added shares in each sector is the sum of returns to labour and capital in the seventh column.

122

Table 7.2 The magnitude of output derived and compound multipliers

Sector number	Economic sector	Derived output multiplier	Compound output multiplier
1	Agriculture	1.90	3.73
2	Food industry	1.94	3.27
3	Petroleum refining	1.33	1.75
4	Quarries & mining	1.72	3.35
5	Non-metal industries	1.66	3.15
6	All other industries	1.45	2.87
7	Electricity & water utilities	1.44	2.52
8	Construction	1.72	3.70
9	Terrestrial & other transportation	1.38	2.71
10	Marine transportation	1.07	1.70
11	Air transportation	1.70	3.23
12	Harbours & harbour authority	1.20	2.92
13	Airport & airport authority	1.43	3.38
14	Communications	1.24	3.28
15	Services	1.40	3.23
16	Trade & general expenditure	2.11	4.71
17	Low-grade hotels & hostels	1.86	3.72
18	Medium-grade hotels	1.87	3.74
19	High-grade hotels	1.84	3.70
20	Restaurants	2.26	4.09
21	Tourist restaurants	1.81	3.17
22	Car rental	1.69	2.95
23	Tour buses	1.62	3.15
24	Domestic flight	1.62	2.80
	Labour cost		3.24
	Average tourism multiplier	1.76	3.50

7.6.3 Regional Level Multipliers

The impact of the two tourist segments on the six districts of Israel is a function of the resources and their interregional trade flows. For example, most of the food for tourist in Eilat at the southern end of Israel is transported from the central regions. The final uses of tourists in the hotels in the north generate demand for goods and services from other regions, such as kitchen utensils, textile goods etc. Thus, the end uses of tourists in one region that does not produce a sufficient quantity (or none at all) of the requested good, generate an import of that good from other regions.

Table 7.3 The shares of primary resources in the VA of the derived output

Sector number	Economic sector	Import CIF	Labour cost	Returns on capital	Total primary resources	VA
1	Agriculture	0.18	0.57	0.25	1	0.82
2	Food industry	0.31	0.41	0.28	1	0.69
3	Petroleum refining	0.76	0.13	0.11	1	0.24
4	Quarries & mining	0.22	0.50	0.27	1	0.78
5	Non-metal industries	0.34	0.46	0.20	1	0.66
6	All othr industries	0.40	0.44	0.16	1	0.60
7	Electricity & water utilities	0.40	0.33	0.37	1	0.70
8	Construction	0.21	0.61	0.18	1	0.79
9	Terrestrial & other transportation	0.09	0.41	0.50	1	0.91
10	Marine transportation	0.83	0.19	−0.03	1	0.17
11	Air transportation	0.40	0.47	0.13	1	0.60
12	Harbours & harbour authority	0.12	0.53	0.35	1	0.88
13	Airport & airport authority	0.08	0.60	0.32	1	0.92
14	Communications	0.32	0.63	0.05	1	0.68
15	Services	0.16	0.56	0.27	1	0.84
16	Trade & general expenditure	0.21	0.80	−0.01	1	0.79
17	Low-grade hotels & hostels	0.15	0.57	0.28	1	0.85
18	Medium-grade hotels	0.15	0.57	0.28	1	0.85
19	High-grade hotels	0.14	0.57	0.29	1	0.86
20	Restaurants	0.18	0.56	0.25	1	0.82
21	Tourist restaurants	0.13	0.42	0.45	1	0.87
22	Car rental	0.09	0.39	0.52	1	0.91
23	Tour buses	0.15	0.47	0.37	1	0.85
24	Domestic flight	0.30	0.36	0.33	1	0.70
	Average tourism multiplier	0.27	0.50	0.23	1	0.73

Table 7.4 Tourism open MRIO model: internal share of each region in its Type I multipliers and derived output due to end uses of international and domestic tourists, 1994

The tourism segment multipliers	Regional end uses	North	Haifa	Centre	Tel Aviv	Jerusalem	South	Each region multiplier
part a: derived output share of each region in its multiplier								
Domestic tourism	1.00	0.83	1.11	0.83	1.03	0.90	0.95	1.77
International tourism	1.00	0.71	0.92	1.11	1.06	0.85	0.69	1.76
Total tourism	1.00	0.77	1.01	0.98	1.05	0.86	0.84	1.76
percentage								
Domestic tourism		47	63	47	58	51	54	100
International tourism		40	53	63	61	49	39	100
Total tourism		44	58	56	60	49	48	100
part b: derived income share in Polenske multiplier of each region								
Domestic tourism	1.00	0.27	0.30	0.27	0.34	0.31	0.30	0.50
International tourism	1.00	0.23	0.29	0.37	0.34	0.30	0.23	0.54
Total tourism	1.00	0.25	0.29	0.32	0.34	0.30	0.27	0.52
percentage								
Domestic tourism		54	61	54	69	63	61	100
International tourism		43	53	69	64	56	42	100
Total tourism		47	56	62	66	57	52	100
part c: derived VA Polenske multiplier share of each region								
Domestic tourism	1.00	0.38	0.44	0.39	0.48	0.44	0.42	0.73
International tourism	1.00	0.33	0.41	0.51	0.51	0.40	0.31	0.78
Total tourism	1.00	0.35	0.43	0.45	0.50	0.41	0.37	0.76
percentage								
Domestic tourism		52	61	53	66	60	58	100
International tourism		42	53	65	65	52	40	100
Total tourism		46	56	59	66	54	49	100
part d: share in employment multiplier of each region								
Domestic tourism	1.00	1.02	1.19	1.02	1.20	1.13	0.97	1.63
International touris	1.00	0.94	1.14	1.15	1.23	1.02	0.93	1.69
Total tourism	1.00	0.98	1.16	1.09	1.22	1.03	0.96	1.67
percentage								
Domestic tourism		63	73	62	73	69	60	100
International tourism		55	68	68	73	60	55	100
Total tourism		59	70	65	73	62	57	100

125

Table 7.5 Tourism closed MRIO model: internal share of each region in its Type II multipliers and derived output due to end uses of international and domestic tourists, 1994

The tourism segment multipliers	Regional end uses	North	Haifa	Centre	Tel Aviv	Jerusalem	South	Each region multiplier
		part a: derived share of each region in its multiplier						
Domestic tourism	1.00	1.34	1.74	1.38	1.82	1.48	1.50	3.39
International tourism	1.00	1.18	1.55	1.84	1.89	1.42	1.13	3.50
Total tourism	1.00	1.25	1.64	1.63	1.87	1.42	1.34	3.46
		percentage						
Domestic tourism		39	51	41	54	44	44	100
International tourism		34	44	53	54	40	32	100
Total tourism		36	48	47	54	41	39	100
		part b: derived income share in Polenske multiplier of each region						
Domestic tourism	1.00	0.33	0.39	0.34	0.46	0.39	0.37	0.76
International tourism	1.00	0.29	0.37	0.46	0.47	0.37	0.28	0.82
Total tourism	1.00	0.31	0.38	0.41	0.47	0.37	0.33	0.80
		percentage						
Domestic tourism		43	51	45	60	51	48	100
International tourism		35	45	56	57	45	34	100
Total tourism		38	47	51	58	47	41	100
		part c: derived VA Polenske multiplier share of each region						
Domestic tourism	1.00	0.54	0.65	0.58	0.76	0.63	0.60	1.31
International tourism	1.00	0.48	0.62	0.75	0.80	0.60	0.46	1.40
Total tourism	1.00	0.51	0.64	0.67	0.79	0.60	0.54	1.37
		percentage						
Domestic tourism		42	50	44	58	49	46	100
International tourism		35	44	54	57	43	33	100
Total tourism		38	47	49	58	44	39	100
		part d: share in employment multiplier of each region						
Domestic tourism	1.00	1.22	1.46	1.24	1.55	1.36	1.15	2.41
International tourism	1.00	1.14	1.41	1.45	1.58	1.24	1.12	2.57
Total tourism	1.00	1.18	1.44	1.35	1.57	1.26	1.14	2.51
		percentage						
Domestic tourism		51	61	52	64	57	48	100
International tourism		44	55	57	61	48	44	100
Total tourism		47	57	54	63	50	46	100

Tables 7.4 and 7.5 present respectively the share of each region in the type I (open model) and in the type II (closed model) multipliers due to end uses of tourists that visit that region. The right-hand column in both tables presents the magnitude of the multiplier of both the national level and each region. Table 7.4 presents the Type I and contains 4 parts, parts a-d, Table 7.5 presents the Type II multipliers and also contains 4 parts a-d. The upper three lines in each of the four parts present the multiplier shares while the three lower lines present these shares presented as percentages of the magnitude of the multiplier. In the following discussion the significant findings are expressed as shares of the multiplier, besides which the same share in percentages is stated in parentheses.

Table 7.4 part a shows the share of each region in the total of the type I multiplier of domestic tourists of 1.77 and of international tourists of 1.76. The magnitudes of the multipliers due to end uses in each region are separately equal because the intermediate direct coefficients were equal. The shares of the other regions in the multipliers of each region are not shown here, but their sum is the difference between the total and each region's share.

- The share of the multiplier of derived output due to final uses of domestic tourists in any of the six regions varies between 0.83 (47 percent) in the North and 1.11 (63 percent) in Haifa.
- The shares of Haifa and of Tel aviv in their multipliers due to domestic tourism, is greater than those of the South and the North.
- The largest share of 1.11 (63 percent) due to domestic tourists in any region was in Haifa as the supplier of all the fuel for both travelling and production in all the branches, since it supplies its own fuel; a little lower share of 1.03 (58 percent) in Tel Aviv, again a high share since it supplies its own services being the supplier of major services to all the other regions and does not have to buy them from other regions.
- The largest share of 1.11 (63 percent) of the derived output multiplier duc to the international tourists is in the Centre, where the international airport is located; and is a little smaller share of 1.06 (61 percent) in Tel Aviv. These figures indicate that those two regions produce for themselves more in response to their own direct end uses.

Table 7.4 (part b) presents the Polenske labour cost multiplier, of which the total of 0.52 is equivalent to the income multiplier of all the foregoing quoted single-region multipliers in the cited articles.[30] The multiplier of 0.54 due to the international tourism is greater than the one of 0.50 due to domestic tourism, especially because of the high import content of the fuel that the domestic day trippers use.

However, in domestic tourism as in the case of the output, the magnitude of the shares in the multiplier varies slightly between the regions, 0.30 (61 percent) in Haifa and 0.34 (69 percent) in Tel Aviv. However a noted difference from the shares in the output multiplier is that the income in the remoter regions is larger in percentage terms: 54 percent in the North, 61 percent in the South and 63 percent in Jerusalem. This is explained by a greater share of labour cost in these regions, because the number of employed persons is larger as shown in part d below.

The shares due to international tourism that stand out were in the Centre of 0.37 (69 percent) and in Tel Aviv of 0.34 (64 percent), but there is a smaller percentage increase of family income in the North, in the South and in Jerusalem. The conclusion is that the domestic tourism generates in these regions more employment and income per 1 NIS of output.

Table 7.4 (part c) presents each region's share in the derived value added multiplier of the open model. The sum of Labour Cost + the OVA not presented here is the VA which is the contribution to the GDP. The VA at the national level was 0.76 due to each 1 NIS of final uses in the open model. The VAs the more prominent regions due to each region's end uses of domestic tourists were 0.44 (61 percent) in Haifa , 0.44 (60 percent) in Jerusalem and 0.48 (66 percent) in Tel Aviv, while those of international tourism were 0.51 (65 percent) in Tel Aviv and 0.51 (65 percent) in the Centre. The conclusion here is parallel to the one made above about the greater impact of family income.

Table 7.4 (part d) present the multiplier for the number of employed persons in the open model. The national level totals of the mare smaller than those of the output multipliers, but the regional shares of the North, the South and of Jerusalem were even larger than those of family income in part b. An explanation of this is that the weighted average labour cost per employed person in the extreme regions is smaller.

Table 7.5 (part a) presents the shares in the type II multiplier of the compound output (closed model) due to final demand in each of the regions. Its monetary magnitude is greater proportionately in all the regions than in the derived output (open model). However, in the case of domestic tourists, the shares and percentage shares of 1.74 (51 percent) in Haifa and of 1.82 (54 percent) in Tel Aviv were more than half of the multiplier of the derived output, but smaller than in the open model. However since the percentage shares of the extreme regions were also smaller, the ratio between the shares of the central to the extreme regions was not changed.

In the case due to international tourists, the shares and percentage shares of 1.84 (53 percent) in Centre and of 1.89 (54 percent) in Tel Aviv were more than half of the multiplier of the derived output, but smaller than in the open model, but the percentage shares of the remoter regions were also smaller, such that the ratio between the shares of the central to the extreme regions was not changed.

A conclusion here is that the percentage shares of each region's compound output, due to final uses of tourists in it, decline while those of other regions increase. However, it should be noted that the absolute value of the output increases in all the regions, but more so in the other regions.

Part b presents the results of the income multiplier of the closed model. The multiplier of 0.80 varies slightly between 0.76 of domestic tourists to 0.82 of international tourists. However, the percentage shares of the central regions Tel Aviv, Centre and Jerusalem due to domestic tourism are in percentage terms larger than those in the compound output.

Part c presents each region's share in the derived multiplier of 1.37 of the compound value added in the closed model at the national level. This means that the compound output generated a greater VA than the end uses as a contribution to the GDP of Israel. The results of the distribution are proportionately parallel to those in part b.

Part d The national level multipliers of the closed model are relatively smaller than the output multipliers due to the fact that the household component of wages is very small indeed, and does not generate much extra employment. The percentage of employment shares in all the regions are smaller than in the open model; but the actual numbers of employed persons has increased by about one half.

7.7   Conclusions

This chapter reports the major findings of a research project of the impacts of international and domestic tourism expenditure in 1994 on the economy of Israel at both the national level and regional levels. A MRIO model was used to estimate the impacts simultaneously at 3 levels: 1. The end uses: the direct expenditures of the tourists; 2. The indirect derived output: The indirect impact (inclusive of the direct end uses) between sectors to supply the goods and services that are used as resources by the sectors that respond to the direct end uses; 3. The compound outputs (inclusive of the derived output): The added induced impact due to the productive repercussions that are due to the household consumption of the persons employed in the direct and the indirect production activities.

The contribution to employment was estimated (direct + indirect + induced) that the compound number of employed persons were 7.5 percent of the total labour force of 1.87 million.

The derived output (open model) that was produced in each of the six regions due to end uses of domestic tourists was between 47 percent in the North to 63 percent in Haifa. This means that about one half up to almost two thirds of the derived output due to end uses is produced in each region.

The derived output (open model) that was produced in each of the six regions due to final uses of international tourists there, was between 39 percent in the North to 63 percent in Centre , this means that the remoter regions of North and South produce relatively less than due to the final uses.

The compound output (closed model) due to direct expenditure of tourists in each region was in absolute terms larger than the derived output in all regions. It is evident in the case of domestic tourists, that Haifa and Tel Aviv produced relatively more than any other region, of the derived and the compound output due to their direct expenditure. In the case of the international tourists the Centre and Tel Aviv produced relatively more than any other region in response to their own direct end uses. However, the shares of all regions in the compound output due to end uses in any region was smaller in percentage terms. The magnitude in absolute terms of the compound output was more or less double.

The household incomes and the derived VA (open model) due to domestic tourism in the North and South regions were proportionately larger than the output because the increase in the number of employed persons was relatively larger than that of the output. However, there was a relatively smaller increase in those regions, due to international tourists. The percentage shares of all the regions in the compound output were smaller, but the ratio between them has remained the same.

The above results lead to the following conclusions: First, the sum of the VA due to final uses was 2.2 percent, that due to indirect output was 4 percent and that due to the induced impacts was 7 percent of the of GDP of 223 billion NIS, while the number of the employed persons were respectively 3 percent, 5 percent and 7.5 percent of the labour force of 1.87 million.

Second, the differences in the three levels of impacts within and between the regions where the final uses originate illustrates the need of studies such as this. The end uses of incoming foreign tourists generate most of the derived output in the central regions of Israel, but the proportionately greater impacts of domestic tourism in the outlying regions of the North and the South balances out this lopsided impact. This is a significant finding in the context of tourism-based economic development.

Third, analysis of multiregional impacts through the use of a MRIO model enables researchers to estimate simultaneously the magnitude of the impacts within each region, the reverberating impacts in the other regions and the returning impacts to the originating region due to the other regions' demand from it.

Fourth, including indirect + induced impacts in the multiplier estimates illustrates that the share in the compound multipliers of each region is larger than the end uses of tourists who visit it. But the other regions also produce output due to end uses in that and any other region. Thus, any increase in output in one region encourages an investment in other regions in order to supply the needs of the initiating region. This conclusion explains why there is a need for an investment in the Central regions as a result of an investment in the peripheral regions, and also why the rate of development of the peripheral regions is slower than predicted and faster in the central regions. The explanation is that regional economic development plans for investments in the peripheral regions do not account for the need for the extra investment in the Central regions. This also causes a faster rate of growth in the Centre due to both the investment for its output as well as that due to demand of the other regions. The outcome is that faster growth is generated in the centre and the investments in the remoter regions are unlikely to be sufficient to improve their condition significantly.

What are the policy implications of those findings? Our results suggest the following guidelines for regional economic development:

First, an attempt should be made to transfer to the remoter regions activities that have strong IO linkages between the remoter region to the central regions;

Second, a successful policy would need to promote activities with strong IO linkages in the region itself;

Third, there is a need to ensure that as much VA as possible is added locally before demand leaks out;

Finally, there would seem to be a need to exploit underused and unused local resources. These normative recommendations raise the issue of suitable investment policy for effecting these measures.

These recommendations raise the issue of what constitutes a suitable investment policy. How can the state activate the policy? More research is needed to identify the required procedures, because policy decisions by government only pave the way and point out the regional objectives, but private investors are the ones to contribute the larger share of any investment. Thus it is necessary to initiate a research that will define the type of projects that should attract government participation and those to be initiated by private investors.

Notes

1. B.H. Archer (1976), 'The Anatomy of a Multiplier', *Regional Studies*, vol. 10, pp. 71–7.

2. J. Liu and T. Var (1982), 'Differential Multipliers for the Accommodation Sector', *Tourism Management,* vol. 3, no. 3, 177–87.

3. L. Briguglio (1993), 'Tourism Multipliers in the Maltese Economy', in I. Johnson , P. and B. Thomas (eds), Perspectives on Tourism Policy, Mussel Publishing, London.

4. J.E. Fletcher (1989), 'Input Output Analysis and Tourism Impact Studies', *Annals of Tourism Research*, vol. 16, no. 4, pp. 514–29.

5. T.W Blaine, 'Input Output Analysis: Application to the Assessment of the Economic Impact of Tourism', in M.A. Khan, M.D. Olsen and T. Var (eds), *VNR'S Encyclopedia of Hospitality and Tourism*, Van Norstad Reinhold, New York, (1992); chapter 10; D.E. Lundberg, M. Krishnamoorthy and M.H. Stavenga, *Tourism Economics*, J. Wiley (1995); S. Wanhill, 'The

Measurement of Tourist Income Multipliers', *Tourism Management*, vol. 5, no. 14 (1994), pp. 281–3.

6. Fletcher, op. cit. ref. 4.

7. Blaine, op.cit. ref. 5.

8. D. Freeman H. Talpaz, A. Fleischer, O. Laufman, 'A multi-Regional Input Output Model for Israel and Extensions: Methodology and Experience', in D.E. Boyce, P. Nijkamp, and D. Shefer (eds), *Regional Science Retrospect and Prospect*, Springer Verlag (1990).

9. W.H. Miernyk, *The Elements of Input Output Analysis*, Random House, New York (1965).

10. K.R. Polenske, 'The Implementation of a Multi-Regional Input Output Model for the United States' in A. Brody and A. P. Carter (eds), *Input Output Techniques*, North Holland, Amsterdam (1972).

11. D. Pasquale and K.R. Polenske, 'Output, Income and Employment, Multipliers', in S. Pleeter (ed.), Economic Impact Analysis, Martinus Nijhoff, Amsterdam (1977), chapter 5, pp. 85–113.

12. See Lundberg et al. op. cit. Ref. 5, and Miernyk, op. cit. Ref. 9.

13. See Tourism and Hotel Services Statistical Quarterly, published by the Central Bureau of Statistics, Jerusalem.

14. Tourism 1994, publication no. 1010, and Tourism 1989–1990, special bulletin no. 901, Central Bureau of Statistics, Jerusalem.

15. Tourism 1994, publication no. 1010, and Tourism 1989–1990, special bulletin no. 901, Central Bureau of Statistics, Jerusalem.

16. A survey performed by Taskir Company for the Ministry of Tourism 1993.

17. 'Tourist Hotels – Income, Expenditure and Product 1987–1988' and 'Tourist Hotels – Income, Expenditure and Product 1991–1992', Central Bureau of Statistics, Jerusalem.

18. see op.cit. ref. 13 and ref. 14.

19. Dahaf institute, Domestic Tourism, Current, Desired and Expected, Ministry of Tourism, Jerusalem (1991).

20. Mertens Hoffman Consultants, A Survey of Domestic Tourism, Ministry of Tourism, Jerusalem (1994).

21. Time Use In Israel, a Time Budget Survey 1991/2, Central Bureau of Statistics, special series no. 996)1995), Jerusalem.

22. D. Freeman and M. Honigbaum, 'The Impact of Incoming Tourism on the Economy of Israel – a Multi-Regional and Multi-Branch Study of Segments of Tourism', Ministry of Tourism, Jerusalem August 1995.

23. Jonas Nordstrom, Tourism Satellite Accounts for Sweden, 1992–3, Tourism Economics, vol. 2, no. 1 March 1996.

24. Input Output Tables 1988, CBS, special bulletin 972, jerusalem 1994.

25. Survey of Trucks 1990, CBS special bulletin no. 924, jerusalem 1993.

26. D. Freeman, O. Zeif and J. Freeman, 'The Impacts of Incoming and Domestic Tourist Expenditures on the Israeli Economy', Ministry of Tourism of Israel, Jerusalem, 20.5.96.

27. See ref. 9; this multiplier is the output multiplier in the foregoing quoted articles, which is how Miernyk called it.

28. See ref. 10, the MRIO multipliers follow the ones defined by K. Polenske.

29. Fletcher, op. cit. ref. 4.

30. The national level total of the Polenske multiplier is equal, by definition, to the Income Multiplier in the quoted single-table studies (before deduction of leakages by Fletcher,op.cit. ref. 4, Wanhill, Lundberg, Blaine, op. cit. Ref. 5).

8 The Impact of Road Infrastructure on Productivity, Employment and Regional Inequalities in Europe

PIET RIETVELD AND FRANK BRUINSMA

8.1 Introduction

Structural changes are taking place in the world economy, a major one being the process of increasing openness of the national economies. A closer look at the economies in the EU reveals that the growth of international trade expresses itself especially in the trade relationships *within the EU*. This strong growth in intra-EU trade implies an increase in the demand for the transport infrastructure serving long distance transport.

Although from an environmental point of view rail transport, inland navigation and short sea shipping would be the most suitable modes of transport to serve the market for international transport, it appears that a substantial part of international transport is taking place via roads.

The road system in the EU is not without problems, however. In the 1980s European governments have invested relatively little in roads, whilst road transport continued to grow. This has led to a substantial level of congestion near the large metropolitan areas. Another problem is that in the peripheral parts of the EU the road system is still relatively underdeveloped. For these reasons there has been a substantial interest recently into the importance of road construction for the European economies. Can the large investments needed to overcome the above problems be justified on the basis of their positive contribution to economic development?

In the present chapter we will first discuss the contribution of roads to the productivity of the economies (Section 8.2). In Section 8.3 the impact of roads on employment will be analysed. Regional inequalities will be highlighted in Section 8.4. Section 8.5 concludes. We will focus on the economic importance of roads at the European level. For a broader discussion of issues related to transport infrastructure we refer to Bruinsma (1994); Vickerman (1995); Leitham (1996); Rietveld and Bruinsma (1998); and Shefer and Shefer (1998).

8.2   Infrastructure and Productivity

A major contribution to the study of the productivity increasing role of infrastructure was given by Aschauer (1989). In his empirical studies of production functions for the US he found rather high values (about .40) of the infrastructure elasticity of production. This induced a large number of studies of the same character for other countries, and with slightly different specifications usually supporting the validity of the approach but leading to considerably lower estimates of this elasticity (see for example Munnell 1993, and OECD 1995). These studies usually contain one indicator of the total infrastructure stock without distinctions between various infrastructure types. Thus these studies do not even distinguish between transport infrastructure and other infrastructure types, let alone that they would distinguish between different transport infrastructure types.

One should not forget, however, that in Europe already in the 1980s several studies had been carried out on the contribution of infrastructure to productivity where much attention was paid to various infrastructure types. For example, Blum (1982) studied the contribution of various types of transport infrastructure to regional productivity in Germany, Andersson et al. (1989) did the same thing for Sweden, Nijkamp (1986) for The Netherlands, and Biehl (1986) contains the results of a broad EU wide study on this issue. For example Blum found clearly significant contributions of the capacity of both long distance highways and other roads on regional production. The fact that these studies give a detailed treatment of various infrastructure types in the production function does not mean to say that the 'early' European studies are in all respects superior to the stream of research induced by Aschauer, because most of them have a serious drawback: they are based on incompletely specified production functions since private capital and/or labour are not always included.

A particular feature of the road system is that it has a network character. The opportunities to increase productivity depend on where exactly the road construction takes place. If it concerns a missing link or an extension of a link in a congested network, the effect may be large. If it is only an extension in a region with low development potential, the effect on the national economy may be negligible. This network character has largely been neglected in the literature. The usual approach is that infrastructure is measured as a capital stock, either in terms of the total amount of money invested, or in terms of the length of a network. A better approach would be to focus on the *services* provided by the infrastructure stock. An example of this can be found in Johansson (1993) and Forslund and Johansson (1995) who specify a production function with accessibility to major export nodes as one of its components. Thus, accessibility is interpreted here as an indicator of the services provided by a transport network.

An attractive consequence of the approach of Forslund and Johansson is that this allows one to use directly the production function model for

136

the economic evaluation of road expansion schemes. The usual approach of cost-benefit analysis which deals with value of time of users, and the valuation of external effects of transport is thus complemented with an analysis of the contribution of road infrastructure to higher productivity in the economy. Forslund and Johansson show that estimates of the rate of return on investments in roads as measured by standard CBA studies are reasonably well correlated with estimates based on the production function technique ($R^2 = .50$). It is important to emphasize here that the two concepts of the rate of return do not measure exactly the same thing. In cost-benefit analysis it includes both the benefits of consumers and the external costs, elements that are lacking in the production function approach. The two concepts overlap in as far as business traffic and freight traffic are concerned. Because of this partial overlap the outcomes of the two approaches cannot simply be added. Further reflection and research are needed to determine how this method can be used to give estimates of broader economic effects that are not included in traditional cost-benefit analyses without double counting positive effects of road construction.

We conclude that in a large number of studies on the contribution of infrastructure to productivity it is found that infrastructure does play a significant role.[1] Most of these studies do not lead to elasticities as high as those reported by Aschauer, however. It should be noted that the number of studies where different types of infrastructure are distinguished is small. As a consequence, these results do support investment efforts in the field of infrastructure, but do not help one to determine what type of infrastructure is needed, neither are they useful to distinguish good from bad projects within a certain infrastructure type. Recent work of Forslund and Johansson (1995) seems to provide an interesting possibility to link the production function approach to the standard practice of cost-benefit analysis.

8.3   Infrastructure and Employment

Many studies on the locational preferences of entrepreneurs lead to the conclusion that accessibility by road, or, more in particular, location near an access point of an express way are among the highest valued locational factors mentioned. As an example, we refer to Table 8.1 which contains the results of a survey of 1250 Dutch firms in the Randstad. Among the six most important locational factors four relate to transport and communications, the most important one being 'accessibility by road'. This type of result underlines that transport infrastructure is quite important for locational decisions.

Nevertheless, it would be superficial to conclude on the basis of these survey results that infrastructure is a basic determinant of regional or national employment. An important reason is that the perspective used by the respondents is clearly very local. This can already be observed

137

from the high score (rank 2) for parking facilities, which is an infrastructure type that is only useful when it is located very near to the site of the establishment. Another indication of the importance of the spatial scale in the valuation of location factors is that Schiphol airport and Rotterdam seaport get low scores. These seem to be facilities that are useful for all locations in the Randstad (they are never more than some 80 km removed from any place in the Randstad) which is a satisfactory distance for most firms, so that seaports and airports receive low scores.

Table 8.1 Reported importance of location factors by Dutch firms located in the Randstad

	score
accessibility by road	9.0
parking lots visitors	8.4
education employees	8.1
telecommunication facilities	7.9
representativeness of building	7.3
accessibility by public traffic	6.7
price/rent building	6.7
load/unload facilities	6.1
expansion possibilities building	5.8
status of immediate environment	5.8
telecommunication services	5.3
distance to suppliers	3.8
access logistic services	3.4
quality natural environment	3.2
proximity to airport	3.1
availability educational centres	3.0
presence of multinational firms	2.9
proximity to seaport	2.6
proximity to distribution centre	2.4
presence of similar companies	2.4
proximity to customs warehouse	2.2
presence of knowledge centre	2.1
opportunities combined transport	2.0
proximity inland waterways	1.6
opportunities for rail transport	1.1

Source: NSS (1991).

It appears indeed that a large majority of firms that relocate do so at a very short distance. In a study on locational behaviour of firms (more than 10 employees) in the Eastern part of the Netherlands, Bruinsma et al. (1997) found that 75 percent of the firms that relocated did so to a place in the same municipality. A closer inspection reveals that in the relocation process 42 percent of the firms remained at approximately the same distance from the nearest ramp of a highway, 41 percent moved to a place nearer to a highway ramp, and 16 percent moved to a location further away. This means that a considerable part of the firms relocate to locations nearby, not leading to a noticeable change in distance to a highway. For those firms where distances do change, there is a stronger tendency towards highways than away from it (41 percent versus 16 percent). Thus relocated firms tend to have somewhat smaller distances to highways than firms that did not move during a certain period.

We conclude that the relocation of firms is a complex process, depending on the need of firms to relocate and the availability of new sites. In general the main reason of firms to relocate is internal growth and the lack of possibility to expand on its site. The question where to relocate to is of a second order, it directly follows from the decision to relocate. In this stage the supply of new sites becomes of importance. In the Netherlands new sites are to a large extent developed near ramps of highways. As a result we find that dynamic, growing firms tend to relocate nearer to highway ramps.

Another relevant category of firms concerns the new firms (but since we focus on firms with more than 10 employees their number is smaller than the number of relocating firms). It appears that their locational pattern with respect to highways is in between that of the relocated firms and the firms that did not move. Thus also the new firms prefer locations at distances from highways that are somewhat smaller than the distances of the firms that did not move.

These results underline that the rapid growth in the number of firms that is sometimes observed at particular places near (newly created) highways is to a considerable extent the consequence of relocations within regions. These relocations are of course quite relevant at a local level but from a broader regional or national level they are not so important.

Nevertheless, although a large part of relocations of firms is very local, it remains an important question to what extent highway construction can explain interregional differences in growth rates of employment. The above research findings do not exclude the possibility that changes in accessibility owing to road construction give certain regions strategic advantages that lead to a higher than average growth rate of regional employment. The reason is that differential growth rates can take place without relocations of firms, that is, by differences in growth of existing firms and by the creation of new firms. The general conclusions that can be drawn from a number of empirical studies is that the effects are rather small (Rietveld 1995). A recent report of results is given in Bruinsma et al. (1997) for the effects of the development of the Dutch highway network since the last decades. It was difficult to find a positive impact of changes in accessibility owing to road construction on the growth rate of regional employment. Only for employment in the transport sector itself a significant effect was found. This result also holds true for subperiods in the beginning of the 1970s during which the highway system was only partially developed. This is a clear example of how difficult it is to demonstrate convincingly that road infrastructure investments stimulate employment growth at the regional level.

To what extent are these empirical findings in agreement with economic theory? Economic theory contributes to the issue of infrastructure investments in two ways. First, production functions as dealt with above are an important building block of the theory of production of firms. According to this theory an improvement of an external input such as infrastructure can be interpreted as a shift in the production function with the effect that less private inputs are needed to produce the same volume of production. In the standard case of a Cobb-Douglas production technology, this would (in the longer run) lead to a decrease of both private capital and employment. (With other technologies one may arrive at situations that a reallocation takes place between private capital and employment.) This is, however not the complete story, since the increase of productivity would in a competitive environment lead to lower prices, which would stimulate demand. Thus in addition to a substitution effect away from labour towards public capital, one will also have a demand effect leading to an increase of production and hence of employment.

An important factor to be mentioned here is the price elasticity of demand: if it is high one may expect a large increase in production volumes and hence in employment, if it is low, the latter effect will be small. Since different sectors make use of infrastructure with different intensities so that also production costs will change at different rates, shifts will take place between sectors leading to employment growth in sectors with high price elasticities and high intensity of infrastructure use, and decline of employment in other types of sectors. Nothing can be said about this a priori, but there does not seem to be reason to expect overall positive employment effects. There is even a reason to expect a negative effect, because the issue of the finance of the infrastructure is not included in this model. If the infrastructure would be financed by a general income tax, consumptive expenditures would decrease. Or alternatively, if the infrastructure investment would be financed by means of government bonds it might raise the interest rate and savings leading to a decrease of private investment and of consumption.

Another relevant theoretical perspective concerns interregional or international trade theory. Transport infrastructure improvements lead to a decrease in transport costs and hence stimulate interregional trade. The intensity of competition increases with the effect that sectors in certain regions that were formerly sheltered by their isolation are now confronted with cheap imports. The result of such a shift is that consumers buy products at lower prices, but also that employment in these sectors and regions decreases. Of course in the exporting regions one may expect at least a similar increase in employment. Thus, the theory of interregional trade predicts that in each region employment in some sectors will grow owing to the improvement of infrastructure, and other sectors will decline. The balance of the two depends among others on the sectoral structure of the regions. Much depends also on the flexibility of the labour markets. A lack of flexibility would mean for example that those workers who lose their job in a certain sector will not be able to get a job in other sectors which have a potential to grow so that unemployment would increase. For a broader discussion on these issues we refer to Rietveld and Bruinsma (1998).

From a theoretical perspective we may conclude that there is no clear reason why one would expect infrastructure improvements to lead to employment growth at an overall level. Empirical studies on the spatial shifts in employment show that these are predominantly short distance in character. There is little evidence that road construction projects have led to substantial changes in growth rates of regional employment.

8.4   Transport Infrastructure and Regional Equity

In the above section we have shown that infrastructure improvements may lead to shifts of employment between regions. An important question is whether these shifts lead to a more equitable or a less equitable distribution among regions. To address this question we have to take into account economies of scale. Economies of scale in production play an important role in interregional/international trade since they reinforce specialization tendencies. In the presence of economies of scale, regions with an initial advantage may benefit much more from a reduction of transport costs than other regions (Krugman 1991), leading to a process of 'cumulative causation' (Myrdal 1957).

Table 8.2 Hypothetical effects of transport infrastructure improvements on manufacturing

Production in:	production costs	shipping costs: high	medium	low
Core	10	3	1.5	0
Periphery	8	8	4	0
Both	12	0	0	0

Source: Krugman (1991).

A nice example of the trade-offs between transport costs and economies of scale is given by Krugman (see Table 8.2). Production costs in the core (10) are assumed higher than in the periphery (8)

141

because of differences in factor costs. Because of economies of scale, production in two locations would be even more expensive (12). Since the core market is larger than the periphery market, the total transport costs are higher when production takes place in the periphery compared with the case that production takes place in the core. Total transport costs are zero when production takes place in both core and periphery. With high transport costs, international trade is not profitable, and production will take place in both core and periphery (note that 12 is smaller than both 10+3 and 8+8). However, with medium levels of transport costs, total costs of production and transport are lowest when production takes place in the core: 10+1.5 is lower than both 8+4 and 12+0. Here we observe a process of spatial polarization when infrastructure improves. However, a further improvement of infrastructure would lead to a shift of the production to the periphery, because with zero transport costs it would only be production costs that count.

This example is obviously simple and partial, but it nevertheless explains important tendencies in the location of manufacturing activity due to infrastructure improvements (see Table 8.3). With high transport costs production will be dispersed, medium transport costs lead to spatial polarization and low transport costs lead to a shift towards the periphery. The general situation in Europe seems to be that transport costs have already decreased substantially in the course of time so that a further decrease will especially be beneficial for the periphery. This holds true in particular when the decrease in transport costs takes place in the periphery itself. This would make the periphery more attractive as a potential location for manufacturing activities.

Table 8.3 Tendencies in the location of the manufacturing sector as a function of transport costs

transport costs:	high	medium	low
optimal location:	both	core	periphery

The above does not necessarily imply that the periphery will eventually dominate the core. The reason is that the process described in Table 8.3 is specific for each sector or product. It corresponds with the life cycle of products. The eventual shift of production activities to the periphery partly relates to products in the later phases of their life cycle. For new products, the core will often be the more attractive location. Thus we observe a certain division of labour where the core specializes in new products, high tech, R&D and the periphery is specialized in the production of goods in their maturity or satiation phase. Also the command and control activities and distribution activities tend to be attracted by the core.

8.5   Inequalities in Accessibility of European Cities

We now turn from a theoretical discussion on spatial inequality to an empirical one. Within the European Union the road system is generally well developed in terms of density and speeds allowed; exceptions are Portugal, Spain, Greece and Ireland (cf. Vickerman 1995). Outside the EU the quality of the services provided by the road system is lower, an exception being Switzerland. In the countries with already well developed road systems, bottlenecks relate to congestion near the large metropolitan areas, and to physical barriers such as large water crossings for countries like Denmark.

An investigation of the impacts of road construction on accessibilities in Europe was carried out by Bruinsma and Rietveld (1993). In a baseline situation accessibility indices for the road system were computed for 42 large European cities. The accessibility was based on a gravity type concept where both the masses (population size, used as a proxy of economic importance) and the travel times are taken into account.[2] Then the consequences of improvements of road infrastructure on travel times can be computed. Two types of projects have been distinguished: upgrading in peripheral countries such that the speeds feasible in the more developed countries are achieved (we assume a speed increase from 60 to 90 km/h). The second type of project concerns the construction of tunnels and bridges such as between Denmark and Sweden, Denmark and Germany, and the Channel tunnel (completed in the mean time).

In Table 8.4 the effects of road improvement programmes on accessibility have been displayed. It appears that according to road accessibility the cities in the Western part of Germany, the Northern part of France and of the Southern part of the UK and in the Benelux have a high accessibility both in the base line situation and with the improvement of the European road system as mentioned above. The favourable outcome for these cities is the consequence of two factors:

- It is in these regions that a substantial number of large cities are located that are relatively near to each other.
- In these regions the road system is already well developed.

Improvements of the road system in peripheral areas can remove the handicap of low road quality, but it will not help to improve the first mentioned factor. This is the reason why the upgrading of the road system in the peripheral areas only leads to a moderate improvement for the accessibility of cities like Warsaw, Sofia and Lisbon. For the same reason the effect of the construction of bridges and tunnels is moderate.

Table 8.4 Accessibility of European cities by road traffic (1991)

	average acessi-bility (base-line)	improve-ment roads periphery (index)	(changes score)	bridges and tunnels (index)	(changes score)
Paris	100	100	-	100	-
London	94	94	-	95	1
Duesseldorf	78	79	1	78	-
Essen	77	78	1	77	-
Kueln	75	75	-	74	-1
Berlin	74	75	1	74	-
Leeds	74	74	-	74	-
Manchester	71	71	-	71	-
Brussels	70	70	-	70	-
Birmingham	70	70	-	71	1
Frankfurt	70	70	-	69	-1
Rotterdam	69	69	-	69	-
Liverpool	68	68	-	68	-
Istanbul	67	70	3	68	1
Amsterdam	67	67	-	67	-
Hamburg	66	66	-	66	-
Milan	65	65	-	64	-1
Rome	63	64	1	62	-1
Muenchen	63	64	1	63	-
Zurich	63	63	-	62	-1
Lyon	62	62	-	62	-
Budapest	61	64	3	62	1
Turin	61	61	-	60	-1
Newcastle	60	60	-	61	1
Vienna	60	62	2	61	1
Genoa	59	60	1	59	-
Madrid	58	60	2	59	1
Prague	58	61	3	60	2
Marseille	56	57	1	56	-
Barcelona	54	54	-	54	-
Zagreb	54	57	3	55	1
Copenhagen	52	52	-	56	4
Athens	52	55	3	54	2
Belgrade	52	55	3	54	2
Warsaw	51	57	6	56	5
Bucharest	50	54	4	53	3
Naples	49	50	1	49	-
Lodz	49	55	6	54	5
Lisbon	48	50	2	49	1
Sofia	45	49	4	48	3
Stockholm	45	46	1	47	2
Dublin	43	43	-	43	-

An interesting question is how these outcomes for roads compare with those for the other transport modes. In Table 8.5 we give a summary of the consequences of major developments in the rail, aviation and road system during the coming decades (see Bruinsma and Rietveld 1993). It appears that the average accessibility of European cities only increases from 100 in the baseline to 102.8 with road development in peripheral areas, and to 104.7 when tunnels and bridges are added. If we compare these figures with the other major types of transport we observe that with rail and aviation more dynamics can be observed. The reason is that with rail, large investment projects are being implemented in the sphere of high speed connections, and that in aviation higher frequencies lead to shorter waiting times and hence to higher accessibility even though travel speeds remain constant.

Table 8.5 Development of average accessibility and inequality of accessibility of European cities for three transport modes

	average accessibility (baseline)	average accessibility (future)	coefficient of variation in accessibility (baseline)	coefficient of variation in accessibility (future)
road	100	102.7 (improvements in peripheral Europe) 104.7 (idem, plus bridges and tunnels)	.192	.176 (improvements in peripheral Europe) .180 (idem plus bridges and tunnels)
rail	100	118.6 (high speed rail)	.281	.318 (high speed rail)
aviation	100	108.0 (higher frequencies)	.356	.348 (higher frequencies)

What are the implications of the above results for the issue of regional inequalities in Europe? The results of Table 8.5 indicate that inequality in accessibility strongly increases for rail. The reason is that high speed rail projects especially take place in the countries where accessibility via rail is already high. For aviation small changes in the inequality of accessibility are expected. In this respect, investments in the road system are an exception. The improvement of roads in the peripheral parts will have a favourable impact on the inequality of accessibility.

Thus our conclusion reads, that with the indicators used, the improvement of the road system in peripheral Europe will have a moderate effect on accessibility of the cities in these countries. In terms of the inequality in accessibility, road improvements do a better job than improvements in other transport modes. Road improvements in these countries can contribute to smaller inequalities measured by means of accessibility.

One should not forget that trade between countries is not only hampered by underdeveloped road systems, but also by other non-physical effects. Empirical studies in this respect indicate that the non-physical border effects are substantial; even among member of the EU they are not negligible (Bröcker 1984; Rietveld 1993). This is an important reason why most congestion problems in the European highway system take place near the large metropolitan areas and not near the national borders. For example, the traffic intensity on the A12 connecting the Randstad with the major cities in Central Germany has at the Dutch-German border a traffic intensity that is only about 7 percent of the intensity near the Randstad.

An important implication is that the European highway network is serving multiple types of users: both intrametropolitan, interregional and international. Given the traffic share of the first and second types of users, there is some rationale in focusing on those routes that have a clear domestic importance, rather than give priority to roads that have a mainly international orientation. Another implication is that improvement of physical infrastructure is one way to improve accessibility of cities, another way would be to reduce the non-physical border effects. As shown by simulations in Bruinsma and Rietveld, this has quite strong effects on the average accessibility in Europe. However, the rather intangible character of these border effects (they have among others cultural, language and institutional dimensions) makes it difficult to manipulate them in the short run. In the long run they have the potential to play an important role in the changes in accessibility in (peripheral parts of) Europe.

In the analysis up to now we discussed the regional inequality issue from the perspective of accessibility. We concluded that improvement of the road system in the peripheral regions will decrease the inequality of accessibility in Europe. The question is then to what extent this will also lead to an decrease in inequality according to economic measures such as productivity or employment. The answer is clearly related to the issues discussed above on the possible shifts in employment as a consequence of changes in road networks. The improvement of road networks will give benefits to both the central and the peripheral regions, but it is not impossible that the central regions will benefit more than the peripheral regions. Much depends on the potentials of the peripheral regions connected. If their comparative advantages concern goods which are highly demanded in the central regions, peripheral regions will benefit from road improvements.

Of special importance are also the relationships *within* the periphery. Improvements of infrastructure in regions often have quite asymmetric effects within the regions. This holds true especially for airports and rail which imply a polarized pattern of development. With roads the number of points of access is larger which means that if there are positive benefits, they will be spread more equally in space compared with railway lines or airports.

8.6   Concluding Remarks

The conclusion is that the major role of road infrastructure concerns its contribution to consumer welfare and productivity. There is little basis to expect that road construction would boost employment at a European level. Road construction in peripheral regions may lead to a spatial reorientation of employment and this might be beneficial for the peripheral regions in Europe, although higher accessibility may be a risk for regions that have little to offer on the European market. Research results on the impacts of road construction usually do not lead to the conclusion that large interregional employment shifts take place.

Cost benefit analysis (CBA) is a common tool in infrastructure planning. Although many discussions are possible about certain assumptions in CBA, it is nevertheless clear that it provides a reasonable starting point for an evaluation and comparison of investment proposals. In at least one respect it is, however, handicapped: within the philosophy of CBA it is difficult to handle equity issues since the outcome is found by adding costs and benefits without bothering about how the costs and benefits are distributed. Therefore, when equity issues are important it is advised to combine CBA with other types of evaluation such as multicriteria analysis (MCA). MCA is also a useful tool in combination with CBA when intangible environmental aspects play a role which cannot (yet) be tackled in CBA (see also Van Pelt 1993).

A large investment programme in road transport in peripheral areas would accommodate a further growth of mobility in Europe and, hence, endanger the achievement of sustainability goals. However, it would be difficult to deny peripheral regions the possibility to achieve levels of mobility comparable to those in the core regions in Europe. This is another example of the conflict that sometimes exists between sustainable development and international (or interregional) equity.

A moratorium on large road projects in Europe for reasons of sustainability would be difficult to accept for equity reasons, but also from the viewpoint of economic efficiency. Such a moratorium would only be a third best strategy compared with approaches where prices are used to correct for congestion and the various environmental externalities of transport. To deal with the equity issue, tradeable permits of CO_2 emissions may offer a possibility to allow peripheral countries a further economic development without violating targets set at the European level to reduce CO_2 emissions.

A final remark is in order about the relationships between different transport modes. In the present chapter we focused on road transport and ignored rail, inland navigation, short sea shipping and combined transport. It is important to realize that these transport modes may play an important role in solving the present sustainability problems. It is especially at the long distance segment of the transport market that these modalities can compete with road transport. The ongoing process of European integration obviously offers opportunities for these alternative transport modes.

Acknowledgement

This contribution is partly based on the paper 'Road Infrastructure, productivity, employment and social cohesion in Europe presented at a seminar of the European Federation for Transport and Environment, Brussels, 8th December 1995 (published in the T&E report on Roads and Economy, Brussels, 1996). The authors thank Dani Shefer for constructive comments on an earlier version of the chapter.

References

Andersson, A.E., Anderstig, C. and Harsman, B. (1989), *Knowledge and Communications Infrastructure and Regional Economic Change*, University of Umea, Umea.

Aschauer, D.A. (1989), 'Is Public Expenditure Productive?', *Journal of Monetary Economics*, vol. 23, pp. 177–200.

Biehl, D. (1989), *The Contribution of Infrastructure to Regional Development*, EC, Brussels.

Blum, U. (1982), 'Effects of Transportation Investments on Regional Growth', *Papers of the Regional Science Association*, vol. 49, pp.151–68.

Bröcker, J. (1984), 'How do International Trade Barriers Influence Interregional Trade?', in Andersson, A.E., Isard, W. and Puu, T. (eds), *Regional and Industrial Development*, North Holland, Amsterdam, pp. 219–39.

Bruinsma (1994), 'De Invloed van Transportinfrastructuur op Ruimtelijke Patronen van Economische Activiteiten', *Nederlandse Geografische Studies,* vol. 175, KNAG, Utrecht.

Bruinsma, F. and Rietveld, P. (1993), 'Urban Agglomerations in European Infrastructure Networks', *Urban Studies*, vol. 30, pp. 919–34.

Bruinsma, F., Rienstra, and P. Rietveld, P. (1997), 'Economic Impacts of the Construction of a Transport Corridor', *Regional Studies*, vol. 31, pp. 391–402.

Erlandsson, U. and Törnqvist, G. (1991), 'Kontakt och Resemojligheter i Europa 1976 och 1988', Institutionen for Kulturgeografi och Ekonomisk Geografi, Lund.

Forslund, U.M. and Johansson, B. (1995), 'Assessing Road Investments: Accessibility Changes, Cost Benefit and Production Effects', *The Annals of Regional Science*, vol. 29, pp. 155–74.

Healey and Baker (1993), *European Real Estate Monitor,* Healey and Baker, London.

Johansson, B. (1993), 'Infrastructure,Accessibility and Economic Growth', *International Journal of Transport Economics*, vol. 20, pp. 131–56.

Krugman, P. (1991), *Geography and Trade*, MIT Press, Cambridge.

Leitham, S. (1996), *Transport Infrastructure and Industrial Operation and Location*, Napier University, Edinburgh.

Munnell, A.H. (1993), 'An Assessment of Trends in and Economic Impacts of Infrastructure Investment', *OECD, Infrastructure Policies for the 1990s*, Paris.

Myrdal, G. (1957), *Economic Theory and Underdeveloped Regions*, Duckworth, London.

Nijkamp, P. (1986), 'Infrastructure and Regional Development, a Multidimensional Policy Analysis', *Empirical Economics*, vol. 11, pp. 1–21.

NSS (1991), 'Eisen aan de Bedrijfsomgeving in de Randstad,- Beleidsonderzoek en Advies', The Hague.

OECD (1995), 'Investment, Productivity and Employment'.

Rienstra, S., Rietveld, P., Hilferink, M. and Bruinsma, F. (1994), 'Road Infrastructure and Corridor Development', Faculty of Economics, Vrije Universiteit, Amsterdam.

Rietveld, P. (1993), 'Transport and Communication Barriers in Europe', in Cappelin, R. and Batey, P. (eds), *Regional Networks, Border Regions and European Integration*, Pion, London, pp. 47–60.

Rietveld, P. (1995), 'Transport Infrastructure and the Economy', *OECD, Investment, Productivity and Employment*, Paris, pp. 103–19.

Rietveld, P. and Bruinsma, F. (1998), 'Is Transport Infrastructure Effective?', *Transport Infrastructure and Accessibility: Impacts on the Space Economy*, Springer, Berlin.

Shefer, D. and Shefer, D. (1998), 'Transport Infrastructure and Regional Development, a Survey', Technion, Haifa.

Van Pelt, M. (1993), *Ecological Sustainability and Project Appraisal*, Avebury, Aldershot.

Vickerman, R.W. (1995), 'The Regional Impacts of Trans-European Networks', *The Annals of Regional Science*, vol. 29, pp. 237–354.

Notes

1. An important issue that has been rather neglected in research relates to causality: if infrastructure would mainly be supplied to those regions with high productivity (because of high private capital stocks) one would again find a clear relationship between infrastructure and productivity, but the causality would be reversed.

2. Bruinsma (1994) has shown that the accessibilities as measured here are strongly correlated to other accessibility concepts sometimes used (see Erlandsson and Törnqvist 1993, and Healey and Baker 1993).

9 Transport Infrastructure Investments and Regional Development: Literature Review

DAVID SHEFER AND DANIEL SHEFER

9.1 Introduction

In the current era of government budget cutting, austerity programs and deficit reductions, any large expenditure on transport infrastructure will be scrutinized more than ever before for cost-effectiveness and its likelihood of achieving the desired results. This chapter attempts to critically review the literature on the effect of transportation infrastructure on regional development.

Although new transportation infrastructure may clearly reduce travel times, and hence, the cost of doing business in a specific region, its larger effect on the regional economy is much more complicated to predict. Other relevant economic factors that can influence the region's overall economic performance, must prevail in order to attract economic activities to the region. Without the necessary regional business climate, a new transportation linkage may actually hinder growth in the region by making it more cost-effective to move resources, including both human and physical factors of production, from that region to more developed areas.

New transportation infrastructure is not, by itself, a driving force for regional development, but rather, it can induce it when used in conjunction with complementary private investment and other public initiatives and policies designed to raise the region's relative competitive advantage. As an input factor for production, the value of transportation infrastructure can vary from sector to sector and industry to industry. Thus, in order to predict the outcome of a given investment, the industries in a given region must be checked for their sensitivity to transportation costs.

Adequate transportation facilities are a necessary, but not a sufficient, factor for the economic development of a region. The undersupply of transport infrastructure can severely hinder growth; however, allocating resources for the construction and maintenance of oversupplied transport infrastructure is an unnecessary waste of limited public resources that could be used more effectively in alternative projects.

151

The role of infrastructure in regional development has often been misunderstood. While a new investment, such as a major highway, may encourage development in underdeveloped regions, its construction alone is not enough to bring about the desired economic changes. Other factors, such as the economic climate in the relevant region, and relative prices of factors of production, including labour, capital and materials, and agglomeration economies tend to determine the viability of a region more than its basic infrastructure (Vickerman 1991).

Attempting to predict the developmental impacts of new transportation infrastructure is problematic. It entails the uncertainty of predicting future demand for a currently non-existing facility, as well as complexities stemming from external effects on the fortunes of cities and regions (Forkenbrock 1990). The possible impacts resulting in net economic growth and/or the redistribution of economic activities should be carefully distinguished. If economic activity is merely shifted from one region to another, then this cannot be viewed as real economic growth, although it may achieve other, more broadly defined goals, such as development in peripheral regions, population redistribution, etc.

The impact of a new transportation link, such as the Cross-Israel highway (a proposed north-south route, further inland than the main coastal road), on core versus periphery development trends specifically, can be compared to similar examples in Europe. The Channel Tunnel could have great impact, both short and long term, on development patterns in north-west Europe. However, as Vickerman points out, 'the crucial question is whether such infrastructural investment can be the driving force in regional development, independently of other factors, or whether it has only an enabling role', (Vickerman 1987)

A new infrastructure development must also be examined in the context of governmental policies surrounding it, including business incentives and planned linkages to existing networks, in order to accurately ascertain its impact. For example, Britain and France have different goals, and hence, different policies for deriving maximum benefit from the Channel Tunnel. The French are planning to concentrate the Tunnel benefits in the declining region closest to the Tunnel, while the British hope to disperse the benefits as far from the affluent south-east as possible.

The case of the Channel Tunnel, and other examples of corridor development in Europe, show that a new link that improves access to major metropolitan areas may have the potential to both encourage, or hinder, the development of areas peripheral to those metropolitan centres. A further analysis of the users of these new links in their regional economic contexts is needed to more accurately predict net economic outcomes, both around the Channel Tunnel, and adjacent to development corridors in Europe.

152

9.2   Transport and Economic Development

9.2.1   General Concepts: Investment, Accessibility and Efficiency

In basic terms, economic development occurs when income and product generated within an area increase. The classical economic benefits of transportation investments are strictly related to reductions in transportation costs, which, in turn, foster economic development (Forkenbrock 1990) by increasing net local income through cost reductions that exceed the cost of the investment. Increased production requires that either more resources be used or that existing resources be used more efficiently. The single most important resource provided by highway investments is time (Mohring 1965).

It has been shown empirically (Lynde and Richmond 1992) that public capital infrastructure plays an important complementary role in the productivity of the private sector. Recent studies suggest that heavy infrastructure investment in the United States during the 1950s and 1960s may have been a key, previously underrated, factor in the strong economic performance of that period (Aschauer 1990). Most transportation infrastructure is owned by the public sector, due to externalities and natural public monopoly. However, neglect of the public capital stock reduces the potential for economic expansion. Although the services of most publicly-owned capital are freely distributed to private producers, the marginal product of these services is positive, and therefore should be considered as an integral component of the aggregate production function (Lynde and Richmond 1992).

The outcomes of transportation investments on the regional economy manifest themselves through observable and measurable changes in the relative *accessibility* of the region affected. Accessibility can be defined as 'the potential of opportunities for interaction' (Bruinsma and Rietveld 1996). However, it can be a mistake to view accessibility – and its inverse relationship to peripherality – as merely a continuous measure of distance or time. Lack of connectivity implies lack of choice, innovation and intellectual opportunity (Vickerman 1996). This implies that the relationship between transportation infrastructure and regional development is much more complex than a simple matter of road building.

Theoretically, road investments should be made only when they lower transportation costs, and all benefits of a road, and therefore the justification for building it, flow from using it for transportation. Individuals may benefit from a highway without travelling on it, when travel by others increases the income they derive from their resources or increases the purchasing power of that income. Although most highway benefits are derived from lower transportation costs, they can also be represented as increases in the real incomes of individuals in their roles as consumers and producers (Forkenbrock 1990).

A transportation investment contributes to economic development if it significantly reduces transportation costs, thereby improving the net return on mobile resources in the area. By providing a better return than competing locations, mobile resources can be attracted to the impact area of the new facility (Forkenbrock 1990). If any economic activity is attracted from other sites within the defined region, then it cannot be viewed as new economic development. Therefore, the definition of the affected area can play a significant role in the corresponding net impact of a particular investment. Uncertainty about future demand for the facility makes an accurate benefit-cost analysis very difficult.

Setting aside political or social considerations, new infrastructure investment must be guided by the efficiency criterion, and should be made 'when those who will directly or indirectly use the services provided by the facility are willing to pay the cost of its construction, operation, and maintenance' (Forkenbrock 1990). Underbuilding infrastructure can clearly inhibit economic development; however, overbuilt infrastructure can also deter growth. Existing infrastructure may become obsolete due to movements of population or business activity, or as a result of changing demand or technology. The use of under-subscribed facilities causes economic inefficiencies that can increase the overall cost of doing business in an area. Maintaining facilities for which demand has fallen functions as a *de facto* tax on economic activity and is a barrier to economic development (Forkenbrock 1990).

An alternative criterion to economic efficiency for guiding highway investments is that of income redistribution. If the goal of a government policy is to influence investment patterns in a particular area, then infrastructure investment may not be efficient in the traditional sense. It could be said that the government is aiming at 'place prosperity' rather than 'people prosperity'. A state government may wish to spread out economic development, with the hope that improved accessibility will lead to the attraction of economic activity that could balance development across the state. However, trying to spread out development may diminish statewide growth. The state's residents could possibly be worse off overall if resources are spread out as a policy objective.

Good transportation facilities are not enough to ensure that economic development will occur. The area must be able to attract the necessary factors of production, labour, capital and materials. Without these factors, even a good transportation facility will accomplish little. The safest way to engender economic development is to focus on cost savings to users and consumers. Transportation capital can be treated as any other factor of production (Isard 1956), and as a commodity input, can be substituted with other inputs to arrive at an optimal factor combination for a specific industry. Therefore, no single policy can be applied to all industries, and particular industries and sectors must be identified in order to formulate a policy that will advance an overall set of objectives (Shefer 1975).

Transportation services can be considered as intermediate goods in the private production and consumption processes of firms and individuals

154

(Bell and Feitelson 1990). As with other intermediate goods, different industries have different demand schedules. When adequate services are not provided in a timely manner, bottlenecks arise. Analysing the attributes of both transportation services and prospective users is necessary in order to assess which long-term public investments will be more effective than others.

Inefficient or insufficient investment in capital infrastructure precipitates urban decay (Shefer 1990). The efficiency of capital investment is greatest during a period of sustainable growth and development. When the level of public and private investment falls below that required for the satisfactory maintenance and replacement of infrastructure in a certain area, the competitive advantages of that area gradually decline as its productivity erodes. The amount as well as the mix of public and private investment, with a positive input required from both sectors, are crucial for sustainable development (Shefer 1990).

Stated choice models can reveal much about the perceptions carried by business people of their current and potential locations, but are naturally open to bias and exaggeration (perceived time losses due to congestion by firms were found to be much larger than the actual time losses). Transport infrastructure may be important for firms and regions because it influences the status of locations (Rietveld 1994). A possible consequence of reduced transport costs is a tendency to change into a more transport intensive way of production. Infrastructure improvement may improve the functioning of the labour market by extending the area from where people can be recruited to work at a certain location without the need to move (Rietveld 1994).

Analysing transport infrastructure impacts has been problematic. Sometimes, only simple comparisons in time are made (before and after the completion of a project) to determine its impact. Without a control group and an attempt to isolate exogenous variables, this method is extremely limited in usefulness. The quasi-experimental approach of Isserman (Isserman, 1990) uses control regions that are more or less identical to the region where the infrastructure improvement took place. This way changes attributable to the investment can be isolated, at least theoretically. The problem with this approach is in the selection of the control regions, since regions are never completely identical, and all exogenous factors cannot be factored in (Rietveld 1994).

9.2.2 Economic Impacts of Transport Investment

Using a simple model of a regional economy, it is seen that transportation investments can affect the regional economy in two significant ways. First, the transport system affects the movement of goods and people within a region – largely shaping how various components of the regional economy relate to each other. Second, investments in the transportation system can affect the economic ties between a region and the outside world (Huddleston and Pangotra

1990). In this regard, it can either inject additional income into the regional economy (a stimulus) or leak income out of the region (a dampening effect).

The internal and external relationships that influence the patterns of regional economic change can be described by dividing the regional economy into three broad sectors: firms, households (individuals), and government. The transportation system affects these three actors primarily through their cost structure – by reducing the costs of procuring inputs and distributing outputs (Huddleston and Pangotra 1990). In turn, lower prices can allow the firm to become more competitive – both inside and outside of its regional context. Alternatively, the lower procurement and distribution costs may be absorbed into higher profit margins for larger corporate wealth or they may result in higher wages for employees.

Firms may also experience the changes brought about by the transportation investments through the demand side, benefitting from an increased flow of visitors into the region, or from an increase in the overall population base in the area. However, the impacts on regional firms are not all necessarily positive. Firms from outside the region can also compete more intensely within the region because of lower distribution costs. Furthermore, increased sales by one firm may be offset by decreased sales by other firms in the region that did not directly benefit from the transportation improvements.

The impact on households are reflected mainly in the income and employment status of individuals. Households also are major consumers of products produced within the region. When regional firms change their output – and hence their derived demand for labour – income and employment of individuals are affected. Transportation investments can also lower the costs of locally produced goods by increasing competition from firms that import into the region.

This traditional economic analysis ignores the benefits to individuals of reduced travel times to work and commercial centres, considering households as merely inputs into the production process of a region, or as consumers of regionally produced products. It does not incorporate the time saved by individuals (as opposed to firms) directly into projected economic benefits of transportation improvements, neither does it look at the potential tax-base increases brought about by an influx of population due to the greater accessibility to and reliability of travel within the region. Continuing the analysis, the effect on local government of transportation improvements will be seen by revenues from changes in land use in the vicinity of the improvements (Huddleston and Pangotra 1990).

From the neoclassical economic perspective, it is logical to expect that reductions in production costs that are produced by investments in transportation would lead to increased market shares for firms whose accessibility is improved. These increased market shares would translate into increased production by affected firms, leading to enhanced employment and income for the region. However, profits may leak from the region, or may result in little net impact, especially when firms sell to the same market, or purchase inputs from a fully employed economy.

Export income is accrued by a regional economy when goods are shipped out via the physical transportation system, or when tourists visit a region and make non-resident purchases. At the same time, transportation impacts are quickly dampened as the amount of regional importation increases. Money injected into the economy is spent and re-spent. In each cycle of spending, a certain amount leaves the region as payments for imports and other leakages, the net change in the local or regional economy being called the multiplier effect.

The operational influence of improvements in the transportation system on the regional economy involves the impact of transportation infrastructure on how the economy operates. Users are the initial benefactors, including both providers of transportation services (truck lines, etc.) and users of transportation services (firms, individuals). The beneficial aspects either lower costs of production or increase demands for their outputs. Ultimately, user impacts are transferred to non-users. Cost savings by firms may be capitalized into new investment in the region, resulting in direct and indirect impacts on output, employment and income in the economy. Alternatively, the cost savings may be passed on directly to consumers as lower prices or higher wages, leading to higher local consumption. Non-users who own land may also benefit from increased land values. These non-user benefits go together with benefits to the revenue streams of local governments

9.3   Analysing Infrastructure Improvements

Transportation investments affect the cost of production and distribution of regional firms, and the cost of goods consumed by a region's population. It is important to recognize that transportation investments must fit into a broader understanding of the workings of the regional economy and how it relates, in turn, to the external world. While analysing impacts, an attempt should be made to differentiate between the user benefits of an improvement in transportation, and the broader economic impacts that accrue from it. The direct user benefits, such as travel time savings, smoother bottlenecks, savings in vehicle operating costs and reduced accident rates are often incorrectly attributed as economic impacts (Perera 1990). These direct user benefits should be incorporated into a broader regional model in order to accurately reflect their relevance to net economic changes.

Techniques for analysing economic impacts include the traditional benefit-cost analysis – best known for determining the efficient use of available resources, input-output analysis – in which industrial linkages and feedbacks between producing sectors and consumers in the economy are simulated, and the gravity model – which relates economic activity to proximity and access to an urban centre.

9.3.1 Cost-Benefit Analysis

Cost-benefit analysis consists of an accounting of all benefits and costs for each alternative plan and the selection of the alternative that yields the greatest benefits per unit of expenditure (Adler 1987). In practice, however, complications arise because many effects from transportation improvements cannot be easily measured (Perera 1990). The three basic methods employed in benefit-cost analysis are:

- Finding the ratio of the total benefits to total costs for each alternative, with the highest B/C ratio offering the largest return per investment dollar.
- Finding the net benefits (net present value) produced by each alternative by subtracting total costs from total benefits and selecting the alternative that offers the largest net benefit.
- An incremental benefit/cost ratio, in which benefits and costs of each alternative are compared to the next alternative, beginning with the least expensive option. As long as the incremental benefits exceed the added costs, it is best to choose the higher cost option (Perera 1990).

The results of all benefit-cost analyses are sensitive to the discount rates used in order to calculate the net present value of the cost and benefit streams over the lifetime of the project. For example, a typical discount rate to be applied may be the average rate of return that can be expected on private investment before taxes and after inflation. Clearly, subtle differences in projected future economic indicators can influence the benefit/cost ratios of different alternatives.

Traditional cost-benefit analysis is limited in its ability to evaluate broader societal and non-market outcomes of a given project, to compare projects in different sectors and to assess the absolute desirability of a project. An alternative method of plan evaluation, the goals achievement matrix (Hill 1968), addresses these issues by defining both tangible and non-tangible costs and benefits in terms of progress toward desired objectives. The various goals and alternative courses can be weighted according to the community values of different sections of the public. The efficacy of the goals-achievement matrix depends to a large degree on the accuracy and objectivity of the numerical weights assigned to the various objectives and affected groups.

9.3.2 Input-Output Analysis

Input/output analysis involves modelling the economy in a set of linear equations that can be solved mathematically. The estimation of construction costs and other project parameters form the basic input in the I/O model, which then generates the impacts of the construction activity. The next group of impacts to consider are those associated with the operation of the project, including economic, social and demographic impacts of a longer duration. This methodology is particularly useful in the assessment of large scale infrastructure projects whose impacts extend well beyond a clearly defined spatial area (Batey et al. 1992).

The most important step in assessing the economic impact of an improvement in transportation infrastructure is to identify all the potential impacts. Economic impacts can be classified as affecting five main areas:

- Business and industry impacts include the effects of facility construction, right-of-way acquisition, business growth and attraction, effects on the tourism and recreation sector, and the agriculture, mining and forestry industries.
- Residential impacts include the induced effects of employment growth in the regional economy, which may attract additional families to the region, thus creating additional demand for housing.
- The impact on tax revenues includes changes in property values and their revised taxation rates and public service charges which may result in changes in net public expenditures (new taxes minus the cost of providing new public facilities and services).
- Regional and community activity impacts include an assessment of effects on the general pattern of community growth, direct income and environmental conditions. These impacts include effects on adjacent land uses and an evaluation of how the improvement will effect existing land uses.
- A transportation improvement impacts on four general resource types: land, labour, materials and energy. The determination of energy consumption from the direct and induced effects of the project can be estimated from I/O models of energy consumption of similar projects (Perera 1990).

9.3.3   The Gravity Model

The gravity model attempts to relate the spatial distribution of activity around a geographical centre (usually of population, employment or economic activity) through proximity and access to that centre. The basic assumption that the activity rate per unit of opportunity is inversely proportional to distance from the centre and will increase as accessibility improves is consistent with empirical observation. It is basically an opportunity model where the distribution of activity 'is viewed as the successive evaluation of alternative opportunities for sites which are rank-ordered in time from an urban centre' (Lathrop and Hamburg 1965).

A methodology was developed by Hirschman and Henderson (1990) to project and evaluate the potential land use impacts of a proposed limited-access highway extension in the Rochester, New York metropolitan area. In their approach, a gravity model of residential location was used to project potential residential location decisions. An advantage of this approach was that it was sensitive to changes in travel times between residential zones and major places of employment. The basic methodology involved a review of the competitive advantages of the area with and without the highway extension and included surveys of businesses inside and outside the highway corridor. The highway was intended to link Rochester, a large town in upstate New York, to two smaller towns to the west.

It was hoped that the economic development that might occur once the highway was completed would generate enough traffic to make the road necessary. Compared to other, more comprehensive evaluation methods, the use of a gravity model alone would be a good way to assess residential land use impacts of a change in travel times, but may neglect other significant potential impacts of the highway.

The gravity model seeks to gauge the impacts of transportation access on the migration component of population change by calculating accessibility index scores for subregions, that are then used to reallocate projected region – wide growth to the subregions (Hirschman and Henderson, 1990). This method only requires one empirical parameter - and that with a typical value that has been established by previous studies. It allows the analyst to relate changes in travel time in a highway corridor to changes in population. However, Seskin's (1990) analysis points out that this method would not consider other regional development benefits accruing from the highway, such as user benefits and regional economic benefits.

A basic assumption of the gravity model is that the overall regional population would remain constant. It is, in effect, treated as a control for the whole region, and allowed to vary in smaller sub-areas. As a practicality, municipalities are regarded as the sub-areas, with each town getting an accessibility index score. Increases in accessibility scores do not necessarily correlate with population increases, as the gravity model assumes that locales with constrained residential growth would continue to be constrained even after the highway extension. This means that population estimates based on the gravity model may be too conservative, particularly in the long run.

Regarding potential business impacts, it was found to be difficult to make I/O models sensitive to changes in travel times. Thus, a primarily qualitative approach was used in the Rochester study. This entailed a survey of businesses inside and outside the corridor and a review of the competitive advantages of the area with and without the extension. It included a detailed evaluation of such factors as developable industrial land, transportation facilities and financial incentive programs. The business survey included personal interviews with local business persons and elected officials. It was found that the primary industrial benefit of the new highway would have been a strengthening of companies already in the corridor.

During the study, it became clear to the analysts that the proposed new highway corridor had relatively little major retail development. Since a possible reason for this might have been poor access, a separate study was done to estimate the amount of new retail space that could be supported by the area and might be developed if a new highway were built. An analogue corridor was selected as a benchmark by relating the total amount of regional retail development to the population in the analog corridor and extrapolating this information to the study area. It was found that the study area could support nearly double its current retail level, and that a highway interchange providing access from all parts of the area was a virtual necessity to realize the market potential.

The study showed that such factors as financial incentives, additional infrastructure improvements, and a possible bias against the area could have considerable positive or negative impacts on industrial development even if transportation access were improved.

9.3.4 Indirect Economic Benefits

When transportation improvement results in reduced costs to businesses, these businesses receive a competitive advantage that results in increased profits and/or access to new markets. It is clear that improvements to transportation infrastructure have benefits that go beyond those given to highway users for the brief period of time that they actually use the road. Two main effects accentuate this point (Seskin 1990). First, changes in transportation infrastructure can affect the cost of doing business. The dollar benefits resulting from reduced vehicle travel time can also be measured in the form of advantages conferred on users of the new highway relative to those businesses beyond the reach of the highway improvement.

The second reason is the failure to recognize, in traditional benefit assessment techniques, the way in which a change in transportation infrastructure modifies not only the actual highway map, but the *perceptions* of individuals that play an important role in personal and business decisions. There is much anecdotal evidence of how a new highway can affect business location decisions based primarily on new perceptions, often not entirely related to actual travel time savings. These issues necessitate the development of new benefit assessment categories, analysing the larger economic regions through which the improvements pass.

Case studies of transportation improvement projects in Wisconsin, Massachusetts and Indiana show that the more comprehensive framework for evaluation of benefits generated a stream of benefits greater than would have been identified solely by considering traditional user benefits (Seskin 1990). The studies showed that both user benefits and regional economic benefits are sensitive to levels of highway system improvements. These economic development benefits are not solely a function of changes in travel time as traditionally included in user benefit assessments. In all three areas, the research showed that infrastructure improvements can increase regional income and employment in the range of 0 to 3 percent for approximately 20 years after its construction (although particular areas within the region may experience greater growth, the overall regional growth rate was consistently in this range).

9.3.5 Quantifying the Impacts

Business expansion impact assessment quantifies not only the direct but also indirect effects of user benefit savings to area businesses. Origin and destination data are needed, usually obtained through surveying area businesses about the travel patterns of their fleets. A regional economic model can determine the value of indirect and induced impacts on the regional economy (taking as inputs the values of all user benefits attributable to the highway improvement) by modelling the effects of recapturing the dollars that otherwise would be lost to longer trips, more accidents and injuries, and possibly greater vehicle operating costs. The model quantifies the values, both direct, indirect and induced, of business user benefits. Dollars that a business saves due to reduced travel times are assumed to reenter the regional economy as lower costs of doing business, representing real dollars saved by the region's residents (rather than merely a reduction in opportunity costs for motorists travelling in passenger vehicles), and are subject to multiplier effects.

To assess business expansion benefits, one must first determine the magnitude of a marginal change in commercial vehicle hours and miles travelled (the output from a transportation network model from which changes in travel time are determined on the basis of the distribution of actual origins and destinations of area business travel). A regional economic model is then used to determine the indirect and induced effects of business travel time savings. Together with the quantified indirect and induced effects of changes in operating costs and of direct safety benefits, the result is a more comprehensive assessment of the value of user benefits to business than has generally been possible with traditional benefit assessment techniques.

A second group of broad regional benefits that result from transportation improvements are changes in the types of business and the rates at which they are attracted to the region. Transportation access is believed to be an important influence in site selection. Neglecting to quantify and include the value of business attraction benefits as part of the highway evaluation process would result in an unnecessary underestimation of the benefits associated with the project (Seskin 1990). The assessment of business attraction impacts involves weighing both qualitative and quantitative data. First, appropriate target industries and sectors must be identified. Next, a review of the measures of concentration of industries (such as shift-share analysis), and an assessment of relative costs within the region (wage rates, utility rates, capital costs) must be performed with quantitative techniques. A review of available data on recent plant expansions and relocations would indicate which industries are more sensitive to local advantages.

To fully assess the potential business attraction benefits, one would also review the strengths and weaknesses of individual communities within the region to determine the potential for induced economic growth connected to changes in transportation infrastructure. In order to help

162

isolate the effect of the transportation investment alone, several scenarios are usually developed. One scenario assumes a continuation of current economic development activities, another assumes the implementation of some policy felt necessary to induce a higher level of economic growth. The final step of business attraction assessment is modelling the indirect and induced effects of new jobs using the regional economic model.

9.3.6 Assessment Difficulties

Clearly, all potential impacts of a transportation improvement (as outlined above) cannot be isolated and quantified without the use of a cumbersome and massive computer model. These potential impacts should be considered only as they affect the target variables one wants to investigate. The choice of variables to be measured should be determined by the key economic relationships that are influenced by the transportation improvement itself. A good approach, according to Huddleston (Huddleston and Pangotra 1990), is to first estimate those variables affected by the initial stimulus and then use ratios, representing deterministic or empirically estimated relationships, to derive changes in other variables.

Four major evaluation challenges are identified (Huddleston and Pangotra 1990). They include the attribution of any impacts to the improvement itself, the double counting of impacts, consideration of the opportunity cost of resources in alternative uses, and the problem of properly defining the impact area. The problem of attribution relates to properly defining the portion of total changes in impact variables that is solely due to transportation investments that are made. Considering the complexity of regional economic systems, it is difficult to isolate the influence of only one variable (such as transportation investment) among the many variables that influence regional economic change over time.

For example, a major study of the economic impacts of Massachusetts Route 128 is now considered flawed because it made no attempt to connect changes in impact variables to the existence of the highway – the problem being that there is evidence that several exogenous factors that were not considered were significant in explaining many of the economic changes in the region during the same time period (Huddleston and Pangotra 1990). It is increasingly recognized that a good transportation system is a necessary, but not sufficient, condition for economic growth. It needs to be shown that a region has all the economic factors required for self-sustained economic growth, only needing an improvement in transportation infrastructure to fully realize its potential, otherwise, investment in transportation infrastructure may not produce the anticipated results.

Another assessment difficulty is the double counting of impacts. If increased sales are broken down, for example, to increased payments for materials, increased labour income, and increased proprietors income, and then all these changes added together as economic benefits, this would represent a double-counting of actual benefits. This must be avoided by not aggregating changes reflecting different stages leading to the final impact. Another form of double-counting occurs when user benefits are added to non-user benefits without considering the transfer of various benefits (such as decreased commodity prices and increased land values) from users to non-users.

The third assessment difficulty involves consideration of the opportunity cost of resources in alternative uses. Account must be taken of the economic impacts that are foregone because of the withdrawal of resources from alternative uses by the transportation project being assessed. Generally, opportunity cost considerations are extremely difficult to incorporate in impact assessment; however, the implications of this omission should be acknowledged in order to correctly interpret the findings.

The final assessment problem involves differentiating between gross and net impacts. The economic impacts of transportation investment may be positive in some areas and negative in others. They must all be considered, and the target region carefully defined, in order to arrive at the net impact, because new investment may merely transfer benefits from one place to another. The net benefit attributable to the transportation improvement equals the difference in returns to resources employed in the absence of the improvement. This very concern with the transfer of economic activity from one place to another (*e.g.* impact of beltways on CBDs) is one of the primary reasons for undertaking the economic impact assessments. An analysis of the regional economy helps sort out those impacts representing changes in welfare from those that do not. Spatial redistribution of impacts may be ignored, indicating that only aggregate regional impacts are relevant. However, the political reality is such that the preferences of individual communities are based primarily on their local impact, rather than on regional impacts and considerations.

The economic impacts of public investment in transportation infrastructure are usually identifiable in theory, but often difficult to measure in practice. Conceptually, the problem of attribution (correctly identifying the role of transportation in regional change) prevents assigning all changes to the transportation investments that were undertaken, without adjusting for exogenous factors. Double counting of impacts is a serious conceptual problem because using only direct user benefits does not solve the problem and reduces the usefulness of the impact assessment. The challenge in designing economic impact methodology lies in being able to assess the effectiveness of various alternatives in accomplishing multiple objectives.

The focus of impact assessment needs to be on determining whether particular investments are critical for realizing various regional development goals, rather than on establishing a causal relationship between transportation investments and economic growth. Relating the role of transportation to development reveals two distinct viewpoints.

The *passive* view is that the transport sector simply reacts to increased demand generated by growing sectors in a region's economy. This is distinguished from the *active* role, where transportation improvements actually cause development (Huddleston and Pangotra 1990).

9.4   The Channel Tunnel's Role in Regional Development

The building of a Channel Tunnel has been long considered as a possibly great impetus to economic development, both through the short run impacts of construction and over the long run through greater accessibility and competitiveness. The crucial question is whether construction of the Tunnel is enough to be the driving force in regional development – independent of others – or whether it has only an enabling role. Previous studies of major infrastructure investments have either centred on the impact on a single region of a single country, or how a country's competitiveness is changed relative to the rest of the world, not considering the scenario where several regions in several different countries are affected.

The Channel Tunnel is located at the centre of an extended regional economy comprising Britain, northern France, the Benelux countries and the west of Germany. Its economic hinterland is the most prosperous region in Europe, dominated by the major conurbations of Greater London, the Rhine/Ruhr area, and Paris/Ile de France. Several relatively disadvantaged regions exist in this triangle, such as Essex and Kent, the old industrial region along the Franco-Belgian border, and areas of Belgium's and Holland's border with Germany. Despite their geographical centrality in Europe, these regions are all peripheral to the national economies that, due to frontier constraints, have been their main economic links until now.

9.4.1   *Contrasting Governmental Policies in France and in Britain*

The economic impact of the Channel Tunnel will depend to a great extent on the policy responses to it. There is a fundamental difference in the economic and political situation vis-a-vis the Tunnel in Britain and France, and this will manifest itself in likely policy responses and regional impacts (Holliday and Vickerman 1990). In France, the Tunnel is part of a clearly identifiable plan to encourage a disadvantaged region in the national economy. In Britain, the Tunnel must be of a national, not local benefit. Finding the correct policies leading to this more ambitious goal have resulted in governmental indecision and a lack of clear and coordinated initiatives (Holliday and Vickerman 1990). The French strategy of concentration of Tunnel benefits in the declining Nord-Pas de Calais region is impractical and undesirable in Britain, where the policy imperative is to disperse the benefits away from the affluent south-east to more distant regions. The impacts of the Tunnel are not necessarily regionally specific, but can be made more so

165

through policy decisions. With the factor of Governmental regional aid introduced, the potential Tunnel impacts may be altered. Of the seven U.K. regions most affected by the Tunnel, only three received substantial elements of regional aid. In contrast, all of the three most affected French regions (Nord-Pas de Calais, Picardie and Champagne-Ardennes) received some aid in the framework of major regional incentive programs. Perhaps most significantly, additional infrastructure investments in education, training and transport figure prominently in the regions' own development strategy.

The Tunnel will reduce the distance between a disadvantaged region and a metropole, although at the same time will also boost the dominance of the entire region of north-west Europe relative to other regions, not necessarily addressing the region's internal disparities. The growth of the high-speed train network is also double-edged, since, by necessity, only a limited number of stops can be allowed, possibly resulting in a corridor effect, with benefits passing by disadvantaged areas in the heart of the corridor. The role of the TGV in France was to exploit the development potential of existing metropoles, not to create new centres of activity, and judged along these lines, is extremely successful. The city most likely to reposition itself in Europe as a result of the Tunnel and the TGV is Lille. The cities most likely to lose are those in Britain outside the south-east, becoming both increasingly peripheral to the north-west Europe economy and suffering from a lack of clear plans to link them properly to the new transport systems (Channel Tunnel and TGV). The competitive disadvantage in the wake of the Tunnel is compounded by impressions of increasing peripherality.

9.4.2 Long Term Tunnel Effects: Polarization or Decentralization?

In determining long-run effects, one must isolate the relative importance of accessibility in the overall regional economic picture. The production side of a local economy depends on the availability and prices of appropriate factors of production, distinguishing between the immobile factors – such as land for development, road and rail infrastructures, the local environment – and the mobile factors of labour, financial capital, etc. The prime determinant of local competitiveness is clearly the immobile factors (Vickerman 1987). The locational characteristics of the region will also affect how quickly the mobile factors can adjust to any change in differential rates of return that might result from infrastructure investment.

The regions' mobile and immobile factors can be combined (Blum 1982) to give the input potential of the region for a given time horizon. A bottleneck occurs when the input potential is exhausted, limiting further growth without rapidly rising marginal costs. A region dependent on immobile factors will more likely face bottlenecks. Of critical importance is determining which input potentials face bottlenecks and what these bottlenecks are. In Blum's study of counties in Rheinland-Pfalz, Germany, the most significant bottleneck was found to be roads in 14 out of the 36 areas, with other important factors including the availability of sites for development. Transport infrastructure is no guarantee of further growth.

Furthermore, studies centring on Scotland (Chisholm and Hoare 1985) have indicated that any relative differences in transport costs may have the result that only those firms which can overcome such disadvantages by substituting other factors for the relatively expensive transport will locate in these peripheral regions. The regional patterns of trade reflect the way that the industrial mix has already adjusted to locational advantages and disadvantages. In other words, an area with relatively high transport costs might attract industries that are relatively indifferent to transport costs. For this reason, the direct effect of infrastructure improvement on a particular region is difficult to predict. The analysis suggests that there is no immediate advantage to be gained for any one UK region, or for UK regions as a whole relative to other European regions in the context of the Tunnel (Vickerman 1987). Poor accessibility does not appear to be the major bottleneck for development of British industries in the south-east of England.

Recent trends have diminished the importance of transport infrastructure on regional development in the European context, due to the increased proportion of freight comprising high-value goods rather than low-value bulk goods. With the shift from heavy-industry manufacturing to high-tech production, other factors such as quality of life and specialized services have gained importance in locational decision making, at the expense of some of the traditional factors. Transport costs are in any case a small proportion of total costs in the manufacturing industry (3 percent to 6 percent of value added, with growth industries at the lower end of that range), so that changes resulting from the Tunnel are unlikely to be large enough to induce relocation and growth by themselves, although they could affect the decisions of businesses already expanding or considering relocation. If the scope for real transport cost reductions is limited and if elasticities of demand for both freight and passenger traffic are low, the Tunnel may be marginal in its overall economic effect. Development may depend on existing initiatives in affected regions and on the extent to which the Tunnel can be integrated into a more general infrastructure-led growth plan (Vickerman 1987).

The Tunnel and its related infrastructure may have a two-fold effect of polarization and diffusion, with the London-Bruxelles-Paris triangle experiencing the greatest impacts of positive value-added growth, together with the central corridor and its expansion – the French TGV line from Paris to Lyon – with future expansion benefiting Belgium, central and southern Germany and northern Italy. Negative impacts may be felt in regions next to regions with positive impacts at both sides of the Tunnel exits (e.g Normandy), and those areas suffering from increasing relative peripherality. The Tunnel will tighten up the core, inducing negative trends in economically active regions such as southern Italy, northern Germany, Denmark, Pais Vasco and parts of the rest of Spain. In Ireland, the gains in manufacturing should be outweighed by negative impacts on services and tourism (Spiekermann and Wegener 1992).

If Tunnel benefits mostly accrue to the already highly industrialized regions in western Europe, then the concentration of activities and existing spatial disparities in Europe will increase, having a polarizing effect. On the other hand, if the Tunnel can help to equalize accessibility throughout central Europe, then a decentralization of development may occur. The removal of a bottleneck does not necessarily induce economic gains in all adjacent regions. More important than the reduction of transport costs are the image a region receives once it is well integrated into the European high-speed rail network, and an active political response to take advantage of opportunities like the Channel Tunnel.

9.5   Ring-Roads (Orbital Motorways) and Regional Development

The orbital motorway has had a profound effect on how transportation networks fit into their urban and regional contexts. Its impact on the relative accessibility of locations within a metropolitan area can be instrumental in altering residential and commercial patterns, as well as land and office rents. An analysis of orbital motorways is also extremely relevant to the study of the potential impacts of the Cross-Israel highway, which, in effect, will act as half of a ring-road around the Tel Aviv metropolitan area.

The first orbital motorways were planned around cities such as Berlin, Munich and London during the 1930s (Bruinsma et.al. 1993). These were long range projects, some never completed. At that time, it should be noted, traffic congestion was not a problem in Europe. The original motivations to build orbital motorways were a combination of the desire to create monumental artifacts for nationalistic purposes and an affirmation of the architectural movement to reveal and reinforce the organic spatial structure of cities.

The stark rise in European road traffic after the Second World War brought about the creation of orbital motorways to relieve congestion and to directly impact the spatial structure of activities. In general, changes in highway networks lead to changes in the behaviour of network users. These changes include the timing and routing of trips, the choice of transport mode, the choice of origin or destination of trips, and trip frequency. These changes, in turn, have their wider economic and spatial impacts. The magnitude of any impacts depend on various conditions, such as the size of the improvement, the pre-existence of suppressed demand, present levels of congestion and network density, and local economic conditions. Previous studies of the effects of road improvements in general (Bonsall 1992) have revealed that a substantial number of drivers commonly return to the peak period in previously congested areas, that route changes may vary from zero to as large as 60 percent in specific cases, and that short term changes in the choice of origin or destination may be very limited.

Orbital motorways, on the other hand, provide a more specific improvement that makes route choice much more flexible. For example, if traffic were to be blocked on one part of a ring-road, one can still use other parts of the road to reach any destination (Bruinsma et.al. 1993). Orbital motorways have three general types of usage: trips within the urban area, trips from outside the urban area to inside (or vice-versa), and trips with both origin and destination outside the urban area. The effects on intra-urban trips depend strongly on the existing urban transportation network, while the effects on commutation to and from the urban area depends more on the accessibility of the urban area from the surrounding region. The effect on trips both originating and ending outside the urban area depends more on the role of the orbital road in the larger interregional network.

The relative importance of these types of usage varies with different cities and regions. A small radius orbital motorway may have greater importance to local, intra-urban traffic, while a large-radius orbital road may have a larger impact on interregional flows. Therefore, careful attention must be given to the radius of the orbital motorway in order to obtain an unambiguous appraisal of its impacts.

9.5.1 London Orbital Motorway – The M25

The M25 London Orbital Motorway was built between 1975 and 1986, and is located in the green belt around London (see Map 9.1). Its relatively large radius of 26 kilometres gives it the character of an outer ring-road. Studies that correlate trip distances and times indicate that outer ring-roads lead to longer trips in terms of distances travelled, but to shorter travel times, so that average road speeds tend to increase. In terms of accessibilities based on travel times, it has led to relatively large improvements (decreasing travel times by more than 10 percent) in those parts of south-east England through which it passes. However, inner London experiences almost no change in accessibility. Changes in route choice due to the M25 have been found to lead to longer, though quicker, routes. The overall effects on transportation costs may be marginal, depending on the coefficients of time and vehicle operating costs used in the calculations.

In Amsterdam, insufficient office space has led many businesses to relocate in the southern part of the urban agglomeration. Concomitantly, governmental policies were used to encourage the suburbanization of the population (Bruinsma et.al. 1993). Complete residential cities were built at some distance from the large cities of the Netherlands. This led to an increasing imbalance in local labour markets and an increase in commuting distances. The housing program (especially to the north of Amsterdam) and the shifts in employment from the centre of the city to the southern part made an orbital motorway necessary.

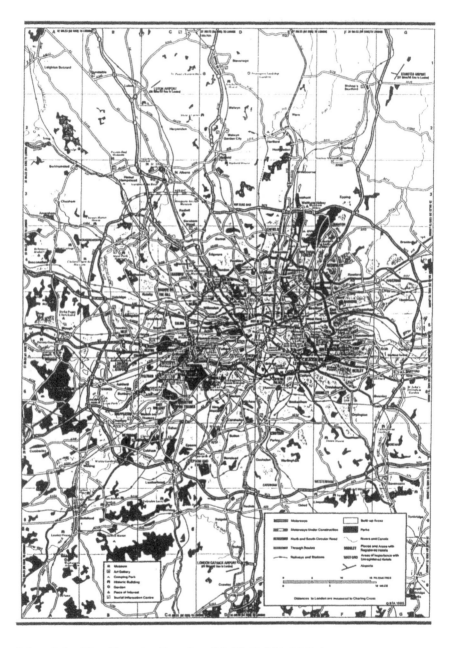

Map 9.1   The Greater London M 25 Orbital Motorway

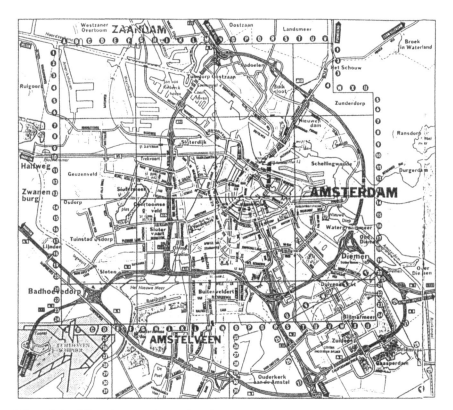

Map 9.2 The Amsterdam Orbital Motorway

9.5.2 The Amsterdam Orbital Motorway

The Amsterdam Orbital Motorway, completed in 1990, was built to address the city's chronic congestion problems. It was constructed in several phases, partly from existing roads (see Map 9.2). In September 1990, the last part of the orbital motorway, the Zeeburger tunnel under the river IJ, was completed, creating a ring-road with a radius of about 5 kilometres. This gives the Amsterdam Orbital Motorway the character of an inner ring-road, as important parts of the agglomeration lie outside the ring-road circle.

The three main functions of the orbital motorway are to improve the accessibility of Amsterdam and the province of North Holland to areas north of the river IJ, to relieve the secondary road network in the Amsterdam region and to create improved conditions for economic development in the Amsterdam region. The first two impacts can be measured in the short-term.

The opening of the Zeeburger tunnel (as the final part of the orbital motorway) led to a huge increase in capacity of the regional road network. The total number of kilometres driven in the Amsterdam

171

region only increased slightly faster than traffic volume for the whole of the Netherlands, due mainly to increasing use of the main road network, with the secondary road network in the Amsterdam region being relieved. For example, the number of kilometres covered by traffic crossing the river IJ on the highway increased by 13 percent, while the number of kilometres by river crossing traffic on other roads decreased by 33 percent (Bruinsma et.al. 1993).

The option of bypassing Amsterdam on the eastern side has led to a major shift in route choice. Of drivers who cross the river IJ, 25 percent have changed their choice of crossing point. The tunnel now carries 19 percent of all motor vehicles that cross the river IJ. Because of this shift to the use of the orbital motorway, Amsterdam's city road network has been substantially relieved. Furthermore, of the drivers who cross the river, 31 percent were able to change their time of departure to more individually preferable times, without the previous fears of congestion. (The number of crossings at morning rush hour, 7 to 9, increased by 16 percent – the 'return-to-the-peak' effect.)

The orbital motorway has led to substantial travel time gains throughout Holland. The largest gains involve journeys between the areas north of the river IJ and the centre of the Netherlands. Improvements can also be seen in travel through older routes due to a general reduction in congestion everywhere.

9.5.3 *Economic Development from the Amsterdam Orbital Motorway*

A study of the impact of the orbital motorway on the economy in the Amsterdam region was performed by analysing rental values in the office sector (they tend to adjust quickly in the short run, while construction activities generally react on a longer time scale), and by surveying experts on firm location and entrepreneurs who would be affected by these changes.

The experts survey on the major location factors for firms in the Amsterdam area showed that other road network extensions have to be considered, as well as investments in telecommunication infrastructures and the attractiveness of nearby living areas and green belts. Subjective factors are of crucial importance, as office developers tend to build close to sites that have proven to be successful. The status or image of an area may outweigh other factors in its selection. In addition, a political decision, such as the prohibition of cars in the inner city area, may enhance the relative attractiveness of sites along the orbital motorway.

It was generally agreed among the experts that firms locating close to the ring-road would experience image and promotional advantages due to their proximity, and furthermore, would be attracted by the potential for expansion into the nearby, available space for industrial and office activities. This could be a major factor for dynamic firms, as 40 percent of the firms in Amsterdam have reported logistic problems caused by lack of space (Bruinsma et al. 1993) in the late eighties.

The spatial distribution of the benefits of the orbital motorway will be difficult to predict. It was expected that those areas joined to the greater urban area by the newest parts of the orbital motorway, the northern and eastern districts of Amsterdam, would gain the most. Specifically, the Northern district, which in the past had suffered an image problem and low perception among entrepreneurs due to its isolation from the rest of the city by the river IJ, was seen to have the potential to reap substantial benefits from the completion of the orbital motorway (provided that adequate public transport connecting the centre of Amsterdam to the district is implemented concurrently).

The Amsterdam orbital motorway was found to have reduced by about 20 percent time losses due to congestion in the Amsterdam area. The effects on office prices, however, are less conclusive. Office prices in zones directly benefiting from the road did not grow faster than in other zones, instead, office prices at locations near already existing parts of the orbital motorway displayed the largest increases. This shows that the ring-road may have merely reinforced the position of zones with an already strong competitive position in the region (Bruinsma et.al. 1993).

9.6 Highway and Corridor Development in the Netherlands

The Netherlands, like several European countries, has witnessed an 'urban-rural manufacturing shift' (Rienstra et.al. 1994) during the past few decades. The Netherlands can be divided into three zones: the Randstad (highly urbanized, with the highest economic and employment growth before 1970, including the four largest Dutch cities), the intermediary zone surrounding the Randstad, and the peripheral zone. After 1970, a shift began from the Randstad to the intermediary zone, consisting of population migration away from the Randstad. This period was characterized by a rate of employment growth in the Randstad below the national average. The intermediary zone benefited from this trend, exhibiting above average rates of employment growth.

The peripheral zone was characterized before the 1970s by a strong emphasis on agriculture and was lagging behind the other zones in economic development. In the period 1970–1990, employment growth in the peripheral region was only slightly lower than the national average, in most periods showing higher growth than that of the Randstad. A shift-share analysis for the different zones between 1970 and 1990 shows that shifts in the Randstad are negative in all five year periods, meaning that the negative development of the Randstad is not caused by its sectoral composition, but by other factors (Rienstra et al. 1994). The shifts are consistently positive in the intermediary zone, indicating that the locational factors are favourable compared with the average. The peripheral zone showed very small relative shifts.

A study of infrastructure construction shows that the growth rate was highest in the peripheral zone, during the period when most of the construction took place (1960–1975). The construction in the intermediary zone was about the national average. However, the strong emphasis on construction activity in the peripheral zone did not lead to a clear improvement of its economic position.

9.6.1 The Accessibility Index

Applying an accessibility index to infrastructure improvements enables one to ascertain the service improvements to users that the improvement provides. Such an index (Bruinsma and Rietveld 1993, 1996) can be defined as:

$$B_i = a\Sigma_j M_j/c_{ij}$$

(9.1)

where:

B_i = accessibility index for region i
a   = constant
M_j = mass of zone j (mass = employment)
c_{ij} = travel time from zone i to j

The travel time is calculated from detailed data on travel speeds on the various links of the network, and computed by means of a shortest route algorithm. Changes in accessibility, by definition, are caused by either changes in mass M or changes in the network. While holding the masses constant, the accessibility indices for the different zones in the Netherlands were calculated:

Table 9.1 Growth of the accessibility index in different zones

	1970	1975	1980	1985	1990
Netherlands (total)	100	113	120	125	130
Randstad	100	112	115	118	122
Intermediary Zone	100	115	122	126	132
Peripheral Zone	100	115	125	133	140

Source: Rienstra, et.al.

Although the accessibility of the peripheral zone grew most strongly, its relative economic position did not improve, strengthening the view that greater accessibility is an enabling factor for economic development, but not sufficient by itself to bring it about. Using a regional labour market model, Rienstra et al. (1994) found that the only unambiguous positive correlation between accessibility and employment growth was in the transport and communication sector. They conclude that the construction of main road infrastructure, with its resulting change in accessibility, does not have a clear impact on the overall employment in a region. Furthermore, accessibility is a function of both the level of physical infrastructure and its quality – including toll policies, parking restrictions, bus lanes, etc. (Berechman 1995). Therefore, new transport infrastructure must be analysed well beyond mere changes in travel times in order to predict future effects on economic development.

Empirical studies of the effect of changes in accessibility on the development of peripheral areas in Europe (Bruinsma and Rietveld 1996) indicate a multi-stage phenomenon. In the first stage, as infrastructure improves and people and resources begin to move more freely, the core region benefits the most. Only in a latter stage, as the overall economic *environment* in the peripheral region has had enough time to develop and exploit the new accessibilities, will the peripheral area start to benefit.

9.7   Conclusions

The purpose of this chapter was to critically review the literature on transport infrastructure in light of the current discussion concerning the most effective policies designed to promote regional development. The various economic processes at work when a new transport infrastructure project is introduced to an economic region were examined both in their theoretical aspects and with empirical examples. Case studies from Europe, including the Channel Tunnel and Orbital Motorways in England and the Netherlands, were examined to help find an empirical basis for studying the possible influence of new transport infrastructure on regional development trends.

The literature on possible economic impacts of the Channel Tunnel illustrates the problems involved with defining impact areas and the possibility of reciprocal impacts on core and peripheral regions. The French are only counting on a positive impact in the area of north-west France adjacent to the tunnel, while the British are counting on more widespread effects throughout Britain. The Channel Tunnel's potential to either exacerbate the domination of the wealthy core of Europe over less developed, peripheral areas *o r* to encourage diffusion and decentralization throughout the continent (depending on other economic factors) is a good point to consider when attempting to predict economic impacts of major infrastructure projects which may affect several regions.

The orbital motorway, or ring-road, has an impact that is easier to quantify. Both an outer ring-road, such as the M25, which encircles the London Metropolitan area, and an inner ring-road, like the Amsterdam Orbital Motorway, which cuts through the middle of the Amsterdam Metropolitan area, have well documented effects of easing congestion and improving access to residents in their respective Metropolitan areas.

The Cross-Israel highway, with its central section passing to the east of the Tel Aviv Metropolitan area, could be expected to act as part of an outer ring-road to the Tel Aviv Metropolitan area, decreasing congestion within the Metropolitan area.

Transportation investment can contribute to economic development by reducing travel time, and therefore the costs, of doing business in a certain area, and by encouraging development by improving the accessibility of a region. These changes in accessibility can be quantified and used to predict movements of population and business activity through the use of a gravity model, which can in turn, be used as part of a more comprehensive regional economic model. However, improved transportation facilities are not enough by themselves to cause economic growth. The area in question must have other conditions necessary to attract new investment, and if not, a new transportation link may actually help drain resources out of the region to a more prosperous one.

Assessing the impact of a transportation improvement is highly problematic. Isolating exogenous factors, avoiding the double counting of impacts, properly defining the impact area and considering the opportunity cost of resources in alternate uses are some of the complexities that must be dealt with in order to obtain a useful assessment of a transportation project. The economic impact of transport infrastructure may be positive in some areas and negative in others, merely causing a redistribution of economic activity with no net change. Some of the impacts of transportation investment involve perception and image of the affected areas, and cannot be quantified.

Public expenditure on infrastructure and private investment, rather than being substitutes for each other, have been shown to be complementary, with both required in order to bring about sustainable growth. In the current age, with the privatization of many traditional public-sector roles in infrastructure development more common, public investment in infrastructure must not crowd-out potential private investment in order to maximize the efficiency of limited public capital.

Investment in transport infrastructure is a necessary, but by no means a sufficient, condition for economic development. If undersupplied, it can severely limit growth, and when oversupplied, it can be a waste of limited resources. New investment in transport infrastructure can only be assessed in a regional context, with the consideration of other economic factors, such as the local business climate, relative prices of other factors of production, and concurrent private investment, in order to predict possible local and regional economic impacts.

References

Adler, H. A. (1987), *Economic Appraisal of Transport Projects*, The World Bank and Johns Hopkins University Press, Baltimore, USA.

Aschauer, D. A. (1990), 'Why is Infrastructure Important?', in Munnell, A. (ed.), *Is There a Shortfall in Public Capital Investment?*, Proceedings of a conference held in June 1990, Federal Reserve Bank of Boston.

Batey, P.W.J., Madden, M. and Scholefield, G. (1992), 'Socio-Economic Impact Assessment of Large-Scale Projects Using Input-Output Analysis, A Case Study of an Airport', *Regional Studies*, vol. 27.3, pp. 179–91.

Bell, M. and Feitelson, E. (1990), 'Bottlenecks and Flexibility: Key Concepts for Identifying Economic Development Impacts of Transportation Services', *Transportation Research Record*, vol. 1274, pp. 53–9.

Berechman, J. (1995), 'Transport Infrastructure Investment and Economic Development', in: Banister, D. (ed.), *Transport and Urban Development*, E&FN Spon, London.

Blum, U. (1982), 'Effects of Transportation Investment on Regional Growth: A Theoretical and Empirical Investigation', *Papers of the Regional Science Association*, vol. 49, pp. 169–84.

Bonsall, P.W. (1992), 'Feasibility of Measuring Responses to Highway Improvement', Institute of Transport Studies, Leeds, UK.

Bruinsma, F., Pepping, G. and P. Rietveld, P. (1993), Infrastructure and Urban Development: The Case of the Amsterdam Orbital Motorway', Research Memorandum 1993–19 (April), Dept. of Economics, The Free University, Amsterdam.

Bruinsma, F. and Rietveld, P. (1993), 'Urban Agglomerations in European Infrastructure Networks', *Urban Studies*, vol. 30, no. 6, pp. 919–34.

Bruinsma, F. and Rietveld, P. (1996), 'The Accessibility of European Cities: Theoretical Framework and Comparison of Approaches', Working Paper, Dept. of Economics, The Free University, Amsterdam.

Chisholm, M. (1985), 'Accessibility and Regional Development in Britain', *Environment and Planning A*, vol. 17, pp. 963–80.

Forkenbrock, D. J. et. al. (1990), 'Road Investment to Foster Local Economic Development', University of Iowa Public Policy Center, Iowa, USA.

Forkenbrock, D.J. (1990), 'Putting Transportation and Economic Development Into Perspective', *Transportation Research Record*, vol. 1274, pp. 3–11.

Forkenbrock, D.J. and Foster, N. (1990), 'Economic Benefits of a Corridor Highway Investment', *Transportation Research A*, vol. 24A, no. 4, pp. 303–12.

Hill, M. (1968), 'A Goals-Achievement Matrix for Evaluating Alternative Plans', *Journal of the American Institute of Planners*, pp. 19–29.

Hirschman, I. and Henderson, M. (1990), 'Methodology for Assessing Local Land Use Impacts of Highways', *Transportation Research Record*, vol. 1274, pp. 35–40.

Hoare, A. (1985), 'Great Britain and Her Exports: An Exploratory Regional Analysis', *Tidjschrift Economic and Social Geography*, vol. 76, pp. 9–21.

Holliday, I. and Vickerman, R.W. (1990), 'The Channel Tunnel and Regional Development: Policy Responses in Britain and France', *Regional Studies*, vol. 24, no. 5, pp. 455–66.

Huddleston, J.R. and Pangotra, P.P. (1990), 'Regional and Local Economic Impacts of Transportation Investments', *Transportation Quarterly*, vol. 44, no. 4, pp. 579–94.

Hutchinson, B.G. (1970), 'An Approach to the Economic Evaluation of Urban Transportation Investments', *Highway Research Record*, no. 314, pp. 72–85.

Isard, W. (1956), *Location and Space Economy*, John Wiley, New York.

Isserman, A. (1990), 'Research Designs for Quasi-Experimental Control Group Analysis in Regional Science', West Virginia University, Morgantown, WV, USA.

Kaplan, M. (1988), 'Infrastructure Needs Assessment: Methodological Problems and Opportunities', in Stein, J.M. (ed.) *Public Infrastructure Planning and Management*, vol. 33, Urban Affairs Annual Reviews, Sage Publications, Newbury Park, California.

Lathrop, G.T. and Hamburg, J.R. (1965), 'An Opportunity-Accessibility Model For Allocating Regional Growth', *Journal of the American Institute of Planners*, vol. XXXI no.2.

Lynde, C. and Richmond, J. (1992), 'The Role of Public Capital in Production', *The Review of Economics and Statistics*, pp. 37-44.

Mohring, H. (1965), 'Urban Highway Investments', in Dorfman, R. (ed.), *Measuring Benefits of Government Investments*, The Brookings Institution, Washington, DC.

Mohring, H. (1993), 'Land Rents and Transport Improvements: Some Urban Parables', *Transportation*, vol. 20, no. 3, pp. 267–83.

Nijkamp, P. (19??), 'Long Term Infrastructure Planning as a Response to Increasing Urban Transport Demand', Unpublished Working Paper, The Free University, Amsterdam.

Perera, M.H. (1990), 'Framework for Classifying and Evaluating Economic Impacts Caused by a Transportation Improvement', *Transportation Research Record,*vol. 1274, pp. 41–52.

Rienstra, S., Rietveld, P., Hilferink, M. and Bruinsma, F. (1994), 'Road Infrastructure and Corridor Development', Paper presented at the 34th European Congress of the Regional Science Association, August, Groningen, The Netherlands.

Rietveld, P. (1994), 'Spatial Economic Impacts of Transport Infrastructure Supply', *Transportation Research A*, vol. 28A, no.4, pp. 329–41.

Seskin, S.N. (1990), 'Comprehensive Framework for Highway Economic Impact Assessment: Methods and Results', *Transportation Research Record*, vol. 1274, pp. 24–34.

Shefer, Daniel (1975), 'A Mathematical Model for the Location of Industry in Developing Areas', *Environment and Planning A*, vol. 7, pp. 251–62.

Shefer, Daniel (1990), ',Innovation, Technical Change and Metropolitan Development: An Israeli Example', in Nijkamp, P. (ed.), *Sustainability of Urban Systems*, Avebury, Aldershot, UK, pp.167–81.

Shefer, Daniel and Voogd, H. (eds) (1990), *Evaluation Methods for Urban and Regional Plans*, Pion Ltd. London.

Spiekermann, K. and Wegener, M. (1992), 'The Impact of the Channel Tunnel on Transport Flows and Regional Development in Europe', Paper presented at the Regional Science Association 32nd European Congress, Belgium.

Vickerman, R.W. (1987), 'The Channel Tunnel: Consequences for Regional Growth and Development', *Regional Studies*, vol. 21, no. 3, pp. 187–97.

Vickerman, R.W., (ed.) (1991), *Infrastructure and Regional Development,* Pion Ltd., London.

Vickerman, R.W. (1996), 'Accessibility, Peripherality and Spatial Development: The Question of Choice', Centre for European, Regional and Transport Economics, University of Kent at Canterbury, UK.

Part C
Regional Development:
Modelling and Policy

10 Employment Forecasting in Fryslân in the Age of Economic Structural Changes

PIET BOOMSMA

10.1 Introduction

In a typical regional economy, thousands of people and businesses conduct a multitude of transactions every day. Ultimately, all of these transactions are interrelated. For policy makers trying to influence the regional economy, good insight into the workings of the economy actually is indispensable. The task of a regional model builder, then, is to identify the key causal paths through which changes in one part of the economy influence other parts of the economy. When enough separate causal paths have been identified, they may be combined to form a complete model of the regional economy. Such a complete model computes direct and indirect effects simultaneously.

Though economic models may include only cause and effect relationships, their forecasts are seldom accurate. This has prompted a lot of joking from critics. The way of defending the use of economic models is that even if forecasts are poor, there are none better, and perhaps a poor forecast is better than none. Econometric theory proposes a number of error sources making economic forecasts diverge from actual values. Generally, four potential sources of error are distinguished: specification errors, conditioning errors, sampling errors and random errors.[1] Sampling errors refer to the fact that the model uses estimates instead of true parameter values. Conditioning errors are the result of the use of inaccurate forecasts of exogenous variables. Specification errors occur when not all relevant explanatory variables are included, when the functional form is incorrect or when there has been a change in regime.

Since the title of this volume assumes a change of regime ('... the age of economic structural changes'), this chapter researches the chances of making a good labour market forecast with a newly developed model of the Frisian labour market.[2] It would lead too far afield to discuss all economic structural changes since the early 1970s and their influences on the Dutch and Frisian economy. The economic structural changes and their effects are taken for granted. The question that will be discussed in this article, is: may a regional econometric model result reasonable forecasts, while econometric theory indicates specification errors due to a change in regime?

Before attempting to answer this question, we first present a short description of the region and subsequently consider some effects of the economic structural changes for Fryslân and describe the construction methodology and content of FREM, an economic model for Fryslân.

10.2 General Characteristics of Fryslân

Fryslân, also known as Friesland, is one of the twelve provinces of the Netherlands. Fryslân is located in the north of the Netherlands (see Figure 10.1) and takes up 9.9 percent of the surface area and 4.0 percent of the population, amounting to about six hundred thousand persons in 1995.[3]

Map 10.1 Map of Fryslân (FR) and the Netherlands

The province of Fryslân is not only associated with the fact that its population has an own language, it is also often associated with a problematic economic situation. Fryslân has indeed a long lasting history of an unemployment rate that is above the national average. Through the years, employment growth has been below the national average. The Frisian economy is further characterized by an overrepresentation of agriculture and traditional manufacturing industries and underrepresentation of high tech industries and business services. The Frisian population comprises relatively to the Dutch average many children and elderly people due to the fact that the annual migration deficit mainly consists of youngsters. The participation rate of women is low, 39 percent in Fryslân with a national average of 47 percent (1994).[4] The average disposable income is 7.5 percent below the national average.[5]

10.3 Economic Structural Changes

The concept of economic structural change has no clear definition. The term is used when trend breaks can be detected; breaks in trends that determine the economic process. These trends may be demographic trends, social trends, environmental trends, trends in technology, internationalization and market structure, but are mostly due to political changes. The unification of Europe, the breakdown of the communist system and the globalization of world trade may be identified as the structural economic changes on a world scale during recent decades, while the increasing public sector until the 1980s and the tendency to counteract this increase thereafter might be considered as a national structural change for the Netherlands. Structural economic changes are expected to have considerable effects on the composition of imports and exports and production patterns.

Whereas structural economic changes have important influences on small open economies like the Dutch, they must also have their influences on the Frisian economy, that forms a part of it. The concept 'industry mix' is frequently used as one of the tools to describe changing production patterns. Table 10.1 shows that the economic structural changes have gone together with large shifts in the industry mix of both the Netherlands as a whole and the province of Fryslân. The general picture is that the relative importance of agriculture and manufacturing industries has considerably declined.

Table 10.1   Industry-mix[1], Fryslân and the Netherlands, 1973 and 1995

	Fryslân		the Netherlands	
	1973	1995	1973	1995
Agriculture[2]	13.6%	8.3%	7.1%	4.7%
Food industry	7.0%	4.2%	4.0%	2.2%
Metal industry	11.6%	7.8%	11.5%	7.2%
OEX-sector	10.5%	8.6%	16.2%	10.7%
Trade	10.2%	13.3%	13.5%	15.3%
Business services	4.3%	8.6%	6.4%	11.3%
Nonmarket sector	10.8%	17.7%	10.8%	19.4%
Building sector	9.5%	6.8%	8.6%	6.0%
Government	9.8%	13.6%	11.1%	13.0%
Residential sector	0.5%	0.7%	0.5%	1.0%
Mining and quarrying	0.1%	0.1%	0.5%	0.3%
Self-employed[3]	12.2%	10.5%	10.0%	9.0%

[1]see for industry classification appendix 1
[2]including self-employed
[3]all industries, excluding agriculture

Besides, the Frisian industry mix has developed more and more towards the national average since 1973. An index for resemblance of sector structure is the mean absolute deviation of regional from national sector shares:

$$100\% - \sum_{i=1}^{n} |(\frac{L_{i,F}}{L_F} - \frac{L_{i,N}}{L_N})| / 2 , \qquad (10.1)$$

where L is employment, F and N are the regions (here Fryslân and the Netherlands respectively) and i (1 to n) represents the i-th industry. The value of the index lies between 0 percent and 100 percent, ranging from total difference to total resemblance.[6] The resemblance index had a value of 87 percent in 1973 and has grown to 91 percent in 1995.

It can be concluded that the industrial structure of the Netherlands has undergone quite a change in the last two decades and the Frisian economy has a growing resemblance to the national average. If the changing industry mix is the consequence of structural economic changes, it is questionable whether an economic model is able to produce accurate forecasts. Thus, if the Frisian economy resembles more and more to the national economy, it is questionable whether a regional model will yield better forecasts than a national model. In Section 10.5 we will examine the qualities of FREM, a regional model for Fryslân, that is presented in the next section.

10.4 Construction and Content of FREM, an Econometric Model of the Frisian Economy

10.4.1 The Model

The Frisian economic model FREM is presented in Appendix 10.3. Figure 10.1 shows a simplified schematic presentation of FREM, while a more elaborate flow chart is found in Appendix 10.2. FREM has been built for labour market forecasting and simulation purposes on a medium term and aims to result good forecasts of developments on the Frisian labour market, given assumed or forecasted Dutch developments. The model comprises a labour demand and a labour supply block. In the labour demand block, employment, production and investment are the main variables. Production and employment have an industrial subdivision, while investments are subdivided into types. The labour supply block consists of natural population, migration and participation, which all have been specified for age and sex.

The model comprises a large number of variables of which 58 are behavioural and 15 are exogenous. The behavioural variables are Frisian employment (12), production (8), investment (3), population/migration (28), participation (6) and unemployment (1) variables. The exogenous variables are national employment (3), real production (3), investment (1), population (1) and unemployment (1) variables; national data on prices (1), wages (1), interest (1) and productive hours in the building sector (1); and finally both national and Frisian data on the housing market (2).

The model has been estimated using data from the period 1973–1990, but for a small number of equations the estimation period had to be lengthened, due to estimation problems arising from definition changes.

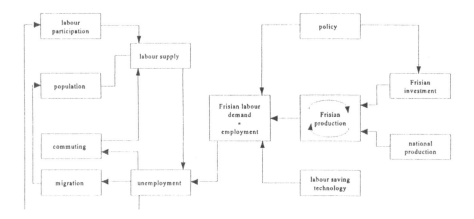

Figure 10.1 Simplified flow chart of the model structure

10.4.2 Bottom-up

During the construction of the model it was tried to do the utmost to accommodate specific regional characteristics and the model has been built bottom-up where reasonably possible. Labour supply is mainly regionally determined. Population structure determines the size and age of the potential labour population, while regional employment possibilities and unemployment rates determine (amongst other things) participation and migration. Labour demand is dependent on regional production, just like business investments. Regional production is less dependent on regional developments. For describing the driving forces of regional production an industrial classification is indispensable.

10.4.3 Sectoral Division

The eleven sectors used in the model have been distinguished for reasons of regional importance, market characteristics and data availability.[7] The sectors agriculture, food industry, metal industry and the OEX-sector (other manufacturing and transport) are typical exposed sectors. These sectors serve an international market and are exposed to international competition. The sheltered sector produces predominantly for the national market and experiences little foreign competition. The sheltered sector mainly consists of services. Market size could even be the guideline for a further disaggregation of the sheltered sector into a nationally sheltered and a regionally sheltered sector. Data availability, however, dictated the choice for the more traditional subdivision into trade and business services. As in FKSEC,[8] three sectors have been distinguished because their process of wage and price formation and output and employment levels are considered to be highly dependent on government policy; these are the residential, mining and quarrying and nonmarket services sectors. Finally, employment in the government sector is fully dependent on government policy.

10.4.4 Estimation Methodology

After the selection of the key variables in the model, the following methodology has been used to specify the model. Economic theory on the various key variables has been the guide in the specification process, while the availability of data of theoretical explanatory variables served as the main restrictive factor. All explanatory variables thus obtained were included in OLS regressions and the estimation period was in principle 1973–1990. Several functional forms have been tested: linear forms, loglinear forms, estimations with ratios, first differences and in period differences with a period of two years. The regressions in first differences and two-period differences served to cause stationarity in non-stationary variables as a way to find significant explanatory variables and correct parameter values. In the ultimate model the variables are predominantly modelled in values and logarithmic forms. When possible, this procedure was followed both for the Frisian and a comparable national equation. The following criteria have been used in the search for a best estimation:

- parameter values are acceptable, which means that the parameters have the expected sign and a size that makes a theoretical interpretation possible.
- parameter values differ between the estimation of the Frisian industry and the Dutch industry only within a certain, explicable, range.
- parameter values are tested by cross-validation: every regression is carried out a few times under omission of a random 20 percent of the cases. The parameter results should remain comparable to each other during this process.
- the estimated parameter values are compared to parameter values of published models of the Dutch economy. Relatively large deviations of the outcomes of the estimations for FREM from other models (in particular, BETA, Athena and FKSEC of the CPB) obtain extra attention.
- the model must be capable of reproducing the most crucial developments in the past. The estimations have a high simulation accuracy; in other words, the mean average percentage errors

(MAPEs) between estimated and actual values within the estimation period are close to 0.
- the estimations have an optimal goodness of fit: R is close to 1.
- t-values, F-statistic and DW-statistic indicate adequacy of the proposed equation. Though the DW-statistic may indicate several problems, equations with autocorrelated disturbances have consequently been adjusted using Cochrane-Orcutts method of iterative least squares.[9]

Finally, after specifying all separate equations, the model has been checked for simultaneity. The simultaneous equations have been re-estimated using the 2SLS procedure.

10.5   Simulation and Forecasts

The performance of FREM has been analysed with the help of two types of simulations. The first simulation consists of (historical) one year forecasts based on actual values for all exogenous variables and all lagged endogenous variables. Forecast errors do not affect forecasts in following years by this method, which will further be referred to as the static simulation. In the other simulation method, the dynamic simulation, each forecast is calculated with actual values for the exogenous variables and values generated by the model for the endogenous variables. The forecast period in the dynamic simulation is five years, so for each simulation year actual values of endogenous variables are at least five years old. Because FREM aims to be a medium term model, we will concentrate here on the results of the dynamic simulation.

Besides by means of graphical presentations,[10] a number of accuracy statistics are employed to judge the simulation results of the model: the mean percentage error, the mean absolute percentage error, the root mean square error and two types of Theil-statistics.[11] If the forecasting accuracy of a regional macroeconomic model is judged, frequently only statistics are presented that can be calculated with the concerning model itself, because competing models are absent. However, comparing forecasts of different models gives the best idea of their relative accuracies. The calculation of Theil-coefficients requires the comparison of the model's forecasts to that of an alternative model. And in fact, alternative models are always available.

The CPB, for instance, uses the naive random walk model as the alternative model. According to the naive random walk model, the forecasted value of each variable equals the actual value in a base year. The base year in the case of the dynamic simulation is t-5 and thus the Theil-statistic of comparison of the model results with the random walk model is:

$$\text{THEIL–RW}_i = \frac{\sqrt{\sum_{t=n}^{(n+v)} (s_{i,F,t} - a_{i,F,t})^2}}{\sqrt{\sum_{t=n}^{(n+v)} (a_{i,F,t-5} - a_{i,F,T})^2}} \quad \text{(Theil-RW-coefficient)} ,$$

(10.2)

in which $s_{i,F,t}$ is the simulated Frisian growth rate, $a_{i,F,t}$ is the actual Frisian growth rate, $a_{i,F,t-5}$ is the growth rate in the base period. The value of the Theil coefficient has a straightforward intuitive interpretation. A value of the Theil coefficient less than, equal to, or greater than one indicates that the model simulation is more, equally, or less accurate than the naive random walk model.

Analogous to the way the Theil coefficient relates simulated growth rates to growth rates in the base year, it is possible to relate simulated values to values generated by applying national growth rates. The application of national growth rates as an alternative to FREM simulations is referred to as the regional share model, for it assumes a constant regional share in all national economic developments. The coefficient that compares the performance of the model simulations to the regional share model is less than, equal to, or greater than one when the model simulation is more, equally, or less accurate than application of national growth figures. This coefficient will be referred to hereafter as the Theil-S-coefficient:

$$\text{THEIL-S}_i = \frac{\sqrt{\sum_{t=n}^{(n+v)} (s_{i,F,t} - a_{i,F,t})^2}}{\sqrt{\sum_{t=n}^{(n+v)} (a_{i,N,t} - a_{i,F,t})^2}} \quad \text{(Theil-S coefficient)}$$

(10.3)

Below, we will look at the simulation qualities of FREM and we will concentrate on the use of the two alternative models that have been mentioned. These two alternatives were the best available. Within the estimation period (1973–1990) 13 dynamic five year simulations are possible. Table 10.2 shows the simulation results on 45 key variables. The forecasts remain on average within a range of about 10 percent of the actual values in the labour demand block of the model and within a range of 4 percent in the labour supply block. Forecast errors appear to neutralize each other: whereas, for example, the mean average percentage errors (MAPE) for all sectoral employment variables are over 1.4 percent, the resulting MAPE for total employment is only 1.1 percent. Frisian unemployment has fluctuated between 5 and 21 percent in the simulation period and the corresponding forecast error between –1.0 and 1.9 percent. A value judgement about the forecast errors is difficult to give, for there are no generally accepted standards for forecast errors on a medium term.

Table 10.2   Simulation accuracy statistics, dynamic simulation, 1978–1990

Variable i	MAPE	Theil-RWi	Variable i	MAPE	Theil-RWi
investment (%)			*fertility rate (Δ)*	1.7	0.09
- non-residential			*migration surplus*	0.1	0.16
buildings	7.0	0.18	*rate (4)*		
- earth, road and					
hydraulic works	11.9	0.32	*population (POP, %)*		
- residential buildings	6.8	0.14	POP total	0.2	0.10
			POP 15-24 yr,women	0.6	0.10
production (%)			POP 15-24 yr, men	0.3	0.07
- food industry	3.4	0.53	POP 25-44, women	0.6	0.20
- metal industry	4.1	0.34	POP 25-44, men	0.3	0.10
- other exposed			POP 45-64, women	0.3	0.25
industries	2.1	0.14	POP 45-64, men	0.3	0.25
- trade	3.3	0.21			
- business services	2.0	0.25	*participation rates (5)*		
- building sector	5.2	0.13	*(PR,Δ)*		
			PR 15-24 yr, women	1.8	0.48
employment (%,5)			PR 15-24yr, men	1.3	0.19
total	1.1	0.13	PR 25-44 yr, women	2.2	0.24
- agriculture (1)	2.1	0.32	PR 25-44 yr, men	0.2	0.25
- food industry (2)	1.5	0.45	PR 45-64 yr, women	3.6	0.17
- metal industry (2)	2.1	0.28	PR 45-64 yr, men	1.3	0.77
- OEX-sector (2)	1.4	0.14	*labour population (5)*		
- trade (2)	4.0	0.19	*(LP, %)*		
- business services(2)	5.0	0.34	labour supply	0.8	0.13
- nonmarket serv. (2)	4.5	0.25	LP total	0.7	0.12
- building sector (2)	3.7	0.21	LP 15-24 yr, women	2.0	0.30
- governm. sector (2)	2.1	0.11	LP 15-24 yr, men	1.4	0.19
- residential sector (2)	8.3	0.32	LP 25-44 yr, women	1.8	0.19
- self-employed (3)	6.3	0.36	LP 25-44 yr, men	0.4	0.12
			LP 45-64 yr, women	3.2	0.17
unemploym. rate (Δ,5)	9.3	0.10	LP 45-64 yr, men	1.2	0.80

Legend for Tables 10.2, 10.3 and 10.4
MAPE = mean average percentage error
Theil-RW = Theil-coefficient for comparison with the naive random walk model
Theil-S = Theil-coefficient for comparison with the regional share model
n = number of cases used in calculations of MAPEs and Theil-coefficients
% = Theil-coefficients have been calculated using growth rates
Δ = Theil-coefficients have been calculated using changes of respective ratios

NA = not applicable
1 employees and self-employed
2 employees
3 excluding agriculture
4 mean absolute error
5 corrected for definition changes
6 no corrections for definition changes. Definition changes apply both to national and Frisian variables.

Table 10.3   Theil-S statistics, dynamic simulation, 1978–1990

Variable i		Theil–S_i		Variable i		Theil–S_i
investment in				*fertility rate*	Δ	0.27
- non-residential				*migration surplus*	Δ	N.A.
buildings	%	0.38		*rate (4)*		
- earth, road and						
hydraulic works	%	0.83		*population (POP)*		
- residential buildings	%	0.49		POP total	%	0.13
				POP 15-24 yr,women	%	0.28
production in				POP 15-24 yr, men	%	0.13
- food industry	%	0.72		POP 25-44, women	%	0.26
- metal industry	%	0.43		POP 25-44, men	%	0.14
- other exposed				POP 45-64, women	%	0.45
industries	%	0.43		POP 45-64, men	%	0.55
- trade	%	0.68				
- business services	%	0.28		*participation rates (6)*		
- building sector	%	0.37		*(PR)*		
				PR 15-24 yr, women	Δ	0.78
employment (5)				PR 15-24yr, men	Δ	0.31
total in	%	0.68		PR 25-44 yr, women	Δ	0.34
- agriculture (1)	%	0.49		PR 25-44 yr, men	Δ	0.29
- food industry (2)	%	0.32		PR 45-64 yr, women	Δ	0.44
- metal industry (2)	%	0.48		PR 45-64 yr, men	Δ	0.81
- OEX-sector (2)	%	0.70		*labour population (6)*		
- trade (2)	%	0.91		*(LP)*		
- business services(2)	%	0.51		labour supply	%	0.59
- nonmarket serv. (2)	%	0.36		LP total	%	0.54
- building sector (2)	%	0.75		LP 15-24 yr, women	%	0.66
- government sector(2)%		0.27		LP 15-24 yr, men	%	0.38
- residential sector (2)	%	0.66		LP 25-44 yr, women	%	0.42
- self-employed (3)	%	1.03		LP 25-44 yr, men	%	0.12
				LP 45-64 yr, women	%	0.46
unemployment rate(6)	Δ	0.78		LP 45-64 yr, men	%	0.56

Legend: see Table 10.2

Theil statistics give more information about the simulation quality of a model, for they compare the model to an alternative. First, we will compare FREM simulations with the naive random walk model. The naive random walk model makes no-change forecasts, but by transforming all variables into growth rates (and in the case of ratios into changes), a naive random walk forecast actually means a constant growth rate for these variables. In the absence of structural economic changes, the naive random walk model might give reasonable forecasts. The Theil-RW statistic compares FREM simulations with naive random walk projections per variable. These random walk projections are not consistent with each other, however. Therefore, the Theil statistics only give an indication of the model quality. Table 10.2 shows that all Theil-RW statistics are below 1, most are even below 0.5. This means that the model outperforms its competitor, the naive random walk, for all listed variables by a considerable margin.

The fact that FREM outperforms the naive random walk model so convincingly strengthens the notions of structural economic change mentioned in Section 10.2. This does not mean, however, that FREM is able to forecast these structural economic changes. Because national developments are exogenous inputs of several parts of the model, it may well be that the essence of the structural economic changes enter the model by means of the exogenous variables.

It would also be very curious if structural economic changes that are determined on a national and international scale could be forecasted in a regional model. What is nonetheless interesting to examine is whether FREM is able to outperform the regional share model, which assumes a constant Frisian share in every national development.[12]

Table 10.3 lists the Theil-S coefficients for the variables under consideration. The table shows that except for the variable 'number of self-employed' again all Theil-S statistics are below 1. For most of the variables, FREM outperforms its regional share competitor still by a fair margin, but it is clear that this margin has diminished, because the Theil-S statistics are all higher than the Theil-RW statistics.

From these results, we conclude that application of national growth rates to (individual) Frisian variables produces better forecasts than assuming constant Frisian developments. This outcome is an extra indication that structural economic changes might enter the model by national exogenous variables. FREM, however, still outperforms its competitors and thus is expected to give extra insights into the development of the Frisian economy on a medium term.

Using historical simulations to check the quality of an economic model is not without its problems, however. There has been some criticism of the use of historical simulations to provide information on model quality.[13] The criticism focuses on the relationship between estimation residuals and simulation residuals. Besides, there are some obvious differences between methods used in historical simulations and in forecasting, for instance concerning the exogenous variables. In historical simulations the exogenous variables are known, while in forecasting they have to be forecasted as well. Finally, global changes in the economic and political environment, may require corresponding changes in the specification of important equations.

To overcome these problems, an ex-post forecast has been carried out for the period 1991–1995. In this period, the relationship between estimation residuals and simulation residuals is much smaller. Besides, the exogenous variables are known and therefore cause no forecasting errors. Global changes in the economic and political environment may still affect the model's accuracy, however, but the extent to which proper forecasts can be made in a time of structural economic changes is exactly what we want to examine.

Five dynamic ex-post forecasts are possible within the period 1991–1995. Because actual data were not available for the whole period for all key-variables, it has not been possible to evaluate the (ex-post) forecasting quality of FREM for all years. Table 10.4 lists the results of the ex-post forecast accuracy. The third column lists the number of cases on which the calculation of MAPEs and Theil-statistics has been based. The general picture from Table 10.4 is that FREM still simulates quite well, but several comments should be made.

Whereas the simulation of the number of self-employed already was no better than the regional share model in the historical simulations, FREM does considerably worse in the ex-post forecast with a Theil-S statistic of 2.41. Neither was employment in trade very well simulated in the historical simulation and its Theil-S statistic has deteriorated further. The simulation of employment in the food industry suffered from a sudden deterioration and was missed by 10 percent on average, even while the production in the food industry was still considerably better simulated compared to the regional share model. The forecast errors of employment in non-market services and the building sector grew too. But the overall performance is not bad at all. All employment errors appear to counterbalance each other and the mean average percentage error of total employment is only 0.6 percent.

The forecast errors also equalize each other in the labour supply block. Most MAPEs for population and participation variables have grown substantially, but, on balance, it turns out that the forecast errors of the Frisian labour population have increased only slightly in comparison to the historical simulations. FREM even improved its forecasting ability of the labour supply relatively to its main competitor, the regional share model. The MAPE of the variable that incorporates all other errors, the unemployment rate, is 10 percent. FREM surpasses the regional share model in forecasting regional unemployment in the ex-post forecast to the same extent as in the historical simulation.

194

Table 10.4 Simulation accuracy statistics, dynamic simulation, 1991–1995

Variable i	n	MAPE	Theil-Si
investment (%)			
- non-residential buildings	2	7.2	0.74
- earth, road and hydraulic works	2	15.5	0.70
- residential build.	2	9.1	0.90
production (%)			
- food industry	4	4.2	0.44
- metal industry	4	7.4	1.09
- other exposed industries	4	0.5	0.07
- trade	4	2.2	0.46
- business services	4	1.0	0.07
- building sector	4	4.8	0.50
employment (%,6)			
total in	3	0.6	0.34
- agriculture (1)	5	1.3	0.25
- food industry (2)	5	10.6	1.02
- metal industry (2)	5	1.4	0.37
- OEX-sector (2)	5	1.4	0.29
- trade (2)	5	6.5	1.08
- business serv.(2)	5	3.5	0.21
- nonmarket serv. (2)	5	7.3	0.68
- building sector (2)	5	7.4	0.52
- governm.sector (2)	5	1.9	0.12
- resident. sector (2)	5	3.6	0.17
- self-employed (Δ 2)	3	9.1	2.41
unemploym. rate(Δ6)	5	10.2	0.76

Variable i	n	MAPE	Theil-Si
fertility rate (Δ)	4	5.5	1.38
migration surplus rate (Δ,4)	4	2.7	N.A.
population (POP,%)			
POP total	5	0.8	0.42
POP 15-24 yr,wom.	5	0.9	0.70
POP 15-24 yr, men	5	0.8	1.40
POP 25-44, women	5	0.8	0.29
POP 25-44, men	5	0.6	0.28
POP 45-64, women	5	1.4	1.60
POP 45-64, men	5	1.1	0.74
participation rates (6) (PR, Δ)			
PR 15-24 yr, wom.	4	2.7	0.85
PR 15-24yr, men	4	3.3	0.67
PR 25-44 yr, wom.	4	3.2	0.67
PR 25-44 yr, men	4	1.8	0.65
PR 45-64 yr, wom.	4	4.0	0.54
PR 45-64 yr, men	4	1.5	0.84
labour population (6) (LP,%)			
labour supply	4	1.1	0.41
LP total	4	0.8	0.43
LP 15-24 yr, wom.	4	2.5	0.41
LP 15-34 yr, men	4	3.6	0.10
LP 25-44 yr, wom.	4	2.7	0.24
LP 25-44 yr, men	4	2.0	0.33
LP 45-64 yr, wom.	4	3.5	0.19
LP 45-64 yr, men	4	1.9	0.21

Legend: see Table 10.2

Again, structural economic changes may have entered the model via the national exogenous variables for the simulations in the period 1991–1995, just as in the historical simulations. Therefore, we conclude that FREM gives extra insight into the developments that may be expected on the Frisian labour market as long as national models are able to forecast the effects of structural economic changes.

10.6 Conclusions

This chapter examines the forecasting power of FREM, an econometric model of Fryslân, at a time of structural economic change. The economic structure both of Fryslân and of the Netherlands as a whole has indeed shown a considerable change between 1973 and 1995, which might have been caused by structural changes, such as the unification of Europe, the globalization of world trade and the increasing public sector in the Netherlands until the 1980s and the tendency to reverse this development thereafter. The examination of forecasting accuracy of FREM in this changing environment has been based on a comparison with two competing models, the naive random walk model and the regional share model.

FREM appears to simulate developments on the Frisian labour market better than its competitors. This judgement is based on 13 dynamic five-year-ahead simulations within the estimation period of most equations of the model (1973–1990), referred to as historical simulations, and 5 dynamic five year ahead simulations for the period 1991–1995, referred to as ex-post forecasts. The valuation statistics have been the mean absolute percentage error and (modified) Theil coefficients.

In historical simulations, FREM outperforms by a wide range the naive random walk model, which assumes constant growth rates. This margin declines when the FREM-simulations are compared to the results of the regional share model, which assumes equal regional and national growth rates. The regional share model, however, is still outperformed by a fair margin except for two variables. The performance of FREM in the ex-post forecasts is comparable to the historical simulations for the aggregated variables labour supply, employment and unemployment. Underlying developments showed a number of larger forecast errors.

That FREM is capable of forecasting labour market developments in times of structural economic changes may be the consequence of exogenous, national variables. The national variables may have incorporated the structural changes. However, the change of regime has not lead to complete redundancy of the model. On the contrary, the overall conclusion is that FREM provides reasonable medium term forecasts and so it may be an important tool for policy makers trying to influence the Frisian economy.

How obvious both competing models that have been used to test the accuracy of FREM may seem, the performance of regional macroeconomic models is seldom or never compared to competing models. The use of both modified Theil coefficients is, therefore, the main contribution of this article.

Appendix 10.1 Sector Classification

Table 10.5 illustrates which industries are included in the eleven sectors that have been distinguished in FREM. The last column gives the corresponding groups of economic activities according to the Standard Industrial Classification of 1974 of the DBS (Statistics Netherlands).

Table 10.5   Sector classification of FREM

FREM Classification	Industries	SIC(SBI)*
Exposed Industries	Agriculture, horticulture and forestry	01/02
1. Agriculture	Food and kindred products industry	20/21
2. Food industry	Basic metal indutry	33
3. Metallurgical	Manufcature of metal products	34
industry	Machinery	35
	Electro technical industry	36
	Manufacture of transport equipment	37
	Manufacture of instruments and optical goods and other industry	38/39
4. Other exposed	Other manufacturing	22-27,29-32
	Fishery	03
	Public utilities	4
	Transportation and communications	7
SHELTERED INDUSTRIES		
5. Trade	Wholesale trade and trade intermediaries	61-64,83.2
	Retail trade	65/66
	Hotels, restaurants, cafes, etc.	67
	Repair of consumer goods	68
6. Business	Banking	81
services	Insurance	82
	Business services and renting of machinery	84/85
OTHER		
7. Non-market	Social services	91,92.9,94,97
services	Health and veterinary services	93
	Cultural, sports and recreational services	95/96
	Private households with wage earning staff	99
	Other services	98
8. Construction	industry	5
9. Residential	sector	83
10. Mining and		1/28
quarrying and	petroleum industry	
11. Governmental	sector	–

*SIC = Standard Industrial Classification, SBI 1974

Appendix 10.2 Flow chart of the model structure of FREM

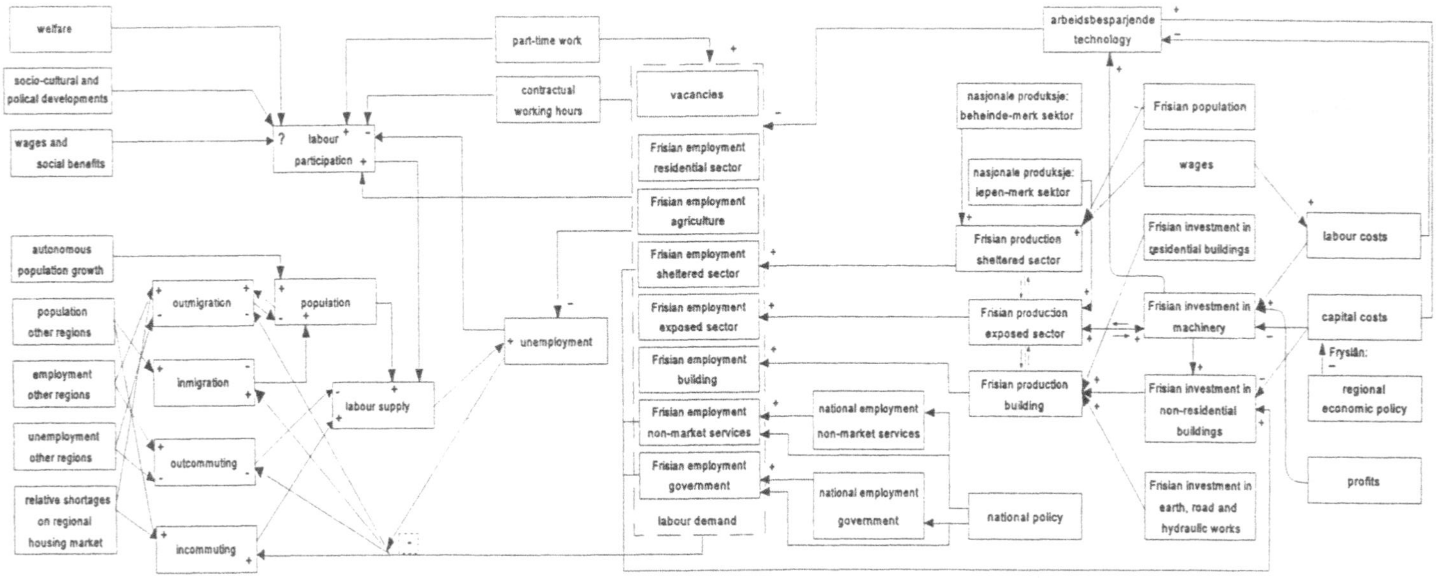

Appendix 10.3 FREM, an econometric model of the Frisian economy

Labour demand model

Employment block

$$L_{F,t} = L_{F,t}^{non-ag} + L_{F,t}^{ag} + L_{F,t}^{se} \qquad\qquad D\text{-}(1)$$

$$L_{F,t}^{non-ag} = L_{F,t}^{ft} + L_{F,t}^{mi} + L_{F,t}^{oex} + L_{F,t}^{tr} + L_{F,t}^{bs} + L_{F,t}^{nms} + L_{F,t}^{bu} + L_{F,t}^{gov} + L_{F,t}^{res} + L_{F,t}^{mq}$$
$$D\text{-}(2)$$

employment by sector

$$L_{F,t}^{ag} = \exp\,[0.99 + 0.90\,*\ln(L_{F,(t-1)}^{ag})] + \varepsilon \qquad\qquad D\text{-}(3)$$
$$\qquad (2.4)\ (21.2)$$

$$L_{F,t}^{ft} = \exp\,[4.29 + 0.60\,*\ln\,(Y/p^Y)_{F,t}^{fi} - 0.027\,*t] + \varepsilon \qquad D\text{-}(4)$$
$$\qquad (423.8)\ (nat.) \qquad\qquad\qquad (-18.3)$$

$$F_{F,t}^{mi} = \exp\,[4.94 + 0.64\,*\ln\,(Y/p^Y)_{F,t}^{mi} - 0.020\,*t + 0.082\,*d_{86}] + \varepsilon \quad D\text{-}(5)$$
$$\qquad (4.9) \qquad (7.8) \qquad\qquad (-15.8) \qquad (5.2)$$

$$L_{F,t}^{oex} = \exp[3.72 + 0.76\,*\ln(Y/p^Y)_{F,(t-1/2)}^{oex} - 0.025\,*t + 0.126\,*d_{86} + 0.049\,*d_{86_{(t-1)}}] + \varepsilon$$
$$\qquad (3.0)\ (4.8) \qquad\qquad\qquad (-8.8) \qquad (4.4) \qquad\qquad (2.0)$$
$$D\text{-}(6)$$

$$L_{F,t}^{tr} = \exp[1.94 + 1.03\,*\ln(Y/p^Y)_{F,t}^{tr} - 0.009\,*t + 0.278\,*d_{86}] + \varepsilon \quad D\text{-}(7)$$
$$\qquad (1.1) \qquad (4.7) \qquad\qquad (-2.3) \qquad (6.8)$$

$$L_{F,t}^{bs} = \exp[1.77 + 1.06\,*\ln(Y/p^Y)_{F,t}^{bs} - 0.125\,*d_{<77} + 0.297\,*d_{86}] + \varepsilon$$
$$\qquad (1.5) \qquad (6.5) \qquad\qquad (-3.7) \qquad\qquad (8.0) \qquad D\text{-}(8)$$

$$L_{F,t}^{nms} = \exp[0.74\,*\ln(L_{F,t}^{nms}) + 0.202\,*d_{86}] + \varepsilon \qquad\qquad D\text{-}(9)$$
$$\qquad (5.2) \qquad\qquad (2.3)$$

$$L_{F,t}^{bu} = \exp[6.41 + 0.42*\ln(Y/p^Y)_{F,t}^{bu} - 0.72*\ln(phh) - 0.022*t] + \varepsilon$$

$$(8.70) \qquad (4.3) \qquad\qquad (-2.8) \qquad\qquad\qquad (-6.7)$$

D-(10)

$$L_{F,t}^{gov} = \exp[-8.08 + 1.36*\ln(L_{F,t}^{gov})]$$

$$(-15.5) \quad (34.3)$$

D-(11)

$$L_{F,t}^{res} = -2781 + 0.0066*POP_{F,(t-1)} + 174*d_{86} + \varepsilon$$

$$(-4.4) \qquad (6.0) \qquad\qquad (3.4)$$

D-(12)

$$L_{F,t}^{mq} = L_{F(t-1)}^{mq} + \varepsilon$$

D-(13)

self-employment

$$L_{F,t}^{se} = L_{F,t}^{non\text{-}ag}*[0.141 - 0.0026*t + 0.82*\Delta(\frac{L^{se}}{L^{non\text{-}ag}})_{F,(t-1)}] + \varepsilon$$

$$(54.0) \qquad (-5.6) \qquad (2.8)$$

D-(14)

$$Y_{f,t}^{fi} = \exp[-3.01 + 1.04*\ln(Y_{N,t}^{fi})] + \varepsilon$$

$$(5.9) \qquad (22.4)$$

D-(15)

$$(Y/p^Y)_{F,t}^{mi} = \exp[0.48*\ln(Y/p^Y)_{N,t}^{mi} + 0.27*\ln(I^{nrb}/p^{I^{nrb}})_{F,(t-1)}$$

$$(13.2) \qquad\qquad (4.7)$$

$$+0.078*\ln(I^{erh}/p^{I^{erh}})_{F,(t-1)} + \varepsilon$$

$$(2.3)$$

D-(16)

$$(Y/p^Y)_{F,t}^{oex} = \exp[-4.92 + 0.65*\ln(Y/p^Y)_{N,(t-1/2)}^{oex} + 0.56*\ln[(Y/p^Y)_{F,t}^{ft} +$$

$$(-7.6) \ (6.1) \qquad\qquad\qquad (3.8)$$

$$+(Y/p^Y)_{f,t}^{tr} + (Y/p^Y)_{F,t}^{bs} + (Y/p^Y)_{F,t}^{bu}]] + \varepsilon$$

D-(17)

$$(Y/p^Y)_{F,t}^{tr} = \exp[-1.61 + 0.94*\ln[(Y/p^Y)_{F,t}^{mi} + (Y/p^Y)_{F,t}^{oex}] + 0.13*\ln(L_{F,t}^{tr})] + \varepsilon$$

$$(-1.8) \ (5.7) \qquad\qquad\qquad\qquad (2.5)$$

D-(18)

$$(Y/p^Y)^{bs}_{F,t}=\exp[-1.27+0.60*\ln(Y/p^Y)^{bs}_{N,t}+0.24*\ln[(Y/p^Y)^{mi}_{F,t}+(Y/p^Y)^{tr}_{F,t}]+\varepsilon$$

$$(-1.9)\ (10.7)\qquad\qquad (2.1)$$

$$D(-19)$$

$$(Y/p^Y)^{bu}_{F,t}=1.06*[(I^{nrb}/p^{I^{nrb}})_{F,t}+(I^{rb}/p^{I^b})_{F,t}+(I^{erh}/p^{I^{erh}})_{F,t}]+323*d_{>87}+\varepsilon$$

$$(80.8)\qquad\qquad\qquad\qquad\qquad (5.8)\qquad D(-20)$$

$$(I^{nrb}/p^{nrb})_{F,t}=\exp[-3.04+0.97*\ln[(Y/p^Y)^{fi}_{F,t}+(Y/p^Y)^{oex}_{F,t}+(Y/p^Y)^{tr}_{F,t}+$$

$$(-1.3)\ (4.0)$$

$$+(Y/p^Y)^{bs}_{F,t}]+0.275*d^{ip1}_F+0.211*d^{ip2}_F]+\varepsilon$$

$$(5.8)\qquad\qquad (5.7)\qquad\qquad\qquad D-(21)$$

$$(I^{rb}/p^{I^b})_{F,t}=\exp[7.58\ -3.07*u_{N,(t-1)}\ -7.05*r^m_{(t-1)}+0.64\ \Delta(I^{rb}/p^{I^b})_{F,(t-1)}+\varepsilon$$

$$(42.0)\quad (-8.2)\qquad (-3.8)\qquad\qquad (5.4)\qquad D-(22)$$

$$(I^{erh}/p^{I^{erh}})_{F,t}=\exp[-5.39\ +1.26*\ln(I^{erh}/p^{I^{erh}})_{N,t}\ -0.025*t+\varepsilon$$

$$(-4.7)\quad (10.0)\qquad\qquad\qquad (-6.0)\qquad D-(23)$$

Labour supply model

Population Block

$$POP_{F,t}=\sum_a\sum_g^{f,m} POP^{g,a}_{F,t}$$

$$S-(1)$$

$$POP^{g,a}_{F,t}=POPN^{g,a}_{F,t}+POPM^{g,a}_{F,t}$$

$$S-(2)$$

Natural Population Block

$$POPN^{g,a+1}_{F,t}=ps^{g,a}_t*POP^{g,a}_{F,t-1}$$

$$S-(3)$$

$$POPN_{F,t}^{g,0} = ps^{g,B} * B_{F,t}^{g}$$

S–(4)

Survival rates

$$ps_t^{m,a} = (100\% - 1.2\%) * ps_{(t-1)}^{m,a} + \varepsilon$$

and

S–(5)

$$ps_t^{f,a} = (100\% - 0.8\%) * ps_{(t-1)}^{f,a} + \varepsilon$$

births

$$B_{F,t} = \sum_{a=15}^{49} POP_{F,(t-1)}^{f,a} * fr_{F,t}$$

S–(6)

$$B_{F,t}^{m} = i_{F,t}^{m} * B_{F,t} = 0.515 * B_{F,t} + \varepsilon$$

S–(7)

fertility

$$fr_{F,t} = 0.030 + 0.59 * fr_{F,(t-1)} - 0.22 * pr_{F,(t-1)}^{f,25-44} + \varepsilon$$
$$\quad\;\;(6.4)\;\;(11.9) \qquad\qquad (-6.4)$$

S–(8)

Migration Block

$$POPM_{F,t}^{c,g} = ms_{F,t}^{c,g} * POP_{F,(t-1)}^{c,g}$$

S–(9)

$$POPM_{F,t}^{a,g} = POPM_{F,t}^{c,g} * \frac{POP_{F,(t-1)}^{a,g}}{POP_{F,(t-1)}^{c,g}} * (1-((1 - ps_t^{a,g})/2))$$

S–(10)

$$ms_{F,t}^{f,0-4} = 0.0016 + 0.780 * ms_{F,t}^{f,30-34} + \varepsilon$$
$$\qquad\quad (3.5) \qquad (11.5)$$

S–(11)

$$ms_{F,t}^{f,5-9} = -0.001 + 1.01 * ms_{F,t}^{f,35-39} + \varepsilon$$
$$\qquad\quad (-2.4) \quad (12.4)$$

S–(12)

$$ms_{F,t}^{f,10-14} = -0.001 + 1.14 \; *ms_{F,t}^{f,40-44} + \varepsilon$$

$$\quad\quad\quad\quad (-1.8) \quad\quad (9.9) \quad\quad\quad\quad\quad\quad\quad\quad S-(13)$$

$$ms_{F,t}^{f,15-19} = 0.003 \; -0.09 \; *u_{F,t-1} \; -0.009 \; *d_{89_{(t-1)}} + \varepsilon$$

$$\quad\quad\quad\quad (3.7) \quad (-15.4) \quad\quad\quad (-9.7) \quad\quad\quad\quad S-(14)$$

$$ms_{F,t}^{f,20-24} = 0.013 \; -0.16 \; *u_{F,t} \; -0.020 \; *d_{89} + \varepsilon$$

$$\quad\quad\quad\quad (2.8) \quad\; (-6.1) \quad\quad (-5.8) \quad\quad\quad\quad\quad S-(15)$$

$$ms_{F,t}^{f,25-29} = 0.017 \; -0.11 \; *u_{F,t} \; -0.010 \; *d_{89} + \varepsilon$$

$$\quad\quad\quad\quad (11.7) \; (-9.9) \quad\quad\; (-5.4) \quad\quad\quad\quad\quad S-(16)$$

$$ms_{F,t}^{f,30-34} = 0.014 \; -0.08 \; *u_{F,t} \; -0.006 \; *d_{89} + \varepsilon$$

$$\quad\quad\quad\quad (10.8) \; (-8.0) \quad\quad\; (-4.1) \quad\quad\quad\quad\quad S-(17)$$

$$ms_{F,t}^{f,35-39} = 0.010 \; -0.06 \; *u_{F,t} \; -0.003 \; *d_{89} + \varepsilon$$

$$\quad\quad\quad\quad (13.1) \; (-9.5) \quad\quad\; (-3.5) \quad\quad\quad\quad\quad S-(18)$$

$$ms_{F,t}^{f,40-44} = 0.013 \; -0.02 \; *u_{F,t} \; -0.002 \; *d_{89} + 0.15 \; dpL_t + \varepsilon$$

$$\quad\quad\quad\quad (8.2) \quad (-4.6) \quad\quad (-3.5) \quad\quad\quad\; (3.3) \quad\quad\quad S-(19)$$

$$ms_{F,t}^{f,45-49} = 0.017 + 0.29 \; *dpL_t + \varepsilon$$

$$\quad\quad\quad\quad (8.2) \quad\quad (4.6) \quad\quad\quad\quad\quad\quad\quad\quad S-(20)$$

$$ms_{F,t}^{f,50-54} = 0.021 + 0.36 \; *dpL_t + \varepsilon$$

$$\quad\quad\quad\quad (7.3) \quad\quad (6.0) \quad\quad\quad\quad\quad\quad\quad\quad S-(21)$$

$$ms_{F,t}^{f,55-59} = 0.023 + 0.36 \; *dpL_t + \varepsilon$$

$$\quad\quad\quad\quad (13.1) \quad (9.9) \quad\quad\quad\quad\quad\quad\quad\quad S-(22)$$

$$ms_{F,t}^{f,60-64} = 0.025 + 0.43 \ {}^*dpL_t + \varepsilon$$

$$(13.2) \quad (10.9) \qquad\qquad S-(23)$$

$$ms_{F,t}^{f,>65} = -0.001 + 0.40 \ {}^*dpH_{(t-1)} + \varepsilon$$

$$(-1.1) \quad (5.9) \qquad\qquad S-(24)$$

$$ms_{F,t}^{m,0-4} = 0.002 + 0.69 \ {}^*ms_{F,t}^{f,30-34} + \varepsilon$$

$$(3.4) \quad (7.6) \qquad\qquad S-(25)$$

$$ms_{F,t}^{m,5-9} = -0.001 + 0.98 \ {}^*ms_{F,t}^{f,35-39} + \varepsilon$$

$$(-2.7) \quad (21.1) \qquad\qquad S-(26)$$

$$ms_{F,t}^{m,10-14} = -0.001 + 1.28 \ {}^*ms_{F,t}^{f,40-44} + \varepsilon$$

$$(-3.7) \quad (19.9) \qquad\qquad S-(27)$$

$$ms_{F,t}^{m,15-19} = -0.001 - 0.04 \ {}^*u_{F,t-1} + 0.003 \ {}^*d_{89_{(t-1)}} + \varepsilon$$

$$(-1.9) \ (-7.2) \qquad (-3.4) \qquad\qquad S-(28)$$

$$ms_{F,t}^{m,20-24} = 0.011 - 0.14 \ {}^*u_{F,t} - 0.014 \ {}^*d_{89} + \varepsilon$$

$$(3.8) \quad (-6.8) \qquad (-4.9) \qquad\qquad S-(29)$$

$$ms_{F,t}^{m,25-29} = 0.022 - 0.15 \ {}^*u_{F,t} - 0.014 \ {}^*d_{89} + \varepsilon$$

$$(13.8) \ (-12.8) \qquad (-8.0) \qquad\qquad S-(30)$$

$$ms_{F,t}^{m,30-34} = 0.013 - 0.08 \ {}^*u_{F,t} - 0.002 \ {}^*d_{89} + \varepsilon$$

$$(14.1) \ (-10.9) \qquad (-2.2) \qquad\qquad S-(31)$$

$$ms_{F,t}^{m,35-39} = 0.010 - 0.06 \ {}^*u_{F,t} - 0.003 \ {}^*d_{89} + \varepsilon$$

$$(19.9) \ (-14.5) \qquad (-6.5) \qquad\qquad S-(32)$$

$$ms_{F,t}^{m,40-44} = 0.015 - 0.02 *u_{F,t} - 0.001 *d_{89} + 0.21 *dpL_t + \varepsilon$$

$$\quad\quad (6.7)\ (-3.3)\quad\quad (-1.0)\quad\quad (3.4) \quad\quad\quad\text{S--(33)}$$

$$ms_{F,t}^{m,45-49} = 0.016 + 0.28 *dpL_t + \varepsilon$$

$$\quad\quad (6.0)\quad (5.4) \quad\quad\quad\quad\quad\quad\quad\text{S--(34)}$$

$$ms_{F,t}^{m,50-54} = 0.014 + 0.24 *dpL_t + \varepsilon$$

$$\quad\quad (12.0)\quad (9.6) \quad\quad\quad\quad\quad\quad\text{S--(35)}$$

$$ms_{F,t}^{m,55-59} = 0.016 + 0.22 *dpL_t + \varepsilon$$

$$\quad\quad (11.8)\quad (7.7) \quad\quad\quad\quad\quad\quad\text{S--(36)}$$

$$ms_{F,t}^{m,60-64} = 0.024 + 0.31 *dpL_t + \varepsilon$$

$$\quad\quad (3.9)\quad (2.6) \quad\quad\quad\quad\quad\quad\text{S--(37)}$$

$$ms_{F,t}^{m,>65} = -0.002 + 0.50 *dpH_t + \varepsilon$$

$$\quad\quad (-0.3)\quad (6.4) \quad\quad\quad\quad\quad\quad\text{S--(38)}$$

migration help variables

$$dpL_t = (\frac{L_{F,t}}{POP_{F,(t-1)}}) - (\frac{L_{N,t}}{POP_{N,(t-1)}})$$

(relative employment chances) $\quad\quad\quad\quad\quad\quad$ S--(39)

$$dpH_t = (\frac{H_{F,t}}{POP_{F,(t-1)}}) - (\frac{H_{N,t}}{POP_{N,(t-1)}})$$

(relative housing market situation) $\quad\quad\quad\quad$ S--(40)

Labour Supply Block

$$LS_{F,t} = LP_{F,t} + CMS_{F,t}$$

$$\quad\quad\quad\quad\quad\quad\quad\quad\quad\quad\quad\quad\quad\text{S--(41)}$$

labour population

$$LP_{F,t}^{g,a} = pr_{F,t}^{g,a} * POP_{F,t}^{g,a} \qquad\qquad S-(42)$$

$$LP_{F,t} = \sum_{g}^{f,m} \sum_{a}^{15-24,25-44,45-64} LP_{F,t}^{g,a} \qquad\qquad S-(43)$$

$$pr_{F,t}^{f,15-24} = 0.437 -0.005 *t -0.018 *d^{ed} + 0.053 *d_{81} + \varepsilon$$
$$\phantom{pr_{F,t}^{f,15-24} = }(69.1) \quad (-5.3) \qquad (-3.8) \qquad\quad (8.4) \qquad\qquad S-(44)$$

$$pr_{F,t}^{f,25-44} = 0.285 + 0.009*t + 0.34*u_{F,(t-1)} + 0.049*d_{89_{(t-1)}} + 0.037\ d_{81} + \varepsilon$$
$$(21.4)\quad (5.2)\quad (2.5)\qquad\qquad (2.5)\qquad\qquad (2.2)\qquad S-(45)$$

$$pr_{F,t}^{f,45-64} = 0.140 +0.221 *u_{F,t} +0.046 *d_{89} + 0.021 *d_{81} + \varepsilon$$
$$\phantom{pr_{F,t}^{f,45-64} = }(19.6)\quad (4.8)\qquad\quad (9.1)\qquad\quad (4.1)\qquad\qquad S-(46)$$

$$pr_{F,t}^{m,15-24} = 0.507 -[0.011 -0.005 *d_{89}] *t + 0.023 *d_{81} + \varepsilon$$
$$\phantom{pr_{F,t}^{m,15-24} = }(123.2)\ (-12.8)\ (2.2)\qquad\qquad (2.9)\qquad\qquad S-(47)$$

$$pr_{F,t}^{m,25-44} = 1.028 -0.059*(w/p^{cons})_t -0.004*d^{aaw} -0.047 *d_{89} + \varepsilon$$
$$\phantom{pr_{F,t}^{m,25-44} = }(78.0)\quad (-4.3)\qquad\qquad (-3.1)\qquad (-29.1)\qquad S-(48)$$

$$pr_{F,t}^{m,45-64} = 0.717 -[0.015 -0.009 *d_{89}] *t +0.060 *d_{81} + \varepsilon$$
$$\phantom{pr_{F,t}^{m,45-64} = }(143.3)\ (-14.2)\ (3.1)\qquad\qquad (6.1)\qquad\qquad S-(49)$$

commuting

$$CMS_{F,t} = cmsr_{F,t} *LP_{F,t} \qquad\qquad S-(50)$$

$$cmsr_{F,t} = -0.0136 + \varepsilon \qquad\qquad S-(51)$$

Unemployment Block

$$u_{F,t} = 0.711 * (\frac{LS - L}{LP})_{F,t} + 0.091 *d_{86} - 0.045 *d_{89} + \varepsilon$$

$$(27.9) \qquad\qquad (8.6) \qquad (-3.1) \qquad\qquad\qquad S-(52)$$

Regression statistics

equation	period	degrees of freedom	DW-statistic	R^2 %	estimation method
D-(3)	1973–1990	16	2.7	96.3	COILS
D-(4)	1973–1990	16	1.5	94.3	COILS
D-(5)	1973–1990	14	2.3	96.3	COILS
D-(6)	1973–1990	11	1.7	93.1	2SLS
D-(7)	1973–1990	14	2.1	93.8	2SLS
D-(8)	1973–1990	14	1.7	98.2	2SLS
D-(9)	1973–1990	16	1.2	96.1	COILS
D-(10)	1973–1990	14	2.1	79.8	2SLS
D-(11)	1973–1990	16	1.9	98.6	COILS
D-(12)	1973–1990	15	2.7	85.7	COILS
D-(14)	1973–1990	16	1.3	67.7	2SLS
D-(15)	1973–1990	16	1.5	96.7	COILS
D-(16)	1973–1990	15	1.8	56.2	COILS
D-(17)	1973–1990	13	1.1	96.5	2SLS
D-(18)	1973–1990	13	1.9	90.6	2SLS
D-(19)	1973–1990	13	1.4	95.7	2SLS
D-(20)	1973–1990	14	2.2	99.8	2SLS
D-(21)	1973–1990	12	2.4	96.3	2SLS
D-(22)	1973–1990	12	1.2	89.1	COILS
D-(23)	1973–1990	15	2.4	84.8	COILS
S-(7)	1973–1990	15	2.2	97.8	COILS
S-(11)	1973–1990	16	2.3	88.6	COILS
S-(12)	1973–1990	16	1.2	89.9	COILS
S-(13)	1973–1990	16	2.4	85.0	COILS
S-(14)	1973–1992	17	1.4	93.7	COILS
S-(15)	1973–1992	17	1.3	71.6	COILS
S-(16)	1973–1992	17	1.5	84.6	COILS
S-(17)	1973–1992	17	1.4	77.5	COILS
S-(18)	1973–1992	17	1.7	82.5	COILS
S-(19)	1973–1992	16	2.1	94.4	COILS
S-(20)	1973–1990	16	1.9	89.3	COILS
S-(21)	1973–1990	16	1.8	67.4	COILS
S-(22)	1973–1990	16	2.1	85.0	COILS
S-(23)	1973–1990	16	1.3	87.5	COILS

equation	period	degrees of freedom	DW-statistic	R^2 %	estimation method
S-(24)	1973–1990	16	0.3	66.8	COILS
S-(25)	1973–1990	16	2.7	76.9	COILS
S-(26)	1973–1990	16	2.7	96.3	COILS
S-(27)	1973–1990	16	2.5	95.9	COILS
S-(28)	1973–1992	17	1.1	74.8	COILS
S-(29)	1973–1992	17	1.7	72.6	COILS
S-(30)	1973–1992	17	1.7	90.6	COILS
S-(31)	1973–1992	17	2.1	86.0	COILS
S-(32)	1973–1992	17	1.9	92.1	COILS
S-(33)	1973–1992	16	1.5	94.4	COILS
S-(34)	1973–1990	16	1.3	62.3	COILS
S-(35)	1973–1990	16	2.4	84.1	COILS
S-(36)	1973–1990	16	2.6	77.2	COILS
S-(37)	1973–1990	16	1.4	25.4	COILS
S-(38)	1973–1990	16	0.3	70.2	COILS
S-(44)	1973–1992	16	1.9	66.6	COILS
S-(45)	1973–1992	15	1.3	97.3	COILS
S-(46)	1973–1992	16	0.6	87.4	COILS
S-(47)	1973–1992	16	1.3	97.1	COILS
S-(48)	1973–1992	16	1.7	98.1	COILS
S-(49)	1973–1992	16	1.8	97.0	COILS
S-(52)	1973–1992	17	1.2	98.6	COILS

Appendix 10.4 List of symbols

a_i = actual growth rate of variable i (actual change in the case of ratios)

a = age

A_i = actual value of variable i

ag = agriculture

B = births (number of persons)

bs = business services

bu = building

c = 5-year cohort

CMS = commuting surplus (number of persons)

cmsr = commuting surplus rate (commuting surplus divided by the total population)

d = dummy

d^{aaw} = dummy for the coming into operation of the AWW (Algemene Arbeidsongeschiktheidswet, General Disability Act) as a supplement to the WAO (Wet op

		arbeidsongeschiktheids– verzekering, Disability Insurance Act) (in 1976)
d^{ed}	=	dummy for statutory change of school-going ages (in 1976)
$d_{<77}, d_{>87}$	=	dummy for revision of the Regional Economic Accounts in 1978 and 1988, respectively
d_{81}	=	dummy for definition change of labour supply in 1981
d_{86}	=	dummy for definition change of employment in 1986
d_{89}	=	dummy for definition changes of labour supply and unemployment in 1989
DF	=	degrees of freedom
dpH	=	difference in housing change (chance in Friesland minus change in the Netherlands)
dpL	=	difference in employment chance (chance in Friesland minus chance in the Netherlands)
DW	=	Durbin-Watson statistic
erh	=	earth, road and hydraulic works
f	=	female
F	=	Friesland
fi	=	food industry
fr	=	fertiliy rate (number of births per woman during the year)
g	=	genus: male or female
gov	=	government sector
gr	=	growth rate
H	=	number of dwellings
I	=	investments
i^m	=	masculinity index (number of males of all births)
ip1, ip2	=	periods that have been distinguished as having clearly different investment premium regimes for Fryslân. The following periods have been distinguished: 1973–1977 and 1981–1984 as periods of moderate investment premiums; the period 1978–1980 as a period of an intensified investment premium regime; and the period after 1984 as a period with relatively low investment premiums. ip1 is a dummy for the period 1973–1984 and ip2 is a dummy for the period 198–1980.
L	=	employment (number of employed persons)
ln	=	natural logarithm
LP	=	labour population (number of persons)
LS	=	labour supply (number of persons)
m	=	male
MAPE	=	mean average percentage error
mi	=	metal industry
mq	=	mining and quarrying
ms	=	migration surplus rate (migration surplus divided by the total population)
N	=	the Netherlands; national
n	=	number

nms	=	non-market services
non-ag	=	all sectors with the exception of agriculture
nrb	=	non-residential buildings
oex	=	other exposed industries
OEX	=	OEX-sector, other exposed industries, see appendix 10.1 Sector classification of FREM
OLS	=	ordinary least squares
p	=	price index (1980 = 100)
pa	=	P/A ratio, the number of workers per labour position/full - time job
phh	=	productive working hours in the building sector (index, 1980 = 100)
POP	=	population (number of persons)
POPM	=	migration (number of persons)
POPN	=	natural population (number of persons)
pr	=	labour participation rate
ps	=	survival chance, which is the same as one minus the mortality rate (number of survivors divided by total number of persons
p_y	=	price level of the output (1980 = 100)
r^m	=	mortgage interest
R	=	region
R^2	=	R bar squared, the adjusted goodness of fit
rb	=	residential buildings
res	=	residential sector
s_i	=	simulated growth rate of variable i (simulated change in the case of ratios
S_i	=	simulated value of variable i
se	=	self-employment
sec	=	sector
sp	=	simulation period
t	=	trend; time; year
Theil-RW	=	Theil coefficient of the naive random walk model
Theil-S	=	Theil coefficient of the regional share model
tr	=	trade
u	=	(registered) unemployment rate
w	=	wages (index, 1980 = 100)
Y	=	production
2SLS	=	two stage least squares
ε	=	error
v	=	number of simulations

References

CBS (Statistics Netherlands) (several years, a), *Enquête Beroepsbevolking,* (Survey of the labour population), Sdu/CBS,The Hague.

CBS (several years, b), *Maandstatistiek van de Bevolking,* (Monthly bulletin of population statistics), Sdu/CBS, The Hague.

CBS (several years, c), *Regionale Gegevens over Arbeid,* (Regional labour statistics), Sdu/CBS, The Hague.

CBS (several years, d), *Regionale Beroepsbevolking,* (Regional labour population), Sdu/CBS, The Hague.

CBS (several years, e), *Sociaal-economische Maandstatistiek,* (Monthly bulletin of socioeconomic statistics), Sdu/CBS, The Hague.

CBS (1996), *Statistisch Jaarboek 1996,* (Statistical Yearbook), Sdu/uitgeverij/CBS, The Hague.

CPB (Central Planning Bureau) (several years), *Centraal Economisch Plan,* (Central Economic Plan), Sdu, The Hague.

CPB (1990), *Athena, Een Bedrijfstakkenmodel van de Nederlandse Economie,* (Athena, A sector model of the Dutch economy), Centraal Planbureau, Monograph, no.30, The Hague.

CPB (1992), *FKSEC, a Sector Model for the Netherlands,* Stenfert Kroese, Leiden/Antwerp.

Eijgenraam, C.J.J. and Verkade, E.M. (1988), 'BETA, Een Bedrijfstakkenmodel van de Nederlandse Economie', (BETA, A sector model of the Dutch economy), Centraal Planbureau, Occasional Papers, no.44, The Hague.

Fischer, P.G. and Wallis, K.F. (1990), 'The Historical Tracking Performance of UK Macroeconomic Models 1978–1985', Economic Modelling, pp. 179–97.

Kennedy, P. (1992), *A Guide to Econometrics,* Third Edition, Blackwell, Oxford UK and Cambridge USA.

Statistisch Zakboek voor het Noorden des Lands (Statistical yearbook of the North), (several years), Bolsward/Leeuwarden..

Statistisch Jaarboek van het Noorden (Statistical yearbook of the North), Kamer van Koophandel (Chambers of Commerce) (several years), Groningen/Leeuwarden/Meppel/Veendam.

Notes

1. Kennedy, p. 269.

2. With this, it is not assumed that other sources of forecasting errors are non-existent.

3. CBS 1996.

4. CBS, c.

5. CBS, e: April 1996.

6. The index is dependent on industry classification.

7. See Appendix 10.1 for a detailed overview of the sector classification.

8. The latest sector model of the Dutch economy (CBS 1992).

9. Ignoring the possibilities of an omitted explanatory variable, an incorrect functional form or a dynamic misspecification. See Kennedy, p. 123 for a description of the Cochrane-Orcutt method of iterative least squares.

10. Correct forecasts of breaks and bending points is one of the indications of the forecasting quality of the model: how many breaks are forecast, how many are missed, how many are wrongly forecast and is there is systematic lag or lead in the forecast breaks?

11. The type of the Theil coefficient used here is also used by the Dutch Central Planning Bureau and is usually mentioned as the modified Theil coefficient. The modified Theil coefficient is a measure that is independent of the level of the variable (CPB 1992, p. 75).

12. We want to reemphasize that caution is needed in the interpretation. Theil statistics compare FREM simulations with constant regional share projections per variable. These projections are not consistent with each other, however.

13. See for example Fischer and Wallis 1990.

11 The Spatial Distribution of Employment in the European Union: 1950-1990

HANS KUIPER

11.1 Introduction

The creation of the European Community (EC) has been the most significant event for the economic, political, and social geography of Europe in the second half of the twentieth century. From its beginnings in the early 1950s with the Treaty of Paris (1952) and the emergence of the European Coal and Steel Community (ECSC), the two Treaties of Rome (1958) setting up the European Economic Community (EEC) and Euratom, on to the Single European Act (1986) paving the way for the Single Market in 1993, and now the tortuous, negotiations over full monetary union at the heart of the Treaty on European Union (Maastricht Treaty), the EC has evolved into an increasingly complex political entity. It is now the dominant influence in shaping the future of twelve European states.

Within the European Community there are vast differences in wealth, incomes, opportunities, lifestyles, politics, traditions, culture, language, landscapes and economic activities. Achieving economic and social cohesion within the Community is therefore an immense task and one whose magnitude is likely to increase as the boundaries of the Community extend to the north and east. This task is nevertheless one that the European Community has set itself (see article 130A of the Single European Act of 1986).

There are many dimensions of inequality. One way in which inequalities can be identified is to examine the level of Gross Domestic Product (GDP) per capita. However, Europe's GDP can be measured in different ways: measured in European Currency Units (ECUs) it gives an indication of the real value of a region's output. Studying these values shows a clear centre-periphery pattern with the richer regions concentrated in the centre, and the poorer regions on the periphery, especially in the south and west.

The fundamental causes of inequality, which affect the degree of competitiveness and the real living standards of the inhabitants of the regions include the scale and nature of employment, the level of unemployment, the activity rate, the degree of education and training of the workforce, levels of investment, levels of research and development expenditure and so on.

Especially the scale and nature of employment in the regions of the European Union is studied over a long period 1950–1990. The European employment strategy is based on interrelated measures to enhance employment creating growth, social solidarity, equal treatment, and special efforts to promote access to jobs for the most vulnerable groups on the labour market.

11.2 The Evolution of Disparities

The European economic integration into a common market and eventually into an economic and monetary union is likely to have important effects for the evolving pattern of regional development throughout the continent. Explaining and predicting the process of regional development is a difficult task because many interrelated factors, including non-economic ones, are at work. By definition, theories and models simplify a far more complex reality into a framework that can be grasped by the human mind. It is apparently due to the complexity of the process that no consistent corpus of doctrine regarding regional development has been established. Different economists look at the process from different perspectives or concentrate on different parts of the total process.

Spatial disparities can refer to:
- disparities between countries,
- disparities between the various regions of each country,
- disparities between the regions of the whole community.

There is a relation between these types of disparities; the last type results from a combination of the first two. The question of growing or declining disparities depends on the way these disparities are measured. Each member country of the Community can influence their internal disparities (second type of disparities) which means that the community policy is strongly dependent on the policy of the member states.

The comparison of spatial disparities is a difficult task. The various indicators of disparity are influenced by the number of regions and the design of the regions.

The issue of the evaluation of disparities is important for the European Community. If the disparities would increase, either as a result of natural forces, or as a consequence of European policy, they might become unacceptably large, decrease the cohesion of the union, and either jeopardize the very achievement of a union or call for powerful correcting policies. On the other hand, if there is a process of convergence, be it natural or favoured by European forces, the cohesion of the community will be strengthened and the need for policies decreased.

11.3 Regional Development Theories

Models explaining the economic development of a set of regions should include a number of factors, as:
- the possibility of a comparative advantage in technology,
- the effects of agglomerations economies,
- the cultural differences among countries (regions),
- the existence of footloose industries,
- the importance of distance,
- the number of inhabitants.

Some well known theoretical approaches, which are useful if regional development has to be explained lead to different conclusions.

Many different views are held about the natural evolution of spatial disparities. They can be found in theories of regional development and in theories of international trade. The views of theorists concerning the expected convergence or divergence of regional differences are very different. The classical and neoclassical theorists believe in the natural disappearance of spatial disparities. They generally assume perfect mobility of production factors between the regions of a given country or between nations. It is easy to argue that both labour and capital will move from low to high wage areas. Outmigration will decrease the supply of labour in low wage areas and exert an upward pressure upon wages in these areas. For symmetrical reasons, inmigration will exert a downward pressure upon wages in high wage areas. Wages will tend to equalize over regions or countries. A similar simple reasoning can be applied to capital movements, which will tend to equalize returns on capital over space. In this neoclassical world there is no room for spatial disparities; and disparities that may have occurred occasionally will be wiped out by movements of factors of production.

On the other hand a large number of economists (e.g. Krugman 1987; following Myrdal 1957 or Kaldor 1970), question the views concerning concentration.

Divergence is stimulated by:
- economies of scale,
- external economies,
- technology and innovation,
- market structures and rents.

As a result of economies of scale, a region, or a country, which happens (for whatever reason) to be specialized in a particular industry will benefit from an increase in production, which will lower its production costs, making it more difficult for other regions or countries to catch up. The question of the evaluation of disparities can be studied empirically to show which of either the convergence or the divergence views is supported by facts.

Two models will be mentioned, a static and a dynamic model, explaining regional development. Location theory, fundamental for the development of regional science, explains the spatial distribution of production activities in an economy.

In these models, explicitly the development and location of different sectors will be explained. Some sectors might be more profitable for a region than others, which would mean that specialization does not equally benefit all regions or nations. The countries or regions specialized in sectors with greater economies of scale and greater spillover effects are likely to benefit more from trade.

11.3.1.1 A static model Tinbergen and Bos defined a number of hypotheses that are necessary in order to create an optimal spatial economic equilibrium. The question that should have been answered was: how can production units of different sectors in different locations be combined, in order to minimize total transportation costs of all relevant products?

In order to answer this general question, models are constructed that determine:
- the number of centres in the economy
- the number and type of sectors located in the centre and
- the location of the centres.

All industrial sectors are ranked according to the number of firms that have to be located; a high number means a low rank. Agriculture is located at each available location. Some hypotheses which are of special interest for this paper concern the organization of the industrial centres. According to the weak Tinbergen hypothesis (WTH) each centre of a certain rank contains all sectors of lower rank. According to the strong Tinbergen hypothesis (STH) a system of centres contains centres of all ranks. In order to calculate optimal location patterns, distance should be introduced in the models. In the first models (Paelinck and Nijkamp 1975) a discrete distance measure is used. Optimal solutions mostly showed concentrated centres (Kuiper and Paelinck 1984). In order to be able to compute transportation costs in a better way (using more realistic distance measures), a number of new hypotheses concerning the area (its shape and its size), the potential locations and the way distances are presumed, were necessary. An important step was the introduction of 'Manhattan circles' as a location area for all activities (Kuiper et al. 1990). The area is organized around a rectangular network with unit mazes. The radius of the circle is integer. The number of potential locations, depending on the radius R of the circle, equals $2R(R+1)+1$.

Results of the computations of optimal location patterns show high concentrations of firms if a limited number of sectors is considered; these concentrations are located in the centre of the area. If the number of sectors to be produced increases and also the number of firms, big concentrations can be observed in a ring around the centre of the area and if the number of firms is increasing the production centres will be located throughout the area.

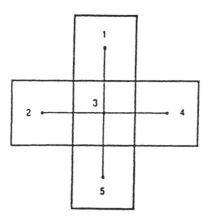

Figure 11.1 A Manhattan circle, R=1

11.3.1.2 A dynamic model The development of output levels of sectors in regions is determined by a number of variables; the general economic development of the country, specific political measures (sectoral or regional), changes within regions concerning for instance the infrastructure, changes in neighbouring regions, changes within sectors concerning production methods, innovations, price levels and consumer preferences, all are influencing regional sector outputs in a different way and all are hard to predict. That means it is very risky to predict output levels of sectors in regions. The best thing to do is try to find general trends in the sectoral development of regions. If stable trends in the past can be found, it could be possible to indicate future development for a relatively short period.

A way of modelling the regional development of sectors in time, is to use the adaptation model FLEUR (Ancot and Paelinck 1983):

$$Y_{rt} - Y_{rt-1} = \alpha\{Y^0_{rt-1} - Y_{rt-1}\} + \frac{\alpha}{2}\{Y^0_{rt} - Y^0_{rt-1} - Y_{rt} + Y_{rt-1}\}$$

where Y^0_{rt} is the output of region r at time t, and

$\quad\quad Y_{rt}^0$ is the equilibrium value of output of region r at time t

The share of region r in the total sector output time t is:

$$S_{rt} \triangleq \frac{Y_{rt}}{Y_t} \text{ and } \Delta S_{rt} = S_{rt} - S_{rt-1}$$

The change of the output share of region r can be modelled (Paelinck 1985) according to next adaption model:

$$\Delta S_{rt} = \alpha \, (S_{rt}^{0} - S_{rt}) \, ,$$

where S_{rt}^{0} is the equilibrium output share of region r and time t.
From this model one can conclude:
Suppose $\alpha > 0$: then the share of region r is increasing
if $S_{rt} < S_{rt}^{0}$, and this share is decreasing
if $S_{rt} > S_{rt}^{0}$; so there is a tendency towards egalization.

Supposing $\alpha < 0$, the share of region r is decreasing if $S_{rt} < S_{rt}^{0}$ and increasing if $S_{rt} > S_{rt}^{0}$ so there is a tendency towards growing apart; the big ones become bigger and the small ones disappear.

According to this model one can expect diminishing inequalities between regions during periods of general economic expansion and widening inequalities during periods of economic recession.

The question of the evaluation of disparities will be studied empirically to show which of either the convergence or the divergence views is supported by facts.

11.4   The Distribution of Employment in Europe (1950–1990)

11.4.1 A Classification of the Regions

In order to study regional differences, first a general picture will be presented, showing the long term trends of sets of regions in the European Union. Studying the employment structure after a classification of regions has been used based on their Gross Regional Products per capita. The set of data consists of the GRP and the population figures of the NUTS1 regions of 9 member states in 1950, 1960, 1970, 1980 and 1990 (the information was found in the NEI (Netherlands Economic Institute) year books and the regional statistics of Eurostat (1985)). A disadvantage of the data set appeared to be the various units that are used; the GRPs in 1950, 1960 and 1970 are expressed in dollars, the GRP in 1980 and 1990 in ECUs. Classification of the regions is realized in 2 steps;

1   the regions are divided into 4 groups in 1950, 1970 and 1990. The European mean value of the GRP is set 100.
    Group 1 consists of regions   > 115
    Group 2 consists of regions   100–115
    Group 3 consists of regions   85–100
    Group 4 consists of regions   <85
2   next the change of the position is studied.

In this way 5 different sets can be distinguished:

1   top regions   •   both in 1950 and in 1990 regions belong to group 1,
2   growth regions   •   regions which realized a relative improvement in 1950–1990 (except a change from group 3 to 2),
3   middle regions   •   regions which stayed in group 2 and 3 during the period,
4   stagnating regions •   regions which realized a relative worsening in 1950–1990 (except from group 2 to 3),
5   backward regions   •   regions belonging to group 4 both in 1950 and in 1990.

In order to illustrate regional trends Table 11.1 shows the development of the mean values of the GRP per capita of the top and backward regions, compared to the mean value of Europe (EUR=100) in 1950–1990.

Table 11.1   Mean GRP-values of top and backward regions

	1950	1960	1970	1980	1990
(1) top regions	168	150	153	153	150
(2) backward regions	49	47	56	56	65
rate (1)/(2)	3.4	3.2	2.7	2.7	2.3

Table 11.1 shows clearly that the disparities between both groups have decreased during the period; only from 1970–1980 was this process stagnating.

11.4.2 The Development of Sectors in Europe

The industrial structure of the European Union is well known. Looking at the broad sectors, the trends over the whole period are shown in Tables 11.2 and 11.3.

The decline in agriculture, the rise and fall of the manufacturing sector and the remarkable rise of service sectors are very clear. In Table 11.3 the development of total employment for a number of branches is presented. In the manufacturing sector two branches decline during the whole observation period; fuel and power products and also textile and clothing, leather and footwear. Another extreme branch is paper and printing products; this sector grew during the period.

Table 11.2 Development of total employment of four branches (millions)

Branch	1950	1960	1970	1980	1990
agriculture, forestry and fishery products	32.4	24.7	15.4	12.3	8.5
industries	34.1	40.1	41.0	36.6	33.4
building and construction	7.4	9.7	11.2	10.3	10.2
services	35.0	43.9	54.3	72.8	87.6
total	108.9	118.9	121.9	132.0	139.7

Table 11.3 Development of total employment by branch 1950–1990 (millions)

Branch	NACE Code	1950	1960	1970	1980	1990
agriculture, forestry and fishery products	B01	32.4	24.7	15.4	12.3	8.5
fuel and power products	B06	3.0	3.3	2.6	2.1	1.7
ferrous and non-ferrous ores and metals, other than radioactive	B13	1.5	1.9	1.9	1.4	1.0
non metallic minerals and mineral products	B15	1.9	2.3	2.2	1.9	1.6
chemical products	B17	1.4	1.9	2.3	2.1	2.0
metal products, machinery, equipment and electrical goods	B24	6.6	9.4	11.0	10.6	10.6
transport equipment	B28	2.9	3.6	4.1	3.5	3.0
food, beverages and tobacco	B36	3.6	4.2	4.1	3.7	3.5
textiles, clothing, leather, footwear	B42	8.3	7.8	6.6	5.0	3.6
paper and printing products	B47	1.7	2.2	2.5	2.5	2.5
products of various industries	B50	3.2	3.5	3.7	3.8	3.9
building and construction	B53	7.4	9.7	11.2	10.3	10.2
recovery, repair, trade, lodging and catering services	B58	14.7	18.5	20.9	24.9	26.8
transport and communication services	B60	6.4	7.1	7.4	8.2	8.1
services of credit and insurance institutions	B69	1.3	1.9	2.8	3.5	4.1
other market services	B74	4.2	5.9	8.2	15.9	24.4
non market services	B86	8.4	10.5	15.0	20.3	24.2
total		109.1	118.4	121.9	131.9	139.8

It is now important to indicate where, and in which regions these sectors are located. The relatively high concentration of growth sectors in a region can explain the disparities between regions. First the groups as defined are considered. Table 11.4 illustrates the development of the shares of sectors of 3 groups. The growth regions, the middle regions and the stagnating regions are indicated as modal regions. In this way, particularly, the differences between the extreme groups are shown clearly.

Although the service sector is very strong in the top regions, especially the commercial service sector, and agriculture is strong in the backward regions, a converging picture is shown in Table 11.4. Table 11.5 shows a more detailed picture of the distribution of the service sector over both extreme groups.

In particular, transport and communication and banking and insurance are much more strongly represented in the top regions. The commercial services explain to a large extent the differences between both groups. The non-commercial services show almost equal shares for both groups.

Table 11.4 Shares of sectors in total employment for 3 groups of European regions in 1950, 1970, 1991

Sector	Agricult.	Industry	Building	Services	Commercial Services	Non-Commercial Services
1950						
top	.10	0.36	0.07	0.47	0.34	0.13
modal	0.24	0.36	0.07	0.33	0.23	0.10
backward	0.50	0.19	0.07	0.25	0.16	0.09
Europe	0.25	0.35	0.07	0.33	0.23	0.10
1970						
top	0.08	0.33	0.09	0.54	0.37	0.17
modal	0.09	0.38	0.09	0.44	0.28	0.16
backward	0.26	0.23	0.13	0.39	0.24	0.15
Europe	0.10	0.37	0.09	0.44	0.29	0.16
1991						
top	0.02	0.19	0.06	0.73	0.48	0.25
modal	0.04	0.26	0.07	0.63	0.42	0.21
backward	0.13	0.16	0.09	0.63	0.40	0.23
Europe	0.05	0.24	0.07	0.64	0.42	0.22

Table 11.5   Share in the service sector of top and backward regions, 1950, 1970, 1991

Sector	Top Regions 1950	1970	1991	Backward Regions 1950	1970	1991	Europe (total) 1950	1970	1991
trade and 'horeca'	0.18	0.18	0.17	0.10	0.14	0.21	0.14	0.16	0.19
transport and communication	0.09	0.08	0.08	0.03	0.05	0.05	0.06	0.06	0.06
banking and insurance	0.03	0.04	0.05	0.01	0.01	0.02	0.02	0.04	0.04
non-commercial services	0.13	0.16	0.25	0.09	0.15	0.23	0.10	0.16	0.22

11.4.4 The Specialization of Regions and the Localization of Sectors

Knowing the development of sectors in Europe and the distribution of the main sectors over groups of regions, a more detailed picture will be presented showing different European regions, and more sectors. The change of the spatial structure of sector development can be described using location coefficients. The location coefficient lc_i, is defined as:

$$ lc_i = \frac{\sum_{r=1}^{R} |S_{ir} - S_r|}{2} $$

where $S_{ir} = W_{ir}/W_i$, the share of region r is employment of sector i,

$S_r = W_r/W$, the share of region r is total employment.

Thus, these coefficients indicate the concentration of a sector by the degree to which the sector distribution diverges from the distribution of total employment across all regions. A value of 0 implies a perfectly spread sector; a high value implies concentration in one region. Table 11.6 shows the location coefficients for a number of economic branches.

Table 11.6 shows a trend towards less concentration for the majority of branches. Agriculture (B01) and food, beverages and tobacco (B36), textile and clothing, leather and footwear (B42) show opposite tendencies. The tertiary sector shows a very clear pattern; all branches have spread over Europe throughout the whole period.

Table 11.6 Location coefficients for economic branches

	B01	B06	B13	B15	B17	B24	B28	B36	B42
1950	0.29	0.44	0.38	0.17	0.26	0.24	0.32	0.13	0.20
1960	0.33	0.40	0.37	0.15	0.24	0.23	0.26	0.12	0.19
1970	0.38	0.28	0.36	0.15	0.23	0.20	0.24	0.11	0.21
1980	0.37	0.26	0.36	0.17	0.23	0.19	0.24	0.14	0.24
1990	0.36	0.19	0.35	0.20	0.21	0.21	0.24	0.14	0.33

	B47	B50	B53	B58	B60	B69	B74	B86
1950	0.25	0.14	0.10	0.14	0.16	0.23	0.15	0.12
1960	0.22	0.12	0.08	0.09	0.13	0.19	0.12	0.11
1970	0.19	0.13	0.08	0.06	0.10	0.17	0.11	0.10
1980	0.18	0.14	0.08	0.06	0.09	0.15	0.11	0.10
1990	0.17	0.15	0.07	0.06	0.08	0.15	0.13	0.09

Source: Ereco (1995), Molle (1980), own computation.

When there is a trend towards lower concentration of branches, the degree to which regions are specialized in certain branches is also likely to show a decreasing trend. The specialization coefficient is used to measure this; SC_r is defined as:

$$SC_r = \frac{\sum_{i=1}^{I} / \sigma_{ir} - \sigma_i /}{2}$$

where

$$\sigma_{ir} = \frac{W_{ir}}{W_r},$$

the share of sector i in the employment of region r

$$\sigma_i = \frac{W_i}{W}$$

the share of sector i in total employment.

High values of SC_r correspond with strong specialization; the value 0 means an average regional structure. Core regions with strong employment structures and lagging regions can deviate from the average region in the same way and therefore generate identical specialization coefficients.

Figure 11.2 shows that the employment generated in the regions in 1990 is more equally distributed compared to 1950. Most regions show declining specialization (that is, show points beneath the 45°line). Appendix 11.1 shows the changes of the specialization coefficient (1950–1990) for each region separately.

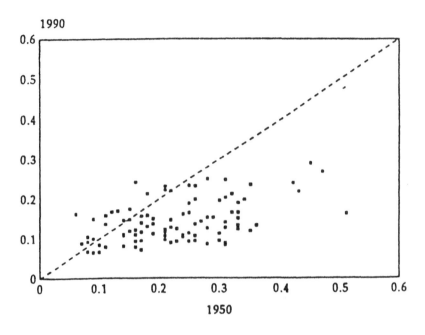

Figure 11.2 The specialization coefficients of European regions in 1950 and 1990

11.5   Conclusions

Achieving regional convergence has been a significant goal of national policy in most of the countries of the EU, and a central goal of EU policy. There is an active policy in the EU designed to generate regional convergence. The issue of whether the economic growth process within Europe is tending to lead to a narrowing of disparities over time (convergent growth) or a further widening (divergent growth) is very important. The chapter focuses on both theoretical and empirical observations, where especially the behaviour of different sectors is important. What happens if a sector is growing? Will it locate to a limited number of regions? And if it is declining? Which sectors are located in a region? Is the region showing many growing sectors or relatively many declining sectors?

When studying theories concerning the regional development of a set of regions it is hard to predict in which direction the economy of a region will go. The models presented give some general tendencies. If an economy is not very developed, the growth will be found in a limited number of locations and regional differences will increase. If the economy is strong, the growth will be distributed over a number of locations; regional differences can both increase and decrease depending on the concentrations of sectors in certain locations. The dynamic model (FLEUR), shows a decline of regional differences where the total sector output is increasing; the sector will be located in different locations. If, on the other hand, total sector output is declining, regional differences will increase; the sector will be produced in a limited number of locations.

The development of total employment in 3 branches in Europe (1950–1990), shows a very clear picture. Employment in agriculture was declining, employment in the service sector was increasing and finally, in the industrial sector it increased during the first 20 years and declined during the last 20 years! Total employment increased throughout the whole period. Looking at the shares of the sectors in total employment for a limited number of regions (top regions – backward regions and modal regions) the mentioned tendency of the 3 sectors can be observed in these regions as well. However, there is an interesting difference between the observations in the first year and the last year. The difference in the employment structure between the top and backward regions in 1950 and 1990 has declined strongly. In 1950, 50 percent of the employment of the backward regions was in the agricultural sector, and 10 percent of the top regions; in 1990, 13 percent in the backward and 2 percent in the top regions.

This means that the differences in the employment structure between the backward and top regions have declined. Especially the service sector has increased strongly in the backward regions. Although, according to the theory and the model one would expect a growing sector to distribute over an increasing number of regions, this increase is very strong. This sector seems to be very footloose. The location of sectors and also the specialization of regions is measured using the coefficients. Sectors B01 (agriculture), B13 (ferrous and non-ferrous ores and metals) and B42 (textiles and clothing) show high location coefficients. These sectors are concentrated in a limited number of regions in Europe. Most sectors show low figures (especially the service sector) so they are represented in many different regions. The specialization coefficients of the European regions also indicate an interesting tendency. In general for almost all regions, over the period 1950–1990, these numbers are declining! This means that the employment structure for the regions shows fewer differences (Appendix 11.1 and Map 11.1).

In this chapter the employment structure of European regions is studied over a long period (1950–1990). A number of general trends seems to be clear. Total employment is increasing and the distribution of employment over the regions shows fewer differences. The chapter does not focus on unemployment figures, although it is an important and well known problem for Europe. In order to be able to solve this problem, it is important for each region to know which sectors are most promising for employment and from this research it seems that the number of sectors suitable to be located in a region is increasing.

The employment structure of the regions shows a more equal picture. That does not mean that prosperity differences are declining. Labour productivity between regions could differ. Some general figures, however, show declining differences between GRP-values of top and backward regions (Table 11.1).

Appendix 11.1 Changes of the specialization coefficient of the European regions

1950↓/1990 →	1: <0.10	2: 0.10–0.20	3: 0.20 – 0.30	4: >0.30
1: <0.10	Schleswig Holstein 57 Niedersachsen Hessen Bayern Picardie Haute-Normandie Rhone-Alpes	Champagne-Ardenne Denmark Austria		
2: 0.10 – 0.20	Rheinland- Pfalz Centre Bourgogne Alsace Friuli-Venezia Giulia Vlaams Gewest East Anglia	Nordrhein-Westfalen Baden-Württemberg Franche-Comté Languedoc-Roussilon Provence- Alpes Côte d'Azur Piemonte Liguria Lombardia Trentino-Alto Adige Veneto Umbria Lazio Campania Noord- Nederland Oost-Nederland Zuid-Nederland Ireland Pias Vasco Cataluna Sverige	Luxembourg (Grand-Duche) Beleares	

Appendix 11.1 (continued)

3: 0.20 – 0.30	Nord-Pas-De-Calais Pays de la Loire Aquitaine Yorkshire & Humberside East Midlands South West North West Scotland	Saarland Basse-Normandie Lorraine Bretagne Poitou-Charentes Midi-Pyrénées Limousin Auvergne Corse Emilia-Romagna Sicilia Sardegna West- Nederland Région Wallone North Ireland Cantabria Comunidad Foral de Navarra Comunidad de Madrid Suomi	Bruxelles Asturias Rioja Cokmmunidad Valenciana Canarias Portugal	
4: >0.30	North Wales	Hamburg Bremen Berlin (West) Ile de France Toscana Marche Abruzzi Molise Puglia South East West Midlands Aragon Castilla-Leon Murcia	Valle d-Aosta Basilicata Calabria Hellas Galicia Castilla-La Mancha Extremadura Andalucia	

Map 11.1 Change of specialization coefficient 1950–1990

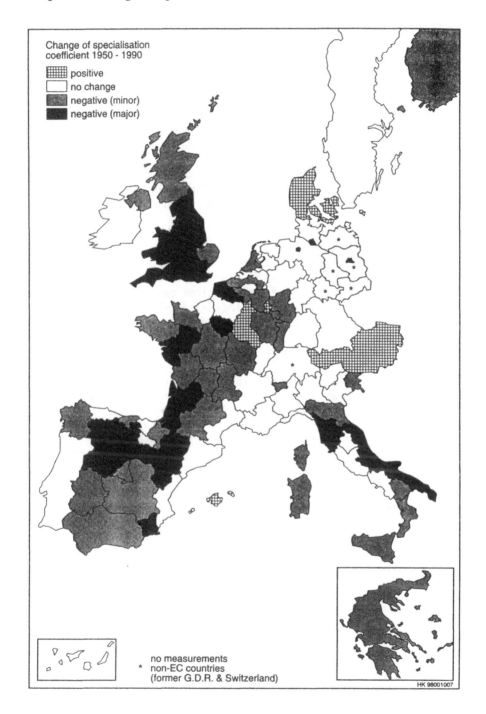

Change of specialisation
coefficient 1950 - 1990

- positive
- no change
- negative (minor)
- negative (major)

no measurements
* non-EC countries
(former G.D.R. & Switzerland)

HK 98001007

References

Ancot, J.-P. and Paelinck, J.H.P. (1983), 'The Spatial Econometrics of the European FLEUR-model', in Griffith, D. and Lea, A. (eds), *Evolving Geographical Structures*, Martinus Nijhoff Publishers, Den Haag, pp. 229–46.

Kaldor, N., (1970), 'The Case of Regional Policies', *Scottish Journal of Political Economy*, vol. 17.

Keeble, D., Offord, J. and Walker, S. (1986), 'Peripheral Regions in Community of Twelve Member States: Final Report', Department of Geography, University of Cambridge, Cambridge.

Krugman, P.R. (1987), *Strategic Trade Policy and the New International Economics*, MIT Press, Cambridge, MA.

Kuiper, F.J., Kuiper, J.H. and Paelinck, J.H.P. (1993),' Tinbergen-Bos Metricised Systems: Some Further Results', *Urban Studies*, vol. 30, no. 10, pp. 1745–61.

Kuiper, J.H. and Paelink, J.H.P. (1984), 'Tinbergen-Bos Systems Revisited', in Pillu, J.M. and Wuesnier, B. (eds), *Modèles Economiques de la Localisation et des Transports*, ENPC, Paris, pp. 117–40.

Kuiper, J.H. and Paelinck, J.H.P. (1992), 'Optimal Tinbergen-Bos Location Patterns of Two Industrial Sectors on a Manhattan Circle (R=1)', in Birg, H. and Schaik, H.J. (eds), *Regionale und Sektorale Strukturpolitik*, Institute für Siedlings- und Wohnungswesen, Münster, pp. 245–63.

Kuiper, J.H., Paelinck, J.H.P. and Rosing, K.E. (1990), 'Transport Flows in Tinbergen-Bos Systems', in Peschel, K. (ed.), *Infrastructure and the Space-Economy*, Springer Verlag, Heidelberg-Bonn, pp. 17–31.

Molle, W.T.M. et al. (1980), *Regional Disparity and Economic Development in the European Community*, Farnborough.

Myrdal, G. (1957), *Rich Lands and Poor*, Harper & Row, New York.

Paelinck, J.H.P. (1985), 'Elements d'Analyse Economique Spatiale', *Editions Regionales Européenne*, pp. 143–83.

Paelinck, J.H.P. and Nijkamp, P. (1975), *Operational Theory and Method in Regional Economics*, Saxon House, Farnborough.

12 Economic Dynamics in the Randstad Holland: Do Agglomeration Economies still Exist?

OEDZGE ATZEMA

12.1 Introduction

The Dutch urban structure is an example of a poly-nucleated urban system (PUS): very large cities are absent and the many medium sized cities are located relatively near to each other. Most of these cities have changed by a process of spatial deconcentration of population and employment. There are 19 city regions in the Netherlands, which are strongly concentrated in the western and southern provinces (see Figure 12.1), but nearly all of the twelve provinces in the Netherlands have at least one urban agglomeration with more then 100,000 inhabitants.[1] Those city regions represent the core of the Dutch economy (80 percent of the national GDP) and they comprise the majority (75 percent) of the Dutch population. Within this PUS, the Randstad Holland is still the most urbanized part, but its dominating position in the national Dutch economy has diminished. Since the mid-eighties the economic performance in the Randstad has improved, but it does not exceed in any way the economic growth in the rest of the Netherlands. Nevertheless, one has to bear in mind that interregional differences in economic growth are small in the Netherlands. Within city regions the process of deconcentration of population and employment persists. Economic growth in the suburban environments exceeds the economic growth in the central cities. Interurban comparison of individual cities shows that the economic growth of the three largest cities in the Netherlands (Amsterdam, Rotterdam and The Hague) is lagging behind the national average; the growth in employment is also negligible.

In this chapter, I will discuss the development of the economy in Dutch city regions, particularly in the Randstad Holland. The central issue investigated in this chapter is related to the performance of those regions in terms of growth of production, productivity and employment. These developments are related to structural economic changes, e.g. changes in sector composition and spatial deconcentration. The chapter raises questions as to the meaning of agglomeration economies within the poly-nucleated urban structure of the Netherlands.

Figure 12.1 City regions in the Netherlands

Source: SEO 1996.

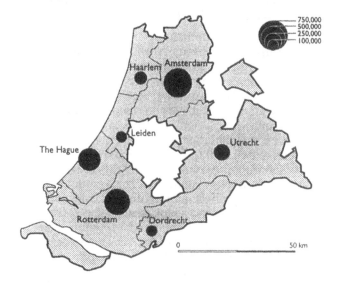

Figure 12.2 Cities and city regions in the Randstad Holland

Source: SEO 1996.

I will start with a general picture of the urban structure of the Netherlands. On the base of a regional division of nineteen city regions, including seven city regions in the Randstad Holland, an investigation will be made of the spatial differences in economic growth and employment growth over the last twenty-five years. The empirical evidence is largely based on the investigations made by the 'Stichting voor Economisch Onderzoek' of the University of Amsterdam (SEO 1996). Furthermore, more recent interregional differences in employment growth are differentiated in structural and location effects. It emerged that the bad performance of the largest city regions is primarily the result of an inefficient local production environment. This shortcoming will influence the evolution of the agglomeration economies in the near future.

12.2   The Dutch Poly-nucleated Urban System

The Netherlands has a long history as a strongly urbanized country with a deconcentrated urban pattern. Since the so-called Golden Ages (sixteenth century) the largest Dutch cities are located in the western part of the country, called *Holland*, but in later centuries most of these cities experienced a moderate or even reduced process of urbanization. A brief overview of their urban-economic history illustrates this development.

The capital city of *Amsterdam* (with a current population of 725,000 inhabitants) became internationally famous in the sixteenth century because of its function as centre of Baltic and colonial trade and a stable market. Since around 1750, the fate of the Dutch urban commercial empire changed considerably, due to a combination of external (e.g. the rise of competitors like Spain and Britain) and internal factors (e.g. the increasingly risk-evading behaviour of their commercial elite and their change from entrepreneurial attitudes towards conspicuous consumption). In this way, Amsterdam has lost economic functions and a large part of its population. The same is true for cities like *Leiden, Haarlem, Delft* and *Dordrecht* (in those days all located near the seashore) which have ancient urban traditions, but at present accommodate less than 150,000 inhabitants each. The traditional city of *Utrecht* (with 235,000 inhabitants) is an exception because of the growth as a national transport and service centre.

It was only in the second half of the nineteenth century that the economic decline of the older cities in Holland changed in their favour, fostered by industrial starts-ups and new trade impulses from the colonies. Besides this economic inspired re-urbanization, some cities developed as economic centres, although their dormant economic functions already existed for centuries. During the nineteenth century, when the Netherlands became a unitary state, *The Hague* (nowadays 445,000 inhabitants) developed into the national government and administrative centre. Later in that century the growth of the city of

Rotterdam (now 600,000 inhabitants) increased strongly when it became an important port of transit for the German economy. Furthermore it became an industrial site of port related industries (such as shipbuilding).

Industrialization affected urbanization outside the Holland provinces as well (Atzema and Wever 1994). Industrial revolution in the Netherlands has not led to such an overwhelmingly concentrated urbanization as in surrounding countries like Germany and Britain. Traditionally, the Dutch economy has a lack of deposits of raw materials (coal, iron ore etc.). This circumstance did not encourage a strong and concentrated process of industrialization. Only in the very south of the Netherlands (around the city of *Heerlen*) coal mining was developed on a relatively small base without many manufacturing industries. These mines were established around 1900 and were closed in 1966 by intervention of the central government. At the same time important reservoirs of natural gas were discovered and exploited in the northern part of the Netherlands (in the province of Groningen).

In other parts of the Netherlands industrialization produced a deconcentrated pattern of urbanization. In the southern part of the country, the city of *Tilburg* became a centre of the textile industry, *Eindhoven* a centre of electronic industry (Philips) and *Maastricht* a centre of ceramic and paper industry. In the eastern part of the Netherlands, the cities of *Arnhem* and *Nijmegen* developed on a more mixed industrial base with some specialization in the synthetic material industry. In *Almelo* and *Enschede* there was a strong emphasis on the textile industry (as in Tilburg), in *Hengelo* on the machinery industry and in *Deventer* on the metallurgical industry. In the agricultural northern part of the Netherlands, the city of *Leeuwarden* became a centre of the food industry, in particular the dairy industry. The other cities outside the Randstad have developed as typical regional centres with mainly administrative and educational functions (*Groningen, Zwolle* and *'s-Hertogenbosch*).

The concept of Randstad Holland is a twentieth century invention. 'Randstad' is the Dutch word for 'rimcity'. The idea of a Randstad is being used since 1924 (Boelens 1998). At that time, town planner Theo van Lohuizen presented a report on an international congress in Amsterdam on population growth in the western part of the Netherlands. He concluded that an urban sphere of influence existed in a ring of cities with a total of three million inhabitants around a green, rural central area ('the Green Heart'). At the same time, the aeronautics pioneer Albert Plesman argued that the perfect location for an airport would be just in the middle of the ring of cities Utrecht, Amsterdam, Haarlem, The Hague and Rotterdam. He was the founder of Schiphol airport and his view was taken up in 1938 by the executive board of KLM to argue that Schiphol was the best location for a national airport (Musterd and de Pater 1992). At that time the name of the Randstad became more popular, although the planning concept of the Randstad was hardly elaborated.

Physical planning by the government in the Netherlands first developed in a reluctant way after World War II. In those days the National Planning Office used the formula of the Randstad to contrast the urban western part of the Netherlands (Holland) with the rest of the country. Besides, the use of the concept had the purpose of safeguarding the Green Heart against further dispersed urbanization. The concept of the Randstad received international attention through the work of Burke (1965) and Hall (1966), who labelled the Randstad as a Green Heart Metropolis and as an unique form of a twentieth-century metropolis.

Nevertheless, until now the notion of the Randstad as a comprehensive metropolitan region has been misleading. The spatial economic coherence between the constituent urban units is very low as well and the constitution of an integrated metropolitan economic-geographical structure is weak (Lambooy 1998). Analysis of commuting trips (Clark and Kuipers-Linde 1994; Van der Laan 1998) and daily activity trips (Cortie et al. 1992) does not show a strong overlap of travel patterns over the borders of the city regions in the Randstad. For most of the inhabitants of the Randstad this concept does not have any economic-functional meaning to their daily life. Or to put it in the words of Van der Laan: 'The urban system of the Netherlands has developed at two related spatial scales. At the local level about two-thirds of the daily urban systems show a multimodal pattern causing functional dualism, reciprocity and complementary. At the regional level of the interaction of the daily urban systems only parts of the north wing of the Randstad are more integrated' (Van der Laan 1998, pp. 224). The daily urban systems used by Van der Laan are quite similar to the city regions which have been presented (see Figure 12.1) and to the northern wing of the Randstad by which he means the city regions Haarlem, Amsterdam and Utrecht (see Figure 12.2).

Nevertheless, one has to keep in mind that these studies deal with the spatial behaviour of people, not of firms. Many firms in the Randstad have commercial relations at distances which transcend the spatial scale of the Randstad. Firms work in quite a different kind of economic reality than people and have a more international expression, especially in an open economy like the Dutch economy. De Smidt (1992) and Shachar (1994) have tried to classify the Randstad economy as a 'world city'. By turning the Randstad from a physical planning concept into economic and social reality and considering the various urban centres within the Randstad as a complete, single functional urban region, it became clear that the Randstad ranks highly in the urban hierarchy of Europe. But it remains questionable whether the Randstad functions as an urban region as such. I conceive the Randstad as a geographical collection of city regions with different economic structures and without strong functional interconnection. From an international perspective the concentration of financial services in Amsterdam and the 'mainports' of the harbour of Rotterdam and the airport Schiphol are the most important anchors for the global position of the Randstad economy

(Lambooy 1993). But the international position of these economic functions are precarious with respect to the continuous extension of important European financial centres like London and Frankfurt and the rise of multimodal distribution centres elsewhere in Europe (Shachar 1994).

Besides, the spatial structure of cities, city regions and of the entire urban system showed a loss of hierarchy, even with respect to firms (Lambooy 1969). Enterprises develop other location patterns, due to larger markets and new enabling technologies, and are leaving the cities with the concomitant result of declining employment. However, the result is not an amorphous spatial structure, but a selective dispersal from the larger cities towards suburbs, smaller cities within the same urban region, but also to medium sized cities further away: it evolves into a *poly-nuclear urban system* (PUS). The difference between 'urban' and 'rural' vanished. The physical characteristics of houses, shops and offices became less specific; an *urban field* emerged (Friedman and Miller 1965). The evolution of global markets, of IT technologies and of the European integration, will influence the spatial behaviour of firms (Bailly and Lever 1996) and it has been up until now an open question whether these developments will lead to a further desurbanization or a re-urbanization of the Northwest European urban landscape (Cheshire 1995). The reason for this is, as Shachar stated: '... the theoretical link between economic restructuring processes and urban development is not clear enough.' (Shachar 1994, p. 398).

I will try to develop a connection between economic restructuring and urban development by focusing on the renewed interest in the functioning of agglomeration economies. According to Richardson 'agglomeration economies and diseconomies are the driving force behind the expansion of geographical concentration of economic activity and population within cities' (Richardson 1995, p.124). He also stated that the working of agglomeration economies is still obscure, because it is difficult to measure and analyse. Traditionally, localization economies (sector specific composition of a collection of firms) and urbanization economies (sector diversity of a collection of firms) have been distinguished. Extra economic growth based on localization economies is related to intra-industrial specialization, reduced research costs for industry-specific skills, easy communication facilitating industry-specific innovation and industry-specific public services. Such localization economies are especially proven by agglomerations of innovative industry. This development leads to extra economic growth in combination with increased economic specialization between cities. The effects of the urbanization economies are partially opposite: the richness of ideas, the variety of groups of consumers and the differentiated labour market furthers new economic activities which find themselves on a developing market. Often such firms cooperate with dissimilar firms, for example specialized service industries, which results in a high growth of urban industries together with a great deal of economic diversity. Both aspects of agglomeration economies connect economic growth to urban constellations.

12.3 Economic Growth and Urban Size

The size of an urban region or country is often considered in the Smithian tradition as a principal factor in the explanation of economic growth. The reason for this is the division of labour and the rise of specialized activities. This is based on the logic of the size of the market for demand, as well as the impact of the differentiation of supply. Agglomeration economies lead to lower costs of inputs and to higher qualities of consumer-related cultural and other amenities, resulting in efficient and attractive consumption-oriented environments. Nevertheless, the mechanisms behind this cumulative process of growth tend to be weakening for the urban region as such, due to new technologies and the strong spatial dispersion connected with high mobility. The result of this development might be that the largest cities lose their advantages, whereas the smaller cities in the urban field can gain from their increased access to the principal inputs and markets.

Before looking at the economic growth of cities and city regions, it might be illuminating to give a brief overview of the recent history of the growth of the Dutch economy. The last twenty-five years economic growth in the Netherlands has been lower than in the first period after the second world war. During the fifties and the first half of the sixties economic growth in the Netherlands was based on capital-widening investments (for instance in the petrochemical complex in the harbour of Rotterdam), rapid technical change (for instance the rise of the electronic industry of Philips) and expanding labour input, which was based on relatively low labour costs (Van Ark et. al. 1996). This changed in the seventies and eighties because of a declining growth rate of investments and rising labour costs, together with a rapid decline in annual working hours per person. High labour productivity and low labour participation are well-known characteristics of the present Dutch labour market. Besides this, the level of economic growth shows short term upward and downward movements in the business cycle. Around 1974 a recession started with a trough in 1982. In 1981 and 1982 economic growth even turned negative. The stagnating world trade (a response to the first oil crisis), real wage upswing and an oversized public sector are the most important causes of the sluggish performance of the Dutch economy in that recession period. It became obvious that Dutch manufacturing industries had lost a lot of their international competitive advantages. Traditional branches of manufacturing disappeared to low wage countries and innovative, technically advanced manufacturing industries were scarcely represented in the Dutch economy. Nevertheless, economic recovery started in 1983 as a result of wage moderation. Employers, unions and the Dutch government agreed on the need for wage moderation and soon profitability and investment levels improved. This economic expansion reached a peak in 1989. Growth decelerated again from 1991 onward, partly in line with international developments. In recent years (1995 and 1996) economic growth in de Netherlands shows positive figures compared to other European countries.

Those fluctuations in economic growth affected also the economies of the several city regions, although the differences in economic growth, measured by the mean annual percentages of growth of the gross regional product (GRP), between the period 1970–1982 and the period 1983–1995 are small (2.7 percent respectively 2.9 percent). Nationally the growth figures are 2.6 percent and 3.0 percent. In general, the economies of the Dutch city-regions were less hit by the recession of the early eighties, but show little growth in the upswing period of the second half of the eighties. Figure 12.3 makes clear that large city regions like Rotterdam and The Hague performed badly during the recession period (1970–1982). The petrochemical and other harbour related industries located in the city region of Rotterdam were hit hard by the oil crises and the international trade recession. In the same period the city region of The Hague experienced a general process of deindustrialization. The same is true for the city region of Haarlem, which includes the only blast furnace complex in the Netherlands (Hoogovens). In the seventies the European steel industry had significant market problems and the Dutch Hoogovens were in trouble too. Management introduced several rounds of rationalization of production which affected the production negatively. In the more recent period (1983–1995) the position of these three city regions improved. Moreover, the economic growth in three of the largest city regions (the regions of Amsterdam, Rotterdam and The Hague) is still below the national level. The city region of Utrecht compares favourably with these three large city regions, due to its central location in the Netherlands in combination with the growing importance of producer services in the Dutch economy. In general, it appears that in the Dutch situation also in the period after 1983 on the scale of individual city regions there is no clear connection between economic growth and population size.

To investigate a more precise relation between economic growth and urban size I will examine also the economic growth of nineteen Dutch cities, which traditionally function as the urban nodes of the city regions (see Figure 12.4). The production figures in each city are calculated by the SEO on the base of detailed sector information (31 sectors) of employment. So the division of employment between the cities and their suburban environment is used to desaggregate the available production figures of the city regions. The calculated mean annual percentages of growth of the gross regional product (GRP) of these cities together, are equal in both periods (1970-1982 and 1983–1995), namely 2.0 percent. The economic growth in most cities appears to be lower than the national growth level and the mean growth level of the city regions is lower too. This signifies a steady process of spatial deconcentration of production.

1970–1982

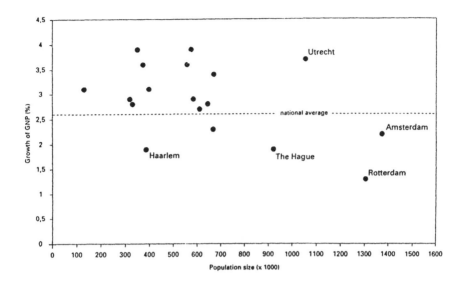

1983–1995

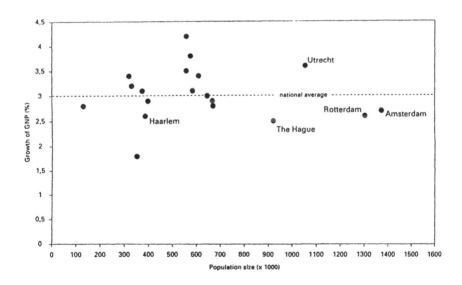

Figure 12.3 Economic growth and population size of city regions in the Netherlands, 1970–1995 (mean annual percentage growth of GRP; city regions ranked by population size in 1995)

Source: SEO 1996.

239

At the top, the three largest cities (Amsterdam, Rotterdam and The Hague) clearly show least economic growth in the recession period. The growth level of the medium sized cities in the south and in the east of the Netherlands is twice as high as in the three largest cities.

The economic growth in the medium sized cities within the Randstad (Utrecht, Leiden, Dordrecht and Haarlem) also exceeds the growth in the largest cities. In the economic recovery period (1983–1995) however, there was less negative connection between economic growth and the cities. This is due to a small upturn of economic growth in the largest cities, particularly in the city of Rotterdam. In recent time this city has shown a remarkable growth of commercial service activities. However this applies least to the city of Amsterdam, although this city was an important (inter)national commercial service centre already. On the other hand some medium-sized cities show a lower economic growth (for example Utrecht within the Randstad and Eindhoven outside the Randstad). In the case of Eindhoven, the city has a one-sided production structure based strongly on the electronic industry of Philips. Similar to the case of Hoogovens, this company executed several reorganizations to become more cost-effective in their production. In the case of Utrecht, the spatial margins of the city have been reached and several firms had to relocate to suburban municipalities within the city region of Utrecht or to other parts of the country.

Figure 12.4 is somewhat deceptive. Without the three largest cities it is very difficult to indicate any connection between economic growth and urban size. Furthermore, it is highly questionable whether the geographical scale of a city is a correct indicator for the relationship between economic growth and the presence of agglomeration economies. In the Netherlands spatial deconcentration of firms and production around cities is a well known phenomenon. The mechanisms behind the cumulative process of agglomeration tends to be weakening for the urban region as such. The absence of a positive relation between economic growth and population size of the cities suggests that those traditional cities may evolve to be an obsolete spatial expression of urbanity. The same is true for the relation between economic growth and the size of the city regions, which indicates that the economic landscape of the Netherlands has developed in the direction of a more extensive urban field.

1970–1982

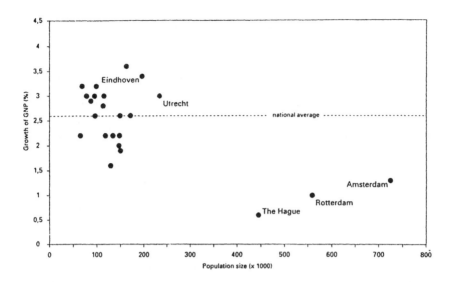

1983–1995

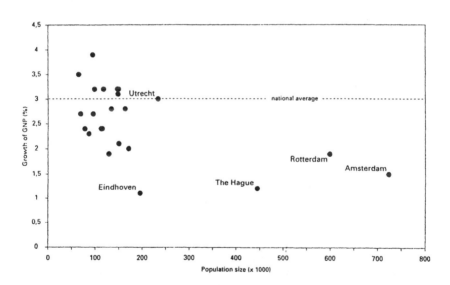

Figure 12.4 Economic growth and population size of cities in the Netherlands, 1970–1995

(mean annual percentage growth of GRP; cities ranked by population size in 1995)
Source: SEO 1996.

12.4   Regional Levelling of Productivity

In theory, the relationship between agglomeration advantages and economic growth affects to the development of productivity. Recently Krugman emphasized the central importance of agglomeration economies and 'increasing returns to scale' for economic development (Krugman 1991; 1995). "Increasing returns to scale' means that due to the location of a set of firms in agglomerations an extra rise of productivity can be expected, as a consequence of the availability of and the access to critical factors, like information, knowledge, finance and sophisticated demand.' Nevertheless Krugman argues that this concept needs to be connected with that of 'market structure': 'In spatial economics (...) you really cannot get started at all without finding a way to deal with scale economies and oligopolistic firms' (Krugman 1995, p.35)'. Arthur (1996) argues that increasing returns are associated with technological developments. Technological changes continuously unsettle the market equilibrium and temporarily create monopolistic characteristics. Their arguments are connected with the positive effects of the increasing market size and firm size as well as the spatial differentiation and specialization of production on the increase of productivity. This last point is the focus of the work of Jacobs (Jacobs 1984). She points at the positive economic impact of a diversifying and specializing process, connected with agglomeration economies of the kind of 'urbanization economies'. These 'urbanization economies' would not apply to cities as such, but more to *regional specialization*. In her opinion, not localization advantages, but urbanization advantages, associated with learning processes and knowledge development, are decisive for entire urban regions to stimulate modern economic development with a high level of productivity.

For the Dutch economy as a whole the increase in productivity is very important to be able to reach a high level of economic growth. Over the last twenty-five years the growth in productivity has resulted in about 80 percent of the growth of the Dutch economy. The increase in international competition has stimulated the shift of labour-intensive industries from the Netherlands towards low wage countries and those industries are replaced by high value production in existing Dutch firms and foreign firms which have invested in the Netherlands. The rising level of technological innovation in trade and industry has also created an increase in productivity. This means partial capital substitution of labour, which is affected by the loss of low value employment in the manufacturing industry. For the greater part, a loss of this kind of employment has been compensated by a growth in relatively low paid employment in the Dutch service sector. According to this sector shift from manufacturing towards service industries, the share of low qualified employment in the total Dutch employment has remained stable as a quarter of the total (Dagevos et. al. 1997). The sector shift towards the services explains why the Dutch economy combines a high level productivity with a growth in employment.

Interregional differences in growth of productivity are small in the Netherlands (see Table 12.1). Generally the growth in productivity in the suburban environments surpasses the increase in the urban centres of the city regions. Because of the lower level of productivity in the suburban environments in 1970, the differences in the development of productivity result in a levelling of the productivity between cities and their surroundings. The same is true for the comparison between city regions, particularly the largest and smaller city regions within the Randstad.

Table 12.1 Growth of productivity and employment in the Netherlands, 1970–1995
(mean annual percentage of growth; employment in man years)

| | Growth in productivity | | Growth of employment | |
	Centre	Suburb	Centre	Suburb
City regions of:				
Amsterdam	2.2	2.6	- 0.8	1.7
Rotterdam	2.2	2.5	- 0.7	0.7
The Hague	2.1	2.4	- 1.2	1.7
Utrecht	2.0	2.4	0.4	2.1
Haarlem	2.1	2.6	- 0.1	- 0.1
Leiden	1.7	2.7	0.9	1.2
Dordrecht	2.4	2.8	0.2	0.4
Within the Randstad	2.2	2.6	0.6	1.3
Outside the Randstad	2.2	2.8	0.4	0.7

Source: SEO 1996.

More detailed analyses (SEO 1996) indicate that the differences in increase of productivity between the cities and their suburban surroundings are related to the sector composition of the production. Cities are specialized in consumer oriented services and in non-commercial services which show a slow growth of productivity. On the contrary, the growth in productivity in advanced producer services, like banking and business services, is greater in the large cities than in their surrounding areas. The same is true for manufacturing industries, although the interregional differences are very small in this respect. Thus, looking at productivity cities show a typical biased production structure: on the one hand, concentrations of high productive advanced producer services and management functions and on the other hand, concentrations of low productive consumer oriented and public services.

Technical advanced manufacturing production is deconcentrated over much of the city regions in the Netherlands.

12.5   Deconcentration of Employment

In contrast to the growth in productivity, there are large spatial differences in the growth of employment. These differences in growth point clearly in the direction of an ongoing spatial deconcentration of employment. That is to say, in the recession period 1970–1982, when employment in the Netherlands decreased in general, the Randstad as a whole, the largest city regions and the largest cities were the greatest losers in absolute as well as relative terms (see Table 12.2). The city regions of Amsterdam, Rotterdam and The Hague lost more than 150,000 man years of employment in 13 years time. Most of this loss of employment was generated by the central cities and only a part of this loss of employment has been compensated by the growth of employment in their suburban surroundings. In the surroundings of the city of Rotterdam, employment in the period 1970–1983 has even decreased. An increase in employment around the medium sized cities in the Randstad has only been experienced by Utrecht and Leiden.

During the economic recovery period after 1983, the growth rate of the Randstad was lagging behind the growth rate in the rest of the Netherlands. All the city regions and the cities showed an upturn in employment again, but the differences in growth between the city regions remained. The growth of employment in the three largest city regions is still below the growth in the city regions of Utrecht and Leiden. Nevertheless, it is remarkable that employment is growing again in the cities of Amsterdam and Rotterdam (not in the city of The Hague). However, it is too early to speak of an 'urban economic renaissance' in the Netherlands, because the growth level of all cities is still below the national level. Besides, the deconcentration of employment to the suburban surroundings continues.

12.6   Sector Shifts of Employment

The Dutch economy has developed into a service economy. This shift is clear when we look at the employment structure: a loss of employment in manufacturing and an increase of nearly five times for employment in the service industry. The increase in employment in commercial services is twice as high as in the public services. In comparison with other western countries the growth of employment in commercial services in the Netherlands is high, mainly as a result of the relatively low growth of productivity (Elfring 1988). More recently commercial services grow as a result of increasing consumer demand for services.

The de-industrialization of employment has struck the Randstad labour market harder than other parts of the country. In the Randstad more employment has disappeared from the manufacturing industry than in the rest of Holland, while because of the history of deconcentrated industrialization a lot more jobs in the manufacturing industry could be found outside the Randstad. De-industrialization of employment is a national phenomenon in the Netherlands, but the speed with which it proceeds is higher in the Randstad than in the rest of the country (Atzema and de Smidt 1992). Within the Randstad there is little regional difference in the process of de-industrialization of employment, that is to say the larger city regions have lost a lot of employment in the manufacturing industries. Nationally employment in the commercial services grows the fastest and an increase of this kind of employment in the rest of the Netherlands exceeds in absolute as well as in relative terms the increase in the Randstad. This reflects the spatial deconcentration of the commercial services in the Netherlands. The same is happening within the Randstad.

The deconcentration of commercial service employment has several causes. Part of the service industries (for instance retail) has moved to the suburban regions along with the relocated ex-urban people who, in general have a stronger purchasing power. The proximity and the accessibility of the customer is also an important location factor for business services (Hessels 1992). Removal of the firm from the Randstad is quite natural, because the infrastructure connections for business traffic by car are worse for intra-urban movements than for inter-urban movements. Moreover, modern telecommunication enables the development of a network over longer distances. Few producer services have a commercial motive to prefer a location central in the city as such, as long as they can choose a location within the national polynuclear urban system. This polynuclear kind of urbanization and the need for accessibility by car account for the spatial dispersed nature of the producer services in the Netherlands (Manshanden 1996). Nevertheless, certain knowledge intensive sectors (advanced producer services like computer services, multimedia and economic consultancy) and those activities which are sensitive to certain location-specific factors (seat of government or an international airport) are still concentrated in some Dutch cities. Besides deconcentration there is also a process of specialization in the Dutch urban system (Atzema and Lambooy 1998).

Furthermore, a distinction can be made in this respect within the Randstad between the northern 'wing' of the Randstad (the combined city regions of Utrecht, Amsterdam, Haarlem and Leiden) and the southern 'wing' of the Randstad (the combined city regions of The Hague, Rotterdam and Dordrecht). Commercial service employment in the northern wing is growing much faster than in the southern wing. In absolute terms, commercial services expand fastest in the city regions of Amsterdam and Utrecht. This is particularly true for the fastest growing part of the commercial service sector, business services. Nevertheless, as mentioned earlier, this sector is also confronted by spatial deconcentration. In the northern 'wing' of the Randstad two growth zones are formed: one stretches out from Utrecht to the west and the other one out from Leiden to the north. Both zones meet south of the city of Amsterdam at the mainport of Schiphol.

Differences in sector composition can easily lead to regional differences in employment growth. Our assumption is that city regions with a concentration of commercial services have an advantage over city regions with manufacturing. This can be tested by a shift and share analysis made for the city regions of the Randstad (see Table 12.3). The analysis shows the amount of jobs, including parttime workers. This is important, because from the early seventies, the share of part-time employment in total employment has grown rapidly in the Netherlands. This share of parttime workers is higher than in any other OECD country (OECD 1993).

The 'real growth' figures in the first column of Table 12.3 underline the differences between the northern 'wing' and the southern 'wing' of the Randstad: about 60 percent of the total employment growth in the Randstad is created in the city regions of Amsterdam and Utrecht. The second column of Table 12.3 shows the 'expected growth', based on the share of the city region in the national employment in 1987. When the difference between the observed growth and the expected growth of a city region is zero, the employment has grown at the same level as the Dutch employment as a whole.

For the Randstad as a whole, the increase in employment lags behind the national level. This meant an ongoing deconcentration of employment in spite of the favourable production structure in 1987. Because the total shift (the difference between observed and expected growth) is negative in the Randstad, the location component is twice as negative as the positive structure component. Especially the city regions of Amsterdam, The Hague and Utrecht had a good point of departure, which means an overrepresentation of commercial services employment. Nevertheless in the city regions of Amsterdam and The Hague the favourable starting-point is overwhelmed by a negative location component. The city region of Rotterdam also has a large negative location component. This region has to deal with a less favourable employment structure (overrepresentation of manufacturing industry) and a very unfavourable location component. The situation in the city region of Utrecht is the opposite. The concentration of commercial services and the location at the fringe of the Randstad has multiple advantages: proximity to the larger city regions, central location in the Dutch market area and sufficient expansion possibilities in the city region.

The two other smaller city regions in the Randstad, the city regions of Leiden and Dordrecht, show a more positive image in comparison to the larger city regions of Amsterdam, Rotterdam and The Hague. In the northern 'wing' of the Randstad the smaller city region of Haarlem does not meet the expectations, due to a negative structure component (the earlier mentioned steel complex) and a large negative location component.

Table 12.2 Growth of employment in city regions, 1970–1982 and 1983–1995 (in '000 man years)

| | 1970-1982 | | | | | | 1983-1995 | | | | | |
| | Centre | | Suburb | | City region | | Centre | | Suburb | | City region | |
	Abs.	%	Abs.	%	Abs.	%	Abs.	%	Abs.	%	Abs.	%
City regions of:												
Amsterdam	-87	-21	29	18	-58	-10	13	4	54	28	67	13
Rotterdam	-66	-19	-5	-3	-7	-14	8	2	34	21	42	10
The Hague	-54	-22	28	21	-26	-7	-9	-5	30	24	21	6
Utrecht	4	3	10	7	14	5	10	3	92	48	102	31
Haarlem	-3	-6	-6	-8	-9	-7	1	2	3	4	4	3
Leiden	4	10	4	7	8	8	6	14	15	25	21	20
Dordrecht	0	0	2	5	2	2	2	5	8	10	10	8
The Randstad	-203	-16	70	8	-133	-6	31	3	246	27	277	14
Rest of NL	-26	-3	-23	-3	-49	-3	97	12	204	24	301	18

Source: SEO 1996.

Table 12.3   Growth of employment in the Randstad, 1987–1993
(according a shift-and-share analysis; '000 jobs)

	Real growth	Expected growth	Difference in growth	Explained by: structure	location
City region of:					
Amsterdam	60.1	65.5	-5.4	13.7	-19.1
Rotterdam	28.1	55.4	-27.3	2.8	-30.0
The Hague	26.1	44.8	-18.7	7.2	-25.9
Utrecht	73.1	44.9	28.2	5.5	22.7
Haarlem	0.8	16.6	-15.8	-2.0	-13.8
Leiden	17.1	13.7	3.5	1.6	1.9
Dordrecht	18.0	9.4	8.6	0.6	8.1
Randstad	223.3	250.3	-26.9	29.3	-56.1

Source: Atzema 1996.

Table 12.4 Migrations of firms in and out of the city regions of the Randstad, 1992–1995
(Number of firms with more than 5 employees)

	In	Out	Net migration N of firms	Employment
City region of:				
Amsterdam	294	568	-264	-7,000
Rotterdam	291	406	-115	-3,000
The Hague	118	354	-193	-6,300
Utrecht	672	595	-31	7,300
Haarlem	85	112	-27	-600
Leiden	150	160	-10	100
Dordrecht	88	181	-93	-3,000

Source: VVK.

The disappointing growth in employment in the three largest city regions of the Randstad (Amsterdam, Rotterdam and The Hague) can be attributed to shortcomings in the production environment. This can be illustrated by figures of interregional migration of firms (see Table 12.4). The Randstad as a whole has lost a net 700 firms in four years. If the corresponding employment of this firm migration, a loss of 12,000 jobs, is put against the total employment growth in the Randstad (148,000 jobs), the total negative effect of firm migration appears to be about 8 percent for the whole of the Randstad. The largest net loss has arisen in the three largest city regions of the Randstad, which show a total net loss of 16,000 jobs by interregional firm migrations. The city region of Utrecht is the only city region in the Randstad with a net positive employment effect of firm migration (7,000 jobs), especially because some larger companies migrated to this region leaving other city regions of the Randstad.

Kemper and Pellenbarg have characterized this spatial pattern of firm migration by using a metaphor of the Randstad as a 'pressure cooker'. In their opinion, the spatial pressure on firms in the Randstad is increasing in such a way that firms decide to move towards the regions outside the Randstad. The main reasons for doing this are the shortage of space in the Randstad to extend growing firms and poor accessibility of firms by car traffic (Kemper and Pellenbarg 1997). With respect to both aspects, firms are better off when they leave the Randstad.

12.7 Conclusions

The empirical information given in this chapter shows that the large cities in the Netherlands display a slower than average national growth of production, productivity and employment. The main reasons for these differences are changes in the composition of the local production structure (de-industrialization and the growth of consumer oriented and non-commercial service industries) and the failure of the urban production environment (the scarcity of representative locations for firms with high quality building facilities in combination with good accessibility by car).

This conclusion does not mean that in the Dutch situation agglomeration economies are not of interest anymore. Firstly, the geographical scale on which one has to examine agglomeration economies in a poly-nucleated urban system is very important. In general, agglomeration economies for many economic activities have to be considered over a group of cities, either the Randstad, but preferably over the wider urban field of the Netherlands. The urban structure of the Netherlands, like Belgium, Switzerland and large parts of Germany, displays poly-nucleation and, hence, different structures of accessibility and urban size. A second remark is that the period of investigation can have an impact on the results. In our analyses there are clear indications of urban economic decline up to the middle eighties, after which the economy of the cities has been changing in economic composition, which can be the basis for better years to come. Certain knowledge intensive service sectors are still sensitive to certain location-specific factors, such as the location of the international airport Schiphol. The largest cities have seen a big change in their economic base, with sectors such as manufacturing and goods-handling activities (like wholesale) leaving for other areas. However, employment in advanced producer services has increased, resulting in a big development of offices in both urban zones crossing the Amsterdam-Schiphol region.

Hence, for certain categories of economic activities agglomeration economies is still a useful concept, but not for general purposes. In the Netherlands, with its poly-nucleated urban structure, a remarkable spatial dispersion of services can be observed. In countries with a dominating national urban city region, like France or Britain, one can probably find a much stronger spatial concentration of producer services. Nevertheless, the Dutch service sector as a whole is increasing as rapidly as in those countries. Large agglomerations, such as London and Paris, show high proportions of fast growing producer services, but at the same time, one can observe the level of costs in those agglomerations of estate buildings and transport. Furthermore, in a mono-centred urban structure the supply of educational and cultural amenities per capita is higher than in a poly-nucleated structure. However, the access is much lower for the rest of the country, which shows that the advantages are more unevenly spread in those countries. In countries with a poly-nucleated structures like the Netherlands, access to amenities and knowledge is more generally available. Agglomeration economies work 'all-round', whereas they are fragmented and apply to the poly-nucleated structure as a total.

For the policy makers, the message can be that the concept of the 'compact city' has not offered the right solution for the urban economic problems until now. Agglomeration economies have to be considered on a larger scale than the compact cities. In the Netherlands, the poly-nucleated structure implies a continuous overlapping of economic activity spaces, leading to land scarcity. Physical planning adds to this scarcity by its attempts to concentrate human occupancy within strict limits of the compact cities. The resulting scarcity and the concomitant high land prices are a factor in explaining the spatial dispersal of land-consuming activities.

Nevertheless, there are several reasons why the Dutch government should stimulate the economy and the employment in the Randstad, especially in the large cities. The most important reason to do so is the existing urban labour market problem. In spite of all success stories about the growth of the Dutch economy there is still a considerable army of unemployed people. In 1995 there were about 500,000 officially registered unemployed persons in the Netherlands (8 percent of the Dutch labour force). Half of them live in the Randstad city regions and nearly 100,000 live in the three largest cities. The unemployment rate in cities like Amsterdam and Rotterdam is twice as high as the national average. The high level of urban unemployment is partly caused by overall shortage of work as a result of low economic growth in connection to the growth of population. More important is the quality of employment. Unemployment in the largest cities is concentrated among the less-educated and foreigners. The recent growth in employment in the large cities fits insufficiently to their labour qualifications. Unemployed persons in the urban nodes lose in the battle of job competition from better educated people living in the suburban areas and from young new entrants on the urban labour market (for instance school leavers). But only partly can this kind of policy be based on the argument that in the Dutch situation the Randstad cities have greater economic advantages. This argument fits specific kinds of firms and employment which is not directly relevant for unemployed people in the cities of the Randstad.

References

Ark, B. van, Haan, J. de and Jong, H.J. de (1996), 'Characteristics of Economic Growth in the Netherlands during the Postwar Period, in Crafts, N. and Toniolo, G. (eds), *Economic growth in Europe since 1945*. Cambridge University Press, Cambridge, pp. 290–328.

Arthur, W.B. (1996), 'Increasing Returns and the New World of Business', Harvard Business Review, July/August, pp. 100–9.

Atzema, O.A.L.C. (1996), 'Overloop van Bevolking en Werkgelegenheid Randstad-Gelderland/ Noord-Brabant', (Overspill of population and employment Randstad-Gelderland/North Brabant), Urban Researchcenter Utrecht.

Atzema, O.A.L.C. and Lambooy, J.G. (1998), 'The Urban Hierarchy of Economic Evolution; Empirical Evidence in the Netherlands', Urban Research Centre Utrecht Document, Utrecht.

Atzema, O.A.L.C. and Smidt, M. de (1992), 'Selection and duality in the employment structure of the Randstad', *Tijdschrift voor Economische en Sociale Geografie*, vol. 83, no. 4, pp. 289–305.

Atzema, O.A.L.C. and Wever, E. (1994), De Nederlandse Industrie., (The Dutch Manufacturing Industry), Van Gorcum, Assen.

Bailly, A. and Lever, W. (1996), 'Introduction', in Lever, W. and Bailly, A. (eds), *The spatial impact of economic change in Europe*, Avebury, Adershot.

Boelens, L. (1998), Randstad Holland: Het had zo Mooi kunnen zijn. *Stedebouw & Ruimtelijke Ordening*, vol. 79, vol. 2, pp. 15–21 (Randstad Holland: it could have been so beautiful).

Burke, G.L. (1965), *Greenhaert Metropolis: planning the western Netherlands*, Mac Millan, London.

Cheshire, P. (1995), 'A New Phase of Urban Development in Western Europe? The Experience of the 1980's, *Urban Studies*, vol. 32, no. 7, pp. 1045–63.

Clark W.A.V. and Kuipers-Linde, M. (1994), Commuting in Restructuring Urban Regions. *Urban Studies,* vol. 31, no. 3, pp. 465–84.

Cortie, C., Dijst, M. and Ostendorf, W. (1992), 'The Randstad a Metropolis?', *Tijdschrift voor Economische en Sociale Geografie,* vol. 83, no. 4, pp. 278–88.

Dagevos, J., Van der Laan, L. and Veenman, J. (1997), *Verdringing op de arbeidsmarkt,* Van Gorcum, Assen (Supplanting on the labour market).

Elfring. T. (1988), *Service Employment in Advanced Economies: A Comparative Analysis of its Implications for Economic Growth,* Gower, Aldershot.

Friedman, J. and Miller, J. (1965), 'The Urban Field', *Journal of the American Planners,* vol. 31, pp. 312–19.

Hall, P. (1966), 'The World Cities', (Chapter 4: Randstad Holland), Weidenfeld and Nicholson, London.

Hessels, M. (1992), *Location Dynamics of Business Services. An Intrametropolitan Study on the Randstad Holland,* Rijksuniversiteit Utrecht, Utrecht.

Jacobs, J. (1984), *Cities and The Wealth of Nations,* Penguin Books, London.

Kemper, N.J. & P.H. Pellenbarg (1997), De Randstad een hoge drukpen. *Economisch Statistische Berichten,* vol. 82, pp. 508-512.

Krugman, P. (1991), *Trade and Geography,* MIT Press, Cambridge, Massachusetts.

Krugman, P. (1995), *Development, Geography and Economic Theory,* MIT Press, Cambridge, Massachusetts.

Van der Laan, L. (1998), 'Changing Urban Systems: An Empirical Analysis at Two Spatial Levels, *Regional Studies,* vol. 32, no. 3, pp. 235–48.

Lambooy, J.G. (1969), 'City and City Region in the Perspective of Hierarchy and Complementarity', *Tijdschrift voor Economische en Sociale Geografie,* vol. 60, no. 2, pp. 141–54.

Lambooy, J.G. (1993), 'The European City: From Carrefour to Organisational Nexus, *Tijdschrift voor Economische en Sociale Geografie,* vol. 84, no. 4, pp. 258–68.

Lambooy, J.G. (1998), 'Poly-nucleation and Economic Development: the Randstad', *European Planning Studies,* vol. 6, no. 4, pp. 457–66.

Manshanden, W. (1996), *Zakelijke Diensten en Regionaal-Economische Ontwikkeling: De Economie van Nabijheid,* Universiteit van Amsterdam, Amsterdam (Business services and regional economic development: the economy of proximity).

Musterd, S. and de Pater, B. de (1992), *Randstad Holland: Internationaal, Regionaal, Lokaal,* Van Gorcum, Assen.

OECD (1993), *The Labour Market in the Netherlands,* OECD, Paris.

Richardson, H.W. (1995), 'Economics and Diseconomics of Agglomeration', in Giersh, H. (ed.), *Urban Agglomeration and Economic Growth,* Springer Verlag, Heidelberg.

SEO (1996), *Steden en Stadsgewesten; Economische Ontwikkelingen 1975–201,* SEO, Amsterdam (Cities and city regions; economic developments 1975-2015).

Shachar, A. (1994), 'Randstad Holland: A "World City"?' *Urban Studies*, vol. 31, no. 3, pp. 381–400.

Smidt, M. de (1992), 'A World City Paradox; Firms and the Urban Fabric, in Dieleman, F.M. and Musterd, S. (eds), *The Randstad: A Research and Policy Laboratory,* Kluwer Academic Publishers, Dordrecht.

Note

1. The only exceptions are the northern province of Drenthe and the province of Zeeland in the southwestern part of the country. The new town Almere (125,000 inhabitants) in the province of Flevoland will be categorized as a part of the suburban surroundings of the city of Amsterdam.

13 Conclusion: Structural Economic Change and Regional Development

DANIEL SHEFER AND PIET RIETVELD

13.1   Unbalanced Regional Growth and Technological Change

In this concluding chapter we review the main issues of structural economic change and investigate their implications for regional development. Also policy aspects are considered because it is important to know the scope for action by regional and national governments that are confronted with the unbalances in the development of the regions.

In the advent of globalization and technological change, constant restructuring and readjustment of the regional economy becomes mandatory. Invariably, technological change and growth in output is accompanied by a noticeable change in the mix, or relative share, of the major sectors of the economy; i.e. agriculture, manufacturing and services. (See Chapter 11 in this volume). Significant changes can also be detected within each one of these major sectors. For instance, in the manufacturing sector, we observe growth together with a continuous increase in the share of the high-technology industrial branches compared with the traditional ones. In the agricultural sector, a continuous change in the capital-labour or capital-output ratios is being observed.

These noticeable changes are accompanied also by a significant improvement in the technology embodied in the new capital formation and the knowledge embodied in labour. Thus, there are differences in the quality and productivity of the various vintages of capital as well as that of labour. All of these dynamic processes manifest themselves in structural changes of the regional economy.

There are two important issues that emerge as a consequence of these on-going structural changes. The first issue is concerned with convergence vs. divergence in the centre-periphery dilemma, and the second, with the concentration vs. dispersal, of population and economic activities over space. What is the impact of technological spillovers on the concentration of population and economic activities? And to what extent does advanced technology induce the concentration of economic activities, or foster the creation of agglomeration economies in some selected points in space? Likewise it is important to ascertain the impact of technological change on the welfare of the inhabitants of peripheral regions relative to those residing in central regions.

The desire to develop peripheral regions exists in many countries throughout the world, particularly in those countries where a wide socioeconomic gap exists between core and peripheral regions. These gaps often exacerbate spatial, social and political unrest in the country. To foster the economic growth of peripheral regions, it is necessary to create employment opportunities that will attract the population to remain and migrants to come and settle in these regions.

Uneven distribution of resources over space, imperfect mobility as well as indivisibility of production factors, and the necessity to economize on scarce resources all induce the concentration of economic activity at discrete and selected points. Consequently, there exist variations among regions. These variations manifest themselves in the levels of economic and social wellbeing of the population in the various regions. In order to reduce the disparities among regions, government agencies devise policies and initiate programs whose main objectives are to increase the employment level, to increase per capita income, and in general to increase the rate of economic growth in the peripheral regions. Different regions offer different opportunities for specialization. Thus, when these opportunities are exploited, they may add to the aggregate income and standard of living of the region's population.

The search for different attributes to satisfy different location needs has resulted in an unbalanced division of industry functions between core and peripheral areas. There is a tendency for large companies to establish only production work, thus, providing mostly low-paid jobs and a few administrative positions in peripheral areas. The expected improvements in the regional economy and in local labour opportunities have often been disappointing, since production branches have been found to create very little, if any, 'spill-over' effects to increase the local multiplier. Multinational corporations that move production operations around the world may be sought by developing countries, but these companies do not offer much more opportunity or job security to the local population than do traditional industries.

Since entrepreneurs strive to maximize profits, they are motivated to invest in regions where the greatest profits can be attained, given some pre-specified level of probabilities of the risk involved due to uncertainties. Profit will be maximized in regions where there is comparatively higher productivity of inputs like labour, capital, and greater efficiency in the transportation and communication networks.

There are multiple issues that are effecting regional structural change. In the sections below we are going to discuss some selected issues, whose ramifications are significant and far reaching.

13.2 Specialization and Free Trade

Specialization and free trade are the manifestation of borderless economy – globalization – which permit division of labour and enhance the comparative advantage of regions. Regional comparative advantage reveals itself in lower input costs (per unit of output) and a higher productivity of each unit of factor of production.

Open economies can also take advantage of an expanded market and through increasing return to scale, enjoy greater production efficiency and a higher rate of economic growth. Greater production efficiency enables industries to expand their domestic market share through import substitution and increase in local consumption. At the same time it allows these industries to compete on the world market, penetrate new foreign markets and increase their export share. (Grossman and Helpman 1990a, 1990b; Porter 1990; Krugman 1979, 1991a, 1991b, 1995)

13.3 Endogenous Economic Growth

The endogenous economic growth models that emerged in the 1980s suggest that firms may invest in new technology through expenditure on research and development if they perceive an opportunity to make a profit. Thus, technological progress could explain the persistent growth of total income and consequently of income per capita or 'standard of living'.

In recent years, industrial innovation has been recognized as a major source fostering economic growth. The resurrection of interest in economic growth models, prompted by the seminal work of Romer (1986) and Lucas (1988), brought to the fore the importance of endogenous technological progress. Endogenous economic growth refers to the industry decision to invest in research and development, or adopt new technology. Technological change and innovation are the engine for economic growth. Thus, it is essential for effective public policy to understand the process by which industry is engaged in innovation activities, or adopt new technology.

Since economic growth is driven to a large extent by technological progress, it is essential for effective public policy to identify the group of industries whose rate of innovation is the largest. There is ample evidence supporting the hypothesis that innovation activities are more prevalent among high-tech industries than in other industrial brunches. Thus, it would be of paramount importance to investigate innovation activities among firms belonging to this specific group of industries. (Romer 1987, 1990; Grossman and Helpman 1991a, 1994; JEP, 1994; Stokey 1995; Nijkamp and Poot 1996; Aghion and Howitt 1998; Shefer et al. 1999).

13.4 High Tech Industries

In the past few decades, the high-tech industrial complex has undergone tremendous expansion worldwide, stimulating a new wave of industrial growth. Policy makers view high-technology industries as crucial components of regional economic growth and an increasingly important part of a regional export base.

Historically, dominant industrial processes and products have gone through phases; for example, the textile industry predominated in the last century; coal and steel rose to preeminence at the beginning of this century; when these stabilized, the car and durable consumer goods industries took off. Each development cycle or 'Kondratieff long wave', exhibiting growth, dominance and, eventually, contraction, has had a profound influence on the social and political environment and on labour-market relations in industrial agglomeration centres.

Recognition of the economic vitality of new high technology industries and their association with prestigious employment opportunities and a high quality of life has led to a flourishing of enthusiasm for high technology industries, as if they were a panacea for all economic problems. Although the majority of high technology industries are located in the major metropolitan centres, both local authorities of peripheral areas and the national government have determined the promotion and geographical dispersion of 'high technology', or 'knowledge intensive', industries to be a high priority. These industries are also attractive because they are thought of as 'clean industries', emitting only small amounts of pollution into the air compared with the older, traditional manufacturing industries.

The literature concerned with location decisions of high-tech industries has varied in emphasis. In most cases, however, studies of high-tech industrial complexes around the world have found that certain regional attributes are attractive for manufacturing branch-location while other criteria are employed for services. Headquarters are usually established either in large urban centres or in medium-sized towns at the edges or urban centres (suburbs) which offer a high quality of life and the proximity of university and research centres. Policy makers interested in developing high-tech industries in outlying regions must take careful note of the high agglomeration tendencies they exhibit and also be warned of the exaggerated expectations often accorded, most notably by politicians, to high-tech industries.

Attempts to attract high-tech industries specifically to those peripheral regions that seem obviously disadvantaged by their distance from urban centres may encounter unsolvable problems. Yet, many policy makers maintain an optimism that high-tech industrial development is possible anywhere because of expanding communications technology which continually increases the industry's 'footloose' and the freedom of not being tied down to a specific source of raw materials or market.

Although advanced technology enables firms to become more 'footloose', their choice of location became more complex and often plant-specific. At the same time, high-tech work force shows signs of being also 'footloose'. This phenomenon manifests itself in the average tenure on a job with a high-tech firm, which is significantly and appreciably shorter than that with a traditional firm. Furthermore, this phenomenon requires a large pool of highly skilled labour that can be found in central regions. A possibility to break through this pattern of dominance by settled central cities is that governments invest in large universities in peripheral regions (see for example Chapter 5 in this volume). This indeed helps to create a pool of qualified workers in the region. To make this policy successful, it is of course necessary that the universities concerned are large enough (spreading expenditures for higher education among too many cities would not create a sufficient mass) and that the regions concerned are sufficiently attractive as residential locations for the highly educated workers.

The valued image of 'high-tech' industry is derived mainly from the well-paid, prestigious and high skilled jobs in research and development. Industries, however, are comprised of many activities, each fulfilling a different function. Production, which demands mostly semi-skilled and unskilled manual labour, is a more footloose activity than is research and development, and hence is likely to locate in peripheral areas. Such differentiation in location has been explained in reference to the 'product life cycle' theory (Vernon, 1966, 1979). This hypothesis presents an historical analysis of the functional stages that a product undergoes before it reaches the consumer; namely: research and development (or innovation), prototype production, mass production, marketing, sales, etc. (see also Chapter 3 in this volume). High-tech economic activities require a structural change in the regional economy that could not be brought about solely from enhanced capital investment in the area. The innovation stage in the product life-cycle, not permitting significant substitution of inputs, emphasizes the accumulation of knowledge and a large pool of high skilled labour associated with research and development to allow the structural changes necessary for 'takeoff' of high-tech activities (Grossman and Helpman, 1991a).

As the product matures, the production process and the product itself become more standardized, and it becomes easier to transfer production operations to a location where labour is cheaper than in the centre. A firm's flexibility in conducting its research and development, marketing and most administration from its home base while moving branch plants to lower-labour cost location forms as production is critical. This flexibility enables firms, especially large corporations that are well endowed to take advantage of national and worldwide opportunities, to expand their markets and to stay ahead of the competition. Branch-plant economies, on the other hand, may boost employment, in the long run, however, they do not develop and diversify into strong, mixed economies that would create the right environment for innovation. An environment that 'breeds' innovation is vital for succeeding in the world of high-tech industry. Pursuing local-based (endogenous) development is perhaps the only way to build a more balanced economy, one that is less vulnerable to plant closures and, perhaps more importantly, that utilizes local inputs, fosters local links and encourages local entrepreneurial and innovation. An alternative path that can be pursued by peripheral regions well endowed with natural or cultural resources is that they specialize in tourism (see the contributions in Chapters 6, 7 and 10). Even though it may appear that the rate of return on investments in tourism is not that high, and that central regions benefit more than peripheral regions, tourism may offer a welcome additional source of income for their residents.

13.5   Innovation and Regional Growth

In recent years researchers have become increasingly aware of the role of industrial innovation and the impact of its diffusion processes on regional development and economic growth. Since economic growth is driven to a large extent by technological progress, it is paramount for effective public policy to understand the process by which industry is engaged in innovation activities. This growing interest resulted from the interrelationship of innovation, competitiveness, and economic growth.

The contribution of innovation to regional economic growth has been widely discussed in the literature. Regional development, as a location where technological innovation takes place, is usually accompanied by new economic activities, market expansion, and technological adaptation. Regions with a high level of innovation have become a destination for highly skilled labour and an impetus for improved social and physical infrastructures. From a technological point of view, advanced economic activities tend to possess a high market value resulting in a competitive advantage, at least during the first stage of the diffusion process. Thus, they enjoy new and at times unique opportunities for the development of firms, expansion of their market share, profitability, and employment growth. Therefore regions that are characterized by a high level of technological innovation, will show a greater acceleration of economic growth (Schmookler 1966; Freeman 1974; Thwaites et al. 1981; Grossman and Helpman 1991b; Davelaar 1991; Feldman 1994; Stokey 1995; Bertuglia et al. 1995, 1997).

The ability of a firm to innovate is contingent, among other things, upon the local innovative milieu, or the economic environment conducive to innovation (see also Chapter 2 of this book). This economic environment includes the degree of cooperation and collaboration among firms and the externalities generated by localization and agglomeration economies. These economies are created by the spatial concentration, or spatial density, of either similar (competitive) or complementary firms, or by the shear size of the regional total number of workers and population (see Chapter 4 of this volume).

Agglomeration economies are perceived as enhancing the innovative capacity of firms. They are considered a cost reducing factors that diminish uncertainty and increase production efficiencies. There are ample theoretical and empirical studies that demonstrate the effect of agglomeration economies on production efficiency. Indeed, modern location theory posits the significant role that agglomeration economies play in explaining the growth of cities. They form the hubs that generate new ideas and technological progress. Agglomeration economies are the principle forces that foster the continuous spatial concentration of people and economic activities in some selected points in space (Shefer 1973; Shefer and Frenkel 1998; Henderson 1988; Kleinknecht and Poot 1992; Carlino and Voith 1992; Glaeser et al. 1992; Jaffe et al. 1993; Giersch 1995; Harrison et al. 1996; Bruinsma and Rietveld 1996; Ciccone and Hall 1996; Black and Vernon 1997).

13.6 Infrastructure and Regional Development

Infrastructure development must be examined in the context of governmental policies, business incentives, and planned linkages to existing networks. The role of infrastructure in regional development has often been misunderstood. While a new investment, such as a major highway, may encourage development in under-developed regions, its construction alone is not enough to bring about the desired economic changes. Other factors, such as the economic climate in the region, and relative prices of factors of production, including labour, capital and materials, and agglomeration economies tend to determine the economic viability of a region more than its basic endowed infrastructure (see also Chapters 8 and 9 of this book).

It has been shown empirically that public capital infrastructure plays an important complementary role in the productivity of the private sector. Recent studies suggest that heavy infrastructure investment in the United States during the 1950s and 1960s may have been a key, previously underrated, factor in the strong economic performance of that period (Aschauer 1989, 1990). Thus, neglect of the public capital stock reduces the potential for economic expansion. The services of most publicly owned capital are freely distributed to private producers. Since the marginal product of these services is positive, these services should be considered as an integral component of the aggregate production function.

Setting aside political or social considerations, new infrastructure investment must be guided by the efficiency criterion. Under-building infrastructure can clearly inhibit economic development. On the other hand, overbuilt infrastructure can add nothing to regional economic growth. Existing infrastructure may become obsolete due to the spatial movements of population or business activity, or as a result of changing demand or technology. The use of under-subscribed facilities causes economic inefficiencies that can increase the overall cost of doing business in an area. Maintaining facilities for which demand has fallen functions as a de facto tax on economic activity.

If the goal of a government policy is to influence investment patterns in a particular area, then infrastructure investment may not be efficient in the traditional sense. It could be said that the government is aiming at 'place prosperity' rather than 'people prosperity'. A state government may wish to spread out economic development, with the hope that improved accessibility will lead to the attraction of economic activity that could balance development across the state. However, trying to spread out development may diminish statewide growth. The state's residents could possibly be worse off overall if resources are spread out as a policy objective.

Inefficient or insufficient investment in capital infrastructure precipitates urban decay. The efficiency of capital investment is greatest during a period of sustainable growth and development. When the level of public and private investment falls below that required for the satisfactory maintenance and replacement of infrastructure in a certain area, the competitive advantages of that area gradually decline as its productivity erodes. The amount as well as the mix of public and private investment, with a positive input required from both sectors, is crucial for sustainable economic growth (Shefer 1990; Forkenbrock 1990; Munnell 1990; Vickerman 1991; Lynde and Richmond 1992; Crihfield and Panggabean 1995; IJTE 1998; Rietveld and Bruinsma 1998).

13.7   Privatization and Deregulation

Privatization and deregulation have been prompted primarily by the constantly increasing costs associated with maintaining publicly owned enterprises. In the last 15 to 20 years, many central and local governments in developed and developing countries have turned their publicly owned enterprises over to private hands. These governments found themselves too financially constrained even to keep allocating meagre resources for the daily operation and maintenance of these enterprises much less make substantial new investments in them. Turning to the private sector is one solution central and local governments have found as a means of insuring that the important public need such enterprises serve continue to be met (Vernon, 1988).

In the early 1980s, all levels of government saw privatizing publicly owned enterprises as an acceptable means of raising money. State-owned enterprises, operating under government policies were often forced to hold down their prices, raise wages of public- workers and at the same time increase the level of services. These policies rendered the operation of state-owned enterprises inefficient. Furthermore, such entities required continuous financial support from the general budget.

At the same time, resistance to increased tax burdens was mounting in several developed countries. An obvious solution to the rapidly growing deficit in government budgets was to sell certain public assets to the private sector. This solution corroborated with the political and economic philosophy held by many of the conservative governments in the early 1980s, such as those of Thatcher in Britain and Reagan in the United States. State-owned enterprises were believed to be less efficient than private firms are. Privatization and deregulation, therefore, were perceived as means of improving competition and, consequently, improving the operational efficiency of public services.

In short, the main objectives of privatization and deregulation are to expose the particular service to a competitive market and to tap new sources of private capital. The underlying philosophy is that market exposure will result in the elimination of monopoly pricing and the establishment of competitive market prices (i.e. prices equal to long run average costs). Prices determined in competitive markets, where government does not interfere, assure the most efficient allocation of resources, thus yielding maximum net benefit to society.

Although privatization is a necessary condition for competition, it is not sufficient, particularly in a situation where government regulation of the service still exists. Therefore, to ensure competition, both privatization and deregulation must exist. There is no doubt that these significant organizational changes in the delivery of services have far reaching repercussions on the economic structure of regions (Yarro 1986;Shefer 1998).

13.8   Information Technology (IT)

Information Technology (IT) and accumulation of knowledge play a vital role in the process of technological change and the spatial diffusion of innovation. Advanced means of communication serve as a vehicle for disseminating knowledge throughout space. Spatial diffusion of innovation is contingent upon rapid and accurate transmission of knowledge and the ability to interact frequently and efficiently among different locations. Therefore, advanced means of communication are a necessary component in the process of regional development and economic growth.

The tremendous advances in communications technology in the last decade have sparked enthusiasm for the theory that physical distance can be reduced in importance and transportation be replaced, to some extent, with information technologies. These technologies are undoubtedly going to influence the way business will be conducted in the future, but exactly how much and in which direction are still subjects for debate. An evaluation of the influence of IT on the peripheral regions' potential share of the 'high-tech pie' must also examine the importance attached by firms to communications quality in making their location decisions. Although advanced means of communications can reduce appreciably the 'friction of space', it is not very clear to what extent face-to-face contact will remain the preferred way of doing business? Or to what extent they will substitute face-to-face interactions?

There is a growing number of scientists, urban economists as well as urban planners, who believe that '(tele)communications are not a substitute for face-to-face interaction, but in fact these forms of information transmission are complements', (Gaspar and Glaeser 1998). Thus improved communications are more likely to enhance the agglomeration and urban concentration then the spatial dispersal of population and economic activities. (Shefer 1988; Shefer and Bar-El 1993).

13.9   Conclusion

There is strong evidence that supports the hypothesis that regional structural changes, derived by globalization and technological progress, do promote the concentration of people and economic activities in space. The continuous division of labour supports specialization and creates the comparative advantage of some selected regions. Thus making them more attractive places to invest and grow. We may therefore tentatively conclude that in the long run, technological change and globalization may further induce concentration of people and economic activities thereby exasperating the already existing gap between central and peripheral regions. It is important to emphasize that this conclusion holds for broadly defined regions. Along with a persistent or even growing gap between central and peripheral regions one may observe at the same time processes of deconcentration within central regions. An example of such a process can be found in Chapter 12 in this volume. These contrary movements at various spatial levels make the theme of divergence versus convergence a challenging theme for research.

References

Aghion, P. and Howitt, P. (1998), *Endogenous Growth Theory*, MIT Press, Cambridge, MA.

Aschauer, D.A. (1989), 'Is Public Expenditure Productive?', *Journal of Monetary Economics*, vol. 23, pp. 177–200.

Aschauer, D.A. (1990), 'Why is Infrastructure Important?', in Munnell, A. (ed.), *Is There a Shortfall in Public Capital Investment?*, Federal Reserve Bank of Boston, Boston, MA.

Bertuglia, C.S., Lombardo, S. and Nijkamp, P. (eds) (1997), *Innovative Behavior in Space and Time*, Springer, Berlin.

Bertuglia, S.C., Fischer, M.M. and Preto, G. (eds) (1995), *Technological Change, Economic Development and Space*, Springer, Berlin.

Black, D. and Vernon, H.J. (1997), 'Urban Growth', National Bureau of Economic Research, Working Paper, No. 6008, Cambridge, MA.

Bruinsma, F. and Rietveld, P. (1996), 'Urban Agglomeration in European Infrastructure Networks', *Urban Studies*, vol. 30, no. 6, pp. 919–34.

Carlino, G.A. and Voith, R. (1992), 'Accounting for Differences in Aggregate State Productivity', *Regional Science and Urban Economics*, vol. 22, no. 4, pp. 597–617.

Ciccone, A. and Hall, R.E. (1996), 'Productivity and the density of Economic Activity', *American Economic Review*, vol. 86, no. 1, pp. 54–70.

Crihfield, J.B., and Panggabean, P.H. (1995), 'Is Public Infrastructure Productive?', *Regional Science and Urban Economics*, vol. 25, no. 5, pp. 607–30.

Davelaar, E.J. (1991), *Regional Economic Analysis of Innovation and Incubation*, Avebury, Aldershort, UK.

Feldman, M.P. (1994), *The Geography of Innovation*, Kluwer Academic Publishers, The Netherlands.

Forkenbrock, D.J. et al. (1990), *Road Investment to Foster Local Economic Development*, University of Iowa: Public Policy Centre, Iowa.

Freeman, C. (1974), *The Economics of Industrial Innovation*, Penguin Books, London.

Gaspar, J. and Glaeser, E.L. (1998), 'Information Technology and the Future of Cities', *Journal of Urban Economics* (forthcoming).

Giersch, H. (ed.) (1995), *Urban Agglomeration and Economic Growth*, Springer, Berlin.

Glaeser, E.L., Kallal, H.D., Scheinkman, J.A. and Shleifer, A. (1992), 'Growth in Cities', *Journal of Political Economy*, vol. 100, no. 6, pp. 1128–52.

Grossman, G.M. and Helpman, E. (1990a), 'Trade, Innovation and Growth', *American Economic Review*, vol. 80, no. 2, pp. 86–91.

Grossman, G.M. and Helpman, E. (1990b), 'Comparative Advantage and Long-Run Growth', *American Economic Review*, vol. 80, no. 4, pp. 796–815.

Grossman, G.M. and Helpman, E. (1991a), 'Endogenous Product Cycles', *Economic Journal*, vol. 101, pp. 121–29.

Grossman, G.M. and Helpman, E. (1991b), *Innovation and Growth in the Global Economy*, MIT Press, Cambridge, MA.

Harrison, B.M, Kelley, E. and Gant, J. (1996), 'Innovative Firm Behavior and Local Milieu', *Economic Geography*, vol. 79, no. 3, pp. 233–258.

Henderson, J.V. (1988), *Urban Development: Theory, Fact and Illusion*, Oxford University Press, New York.

International Journal of Transport Economics (IJTE) (1998), Special Issue on Infrastructure, Investment and Development.

Jaffe, A., Trajtenberg, M. and Henderson, R. (1993), 'Geographic Localization of Knowledge Spillovers as Evidenced by Patent Citations', *Quarterly Journal of Economics*, vol. 108, no. 3, pp. 577–98.

Journal of Economic Perspective (JEP) 1994, Special Issue on: Endogenous Economic Growth, vol. 8, no. 1.

Kleinknecht, A. and Poot, T.P. (1992), 'Do Regions Matter for R & D?', *Regional Studies*, vol. 26, no. 3, pp. 221–32.

Krugman, P. (1995), *Development, Geography and Economic Theory*, MIT Press, Cambridge MA.

Krugman, P. (1991a), *Geography and Trade*, M.I.T. Press, Cambridge, MA.

Krugman, P. (1991b), 'Increasing Returns and Economic Geography', *Journal of Political Economy*, vol. 99, no. 3, pp. 483–99.

Krugman, P. (1979), 'A Model of Innovation, Technology Transfer, and Trade', *Journal of Political Economy*, vol. 83, pp. 253–66.

Lynde, C. and Richmond, J. (1992), 'The Role of Public Capital in Production', *The Review of Economics and Statistics*, pp. 37–44.

Lucas R.E. Jr. (1988), 'On the Mechanics of Economic Development', *Journal of Monetary Economics*, vol. 22, no. 1, pp. 3–42.

Munnell, H.A. (ed.) (1990), *Is There a Shortfall in Public Capital Investment?*, Proceeding of a Conference held in June 1990, Federal Reserve Bank of Boston, Boston, MA.

Nijkamp, P. and Poot, J. (1996), 'Endogenous Technological Change, Long-Run Growth and Spatial Interdependence: A Survey', Unpublished paper presented at the International Seminar on 'Endogenous Growth and Space Economy', pp. 19–20, Amsterdam.

Porter, M. (1990), *The Competitive Advantage of Nations* Free Press, New York.

Rietveld, P. and Bruinsma, F. (1998), *Is Transport Infrastructure Effective?*, Springer, Berlin.

Romer, P.M.(1986), 'Increasing Returns and Long-Run Growth', *Journal of Political Economy*, vol. 94, no. 5, pp. 1002–37.

Romer, P.M. (1987), 'Growth Based on Increasing Returns Due to Specialisation', *American Economic Review*, May 1987 (Paper & Proceedings), vol. 77, no. 2, pp. 56–62.

Romer, P.M. (1990), 'Endogenous Technological Change', *Journal of Political Economy*, vol. 98 (part 2), pp. S71–S102.

Schmookler, J. (1966), *Invention and Economic Growth*, Harvard University Press, Cambridge, MA.

Shefer, D. (1973), 'Localization Economies in SMSs: A Production Function Analysis', *Journal of Regional Science*, vol. 13, no. 1, pp. 55–64.

Shefer, D. (1988), 'The Effect of Various Means of Communication on the Operation and Location of High Technology Industries', in Giaoutzi, M. and Nijkamp, P. (eds), *Informatics High Tech and Regional Development*, Avebury, Aldershot, UK, pp. 168–81.

Shefer, D. (1990), 'Innovation, Technical Change and Metropolitan Development: An Israeli Example' in: Nijkamp, P. (ed) *Sustainability of Urban Systems*, Avebury, Aldershot, UK, pp. 167–81.

Shefer, D. (1998), 'Economic and Social Merits and Liabilities of Privatization and Deregulation of Public Transport', Paper prepared for and delivered to a workshop in the UN University, Aoyama, Tokyo, Japan, 14th October.

Shefer, D. and Bar-El, E. (1993), 'High-Technology Industries as a Vehicle for Growth in Israel's Peripheral Regions', *Environment and Planning C*, vol. 11, pp. 245–61.

Shefer, D. and Frenkel, A. (l998), 'Local Milieu and Innovations: Some Empirical Results', *The Annals of Regional Science*, vol. 32, pp. 185–200.

Shefer, D., Frenkel, A., Koschatzky, K. and Walter, H.G. (1999), 'Targeting Industry for Regional Development in Israel and in Germany – A Comparative Study', Papers presented at the Western Regional Science Association Annual Meeting, Ojai CA, (21–24 March).

Stokey, N.L. (l995), R&D and Economic Growth', *Review of Economic Studies*, vol. 62, pp. 469–89.

Thwaites, A.T., Oakey, R.P. and Nash, P.A. (1981), 'Industrial Innovation and Regional Development', final report to the Department of the Environment; CURDS, University of Newcastle upon Tyne, Newcastle upon Tyne.

Vernon, R. (l966), 'International Investment and International Trade in the Product Life Cycle', *Quarterly Journal of Economics*, vol. 80, pp. 190–207.

Vernon, R. (l979), 'The Product Cycle Hypothesis in a New International Environment', Oxford Bulletin of Economics and Statistics, vol. 41, pp. 255–67.

Vernon, R. (l988), *The Promise of Privatization*, Council on Foreign Relations, New York.

Vickerman, R.W. (ed.) (l991), *Infrastructure and Regional Development*, Pion Ltd., London.

Yarro, G. (l986), 'Privatization in Theory and in Practice', *Economic Policy*, vol. 2, (April) pp. 323–78.

For Product Safety Concerns and Information please contact our EU
representative GPSR@taylorandfrancis.com Taylor & Francis Verlag GmbH,
Kaufingerstraße 24, 80331 München, Germany

Printed and bound by CPI Group (UK) Ltd, Croydon, CR0 4YY
08/05/2025
01864459-0002